Library of
Davidson College

Benjamin Jowett
and the Christian Religion

Benjamin Jowett
and the Christian Religion

PETER HINCHLIFF

CLARENDON PRESS · OXFORD
1987

Oxford University Press, Walton Street, Oxford OX2 6DP
Oxford New York Toronto
Delhi Bombay Calcutta Madras Karachi
Petaling Jaya Singapore Hong Kong Tokyo
Nairobi Dar es Salaam Cape Town
Melbourne Auckland
and associated companies in
Beirut Berlin Ibadan Nicosia

Oxford is a trade mark of Oxford University Press

Published in the United States
by Oxford University Press, New York

© Peter Hinchliff, 1987

All rights reserved. No part of this publication may be reproduced, stored in a retrieval system, or transmitted, in any form or by any means, electronic, mechanical, photocopying, recording, or otherwise, without the prior permission of Oxford University Press.

British Library Cataloguing in Publication Data
Hinchliff, Peter
Benjamin Jowett and the Christian religion.
1. Jowett, Benjamin—Contributions in
doctrinal theology 2. Theology, Doctrinal
—England—History—19th century
I. Title
209'.2'4   BX5199.J/
ISBN 0-19-826688-X

Library of Congress Cataloging in Publication Data
Hinchliff, Peter Bingham.
Benjamin Jowett and the Christian religion.
Bibliography: p.
Includes index.
1. Jowett, Benjamin, 1817–1893. 2. Theologians—
England—Biography. I. Title.
BX5199.J68H56 1987   230'.3'0924 [B]   87-14208
ISBN 0-19-826688-X

Set by Computerised Typesetting Services, Finchley, London N12 8LY
Printed in Great Britain
at the University Printing House, Oxford
by David Stanford
Printer to the University

For

JOHN PREST

in gratitude for much kindness and help,
not least in the writing of this book

Acknowledgements

I wish to thank the master and fellows of Balliol College, Oxford, the British Library Board, the Archbishop of Canterbury and the trustees of Lambeth Palace Library for permission to use archives in their keeping; also the editors of *Theology* and the *Journal of Ecclesiastical History* for permission to incorporate material originally published in those journals.

I am greatly indebted to Professor Denis Noble for his generous and patient help in overseeing the conversion of the text from my own word processor to the format required by the Press.

Contents

1. The Early Jowett — 1
2. Education and Reform — 26
3. The Pauline Commentaries — 45
4. Essays and Reviews — 69
5. Master — 95
6. A Liberal Gospel — 121
7. Disciples — 152
8. Darwinism and Faith — 182
9. After Jowett — 209

Bibliography — 233

Index — 239

I

The Early Jowett

Benjamin Jowett was born in Camberwell on 15 April 1817.[1] He was the son of a not very successful small businessman (first furrier, then printer) and was educated at St Paul's School. He entered Balliol as a scholar in October 1836,[2] and spent virtually the whole of the rest of his life in the college, of which he became master in 1870. His mother lived until 1869 (his father had died ten years before that) and he was a dutiful and affectionate son. But one gets the impression that his home and family were not really among the things which mattered most to Jowett. And since, moreover, he never married, the college was always the focal point of his life.

It was also, in an unusual degree, a factor in the development of his thought. Up to about 1850 most of Jowett's ideas seem to have taken shape through a series of close friendships. He and his friends planned and sometimes produced joint works of scholarship; and in many ways Jowett seems always to have worked best in co-operation with other people. Most of these became his friends because they, too, were members of the college. Though the educational system with which he was involved, whether as pupil or as young don, was conventional and conformist, the college provided him with a wide variety of congenial and clever people who were not. This is not to say that Jowett was devoid of originality. He possessed a fertile mind but he seems to have had particular need of other minds to act as stimulus and catalyst.

After 1854 he became, largely through his own fault, a lonelier person. His closest companions were his pupils (or former pupils)

---

[1] For biographies of Jowett see [E.] Abbott and [L.] Campbell, [*The Life and Letters of Benjamin Jowett*, 2 vols., London 1897] and [G.] Faber, [*Jowett, a Portrait with Background*, London 1957].

[2] Jowett appears in the college register under 1835, when he was actually elected into his scholarship.

rather than his contemporaries—though of course they were still Balliol men. And the role of the college in his life shifted subtly in consequence. Balliol became an instrument in what he hoped to achieve, rather than the context which formed him. He was a professional philosopher and theologian. Because he found the required conformism of Oxford too confining a context for his thought, it became one of his aims to create an academic institution, free from religious tests but nevertheless genuinely religious in spirit. This implied using Balliol as an instrument for his theology and this means that any study of his religious ideas is bound to concern itself with what he was doing in, and planning for, his college.

In fact one of the recurring themes of Jowett's life was his belief that the reform of the university was a religious or theological necessity as well as a practical one. He is chiefly remembered as an academic who was anxious to raise intellectual standards. But that was only one aspect of his concern for reform: the religious aspect was just as important to him. For him and his opponents, indeed, the two were inextricably linked.

Nineteenth-century Oxford had retained much of the form of a medieval university. Beneath the way in which it functioned there lay the tacit assumption that a university was an integral part of the Church; that all teaching was founded upon a religious base so that human learning might express eternal truth; that everyone within the university community should accept that eternal truth; and that it was the function of that community to maintain it.

This essentially medieval idea of the nature of a university was hardly, of course, maintained in its original purity in nineteenth-century Oxford. Oaths and religious tests, academic instruction and examinations, the style of the fellows' lives, and the autonomy of colleges, had altered almost beyond recognition. But there was enough of the substructure left for it to be a reality and, in a sense, it was actually reinforced by certain reforms introduced at the beginning of the century and by the ideas given prominence by the Tractarian movement. It was still very much an organ of the Church. Its teachers were clergymen. Its members were bound to the Church's standards of orthodoxy and were required to attend its worship.

At the same time, there was little real devotional fervour. It would be difficult to regard the daily life of the average undergraduate or don as a reflection of religious commitment. Nor did academic study appear to spring from deep faith. Oxford religion was largely a series of formal exercises and the theory that the university represented the intellectual life of the Church was little more than a theory.

Jowett came to believe that the business of the academic was to enquire after truth and that this ought to be the case in theology as in any other discipline. It was a matter of searching for genuine religious understanding rather than of accepting received opinion. But he was also the kind of person to whom religious feeling and moral behaviour mattered a very great deal. Again and again he felt himself caught in a trap where he was forced to accept formal religious tests which seemed to him, by their very nature, to stifle rather than encourage real religious feeling or genuine intellectual enquiry.

It became his ambition to create an educational institution where the intelligent and critical could pursue their studies in a genuinely religious context. There was no university in England where quite that possibility existed. Even the new universities and colleges which were founded in his lifetime were either self-consciously secular and attempted to exclude religion from their life altogether; or were as determined as any ancient university to insist on religious conformity. F. D. Maurice's enforced departure from King's College London, because he would not accept conventional views about eternal punishment, was a manifestation of such a determination. Jowett wanted a university and a college in which religion and rational enquiry did not conflict; where one would not be forced to conform to a dead ecclesiasticism or become either a rebel or a hypocrite; but where the life and the ethos of the place would actively encourage the spiritual as well as the intellectual development of the young.

When Jowett was an undergraduate the training provided at Oxford was the product of a reform of the examination system undertaken at the very beginning of the nineteenth century.[3] It was

[3] For a description of the system see [S.] Rothblatt, ['The Student Sub-Culture and the Examination System in Early Nineteenth Century Oxbridge', in L. Stone

an essentially conservative rather than radical reform, for all that the precise motivation behind its adoption is not known.[4] Nor is its conservatism surprising. The politically restless, if academically somewhat dormant, Oxford of the eighteenth century had recently become a Tory stronghold of loyalty to Crown and Church, so that by 1797 even Fox himself had almost given up hope of keeping Whiggism alive in Oxford.[5] The ecclesiasticism of Oxford was not only very formal; it was also an expression of a political attitude.

The heart of the reform was the creation of a new honour school in *Literae Humaniores* in which a demanding written examination replaced the last formal (and almost farcical) vestiges of the ancient practice by which candidates for a degree were supposed to display their learning in debate. In spite of a growing recognition that the undergraduates were young adults who could not simply be treated as children, the chief emphasis was now to be placed upon the acquiring of knowledge and of what were regarded as the correct answers. The detailed study of classical texts was what mattered. Excitement about ideas, whether one's own or anyone else's, was less important. Nor was it only in the final examination that competitive ability was recognised. There was an increasing number of prize exercises of one sort and another by which academic achievement was rewarded.[6]

The syllabus required a study of Greek and Roman literature, moral philosophy, logic (chiefly Aristotle), the elements of mathematics and physics, and of religion and the doctrinal articles. Those fellows of colleges who had been appointed to hold the office of tutor—and the appointment was usually in the gift of the head of the college—delivered catechetical lectures upon the prescribed texts, working through a book line by line and then questioning the

---

(ed.), *The University and Society*, Princeton 1974,] pp. 247ff. and [A. J.] Engel, [*From Clergyman to Don: The Rise of the Academic Profession in Nineteenth Century Oxford*, Oxford 1983,] pp. 3ff.

[4] [W. R.] Ward, [*Victorian Oxford*, London 1965,] p. 12.

[5] Ward, p. 5.

[6] Rothblatt, p. 288.

undergraduates about what they had been told. By 1834 catechetical exercises of this kind appear to have taken up two full days of the Balliol undergraduate's working week.[7]

In one sense, educational standards actually declined after the end of the eighteenth century. Such teaching as had been given in professorial lectures on the natural sciences had little relevance to the examination, particularly after mathematics and physics were made a separate school in 1807. Few undergraduates, therefore, bothered to go to the lectures, though Balliol seems to have had a college rule requiring some attendance at them.[8] What one had to do, whether one was reading for a pass degree or for Greats (the other alternative), was to master a body of information, chiefly in religion and humane letters, in which received truth rather than originality was emphasised. If one was clever enough to satisfy the Greats examiners, one might choose to sit a second examination in mathematics and basic physical science.

Another effect of the new examination system was to reveal the weakness of Oxford teaching. The vast majority of fellows of colleges were clergymen, or had undertaken to be ordained within a fixed period of their election. There was no requirement that they should do any teaching or even necessarily engage in study of their own. The catechetical classes given by the tutors were simply insufficient for the purposes of the examination. Nor was the standard of tuition very high, to judge by the reactions of Sir William Hamilton, an undergraduate at Balliol in about 1810 and later one of Oxford's most severe critics.[9] And Robert Lowe (Chancellor of the Exchequer in Gladstone's first administration and a close friend of Jowett's) complained that the catechetical lectures were 'inexpressibly tedious and disgusting to the more forward student'.[10] The whole system must have been as boring for the tutors as for the undergraduates, for they were required to teach a large variety of subjects and were given no opportunity to specialise.

Undergraduates who wished to pass the examination needed

---

[7] Ward, p. 90.
[8] Ward, p. 108.
[9] Ward, p. 82.
[10] Quoted in Engel, p. 40.

more help than colleges provided and were virtually compelled to hire themselves private coaches who would give them personal tuition. R. D. Hampden, the notorious liberal of the future, had achieved the almost unprecedented distinction—some two decades before Jowett himself took the examination—of a double first without the services of a private tutor.[11] Nor were the senior members of the university much interested in the undergraduates at a personal level. Donnish interest in encouraging team games in colleges did not really develop until the Victorian era. Even the tutors did not regard it as part of their duty to cultivate the friendship of undergraduates and, indeed, the undergraduates seem to have had very little respect for the fellows of their colleges. Not until the Oriel of the 1830s was there the kind of close affection between tutors and pupils which was to be such a feature of mid-century Oxford.[12]

Jowett, of course, read Greats which—for all the limitations of the examination and teaching system—was nevertheless one of the few rigorous academic courses available in the England of the first half of the nineteenth century. It is clear that he possessed a keen intelligence and a relatively well-trained one. At nineteen he was probably one of the older undergraduates in the college, though the average age as well as the overall numbers of undergraduates had been rising in the first quarter of the century. If surviving pictures are anything to go by he was rather 'pretty' in his youth. As he grew older he developed a very distinctive appearance and even the serious portraits of him often have something of the caricature about them—not much chin: a rather pompous expression. He was not strongly built, either. Slight, not very tall, with small hands and feet, he cannot have looked the strong, powerful personality that the Jowett legend would lead one to expect.

The master of the college when Jowett went up to Balliol was Richard Jenkyns. Jowett is usually remembered as the master responsible for making Balliol the great centre of intellectual achievement which it was to become by the end of the nineteenth century. But it was really Jenkyns and his predecessor, John Parsons,

[11] Ward, p. 93.
[12] Rothblatt, p. 264.

who laid the foundations upon which Jowett was to build[13]—though not, perhaps in quite the way that they would have wished.

Parsons had been one of the prime movers in the reform of the early years of the century.[14] The college was very small when he became master in 1798—probably not more than thirty-five in total, including fellows and bachelors as well as undergraduates. Its affairs were far from healthy and its scholars and fellows were not people of much academic distinction or ability. Many of them were appointed through an arrangement whereby Blundell's School in Tiverton had acquired not only two scholarships but also the right for those scholars to succeed to vacant fellowships. Since fellows did not stay very long but moved on to college livings, vacancies occurred fairly frequently. A large number of Balliol fellowships had, therefore, come to be filled by men from Blundell's.

By the time Jenkyns took over in 1819, the struggle to improve the quality of fellows had begun and the size of the college had grown to about fifty. Jenkyns was once described by Dean Church as 'an unfailing judge of a clever man as a jockey might be of a horse'.[15] By the time he died in 1854 not only had numbers begun to rise towards one hundred but the report of the royal commission of 1852 said,

Balliol, which now enjoys so high a reputation was at the beginning of the present century regarded as one of the worst Colleges in Oxford. Its Fellowships and Scholarships, which were long bestowed as matters of personal favour, were, we believe, first thrown open to public competition by the exertions of its late and its present Head . . . [so that it has become] . . . the most distinguishing characteristic of this Foundation that it is peculiarly free from all restrictions which might prevent the elections of the best candidates to its Headship, Fellowships, Scholarships, and even to its Visitorship. The result of this has been that Balliol, which is one of the smallest Colleges in Oxford, as regards its Foundation, is certainly at present the most distinguished . . .[16]

[13] [John] Jones, ['Sound Religion and Useful Learning: The rise of Balliol under John Parsons and Richard Jenkyns, 1798–1854', in John Prest (ed.),] *Balliol Studies*, [London 1982,] pp. 89ff.

[14] Rothblatt, p. 286.

[15] [H. W. C.] Davis, [*History of Balliol College*, revised by R. H. C. Davis and R. Hunt, Oxford 1963,] p. 183.

[16] Quoted by Jones in *Balliol Studies*, pp. 117f.

The reform and excellence at which Parsons and Jenkyns aimed was essentially of that conservative kind, emphasising received orthodoxy and success in examinations, which had been embodied in the reforms of early nineteenth-century Oxford. These reforms were not so much a stage on the way towards the drastic overhaul of the university in the mid-Victorian period, for which Jowett himself was to strive so hard, as something undertaken for almost entirely opposite reasons.[17]

Perhaps the least conservative and most creative element within the university in the early nineteenth century were the Noetics of Oriel College. Edward Copleston (provost of the college from 1814 and subsequently—and at the same time—dean of St Paul's and Bishop of Llandaff) was the nucleus of a scintillating group of fellows. The group included Richard Whately, R. D. Hampden, Thomas Arnold, and Edward Hawkins (always, perhaps, a somewhat secondary figure, even after succeeding Copleston as provost in 1828). Generally Whig in political sympathies, their chief concern in the sphere of religion was to provide a sound basis in inductive reasoning for the construction of a natural theology.[18] They sought some means of demonstrating a rationally justifiable connection between what they called the 'facts' of nature and revelation and the 'theories' by which Christian tradition had interpreted them or had derived doctrines from them. But a connection, in that sense, also implied a distinction. Inevitably the doctrines were made to appear less authoritative than the revelation itself and of manifestly secondary importance.

A similar distinction was to become part of Jowett's approach to scripture as he developed it in his contribution to *Essays and Reviews* and he may have derived it through Arnold's *Principles of Church Reform*. In that work Arnold took a typically Noetic line, maintaining that any attempt to formulate a dogmatic position was bound to

---

[17] Rothblatt, p. 303.

[18] For the theology of the Noetics see [P.] Corsi, ['Natural Theology, Methodology of Science and the Question of Species in the Works of the Reverend Baden Powell', Oxford University D. Phil. thesis, 1980]. For links between Whigs, Broad Churchmen, and the question of university reform see R. Brent, 'The Emergence of Liberal Anglican Politics: The Whigs and The Church, 1830–1841', Oxford University D. Phil. thesis, 1984, n.b. pp. 153ff. and 161ff.

create differences of opinion: doctrinal conclusions could never be so conclusively demonstrated as to remove all possibility of disagreement.

Like the Tractarians later, the Noetics made serious and determined efforts to publicise their views and extend their influence in the university and in society at large. The chief vehicle for their opinions was the *London Review*, started in 1828, but it never had anything like the widespread circulation of the Tracts. The Noetics were probably at the height of their influence, at least within Oxford itself, in the years between 1825 and 1829. One of their tactics, an idea of Copleston's which Whately in fact turned into a practical reality, was to take over St Alban's Hall, of which Whately became principal in 1825. Within the independence of the Oxford college system this gave them a means of propagating their ideas about education and theology which could not be obstructed by a reactionary resistance to all change. In a sense, what Arnold was to do at Rugby and Jowett at Balliol were even more spectacular versions of the same tactic—using an educational institution to propagate Broad Church religion.

In spite of their Whig politics and their liberal reputation in religion, the Noetics were far from radical. In fact a generally conservative tendency is detectable in much of what they thought and did. Though their views on dogma led them to insist, for the most part, that any authority possessed by the Thirty-nine Articles was not a divine one and though many of them supported the admission of dissenters to the university, they were by no means straightforwardly in favour of change. Copleston had had much to do with the framing of the examination system at Oxford. Whately, though opposed to establishment, believed that every member of the Church of England should be required to leave if he would not accept the literal sense of the Thirty-nine Articles.[19] Hawkins proposed in 1830 that a declaration of loyalty to the Church of England should be substituted for subscription of the Articles, a suggestion which, curiously enough, was to be repeated at Balliol in the 1850s by Robert Scott, not at all a man of the Noetic cast of mind.[20] And in

[19] Corsi, p. 119.
[20] Corsi, p. 141.

the 1840s Copleston would exchange sympathetic letters, complaining about the iniquities of Tractarian tutors, with Richard Jenkyns, Scott's conservative predecessor as master of Balliol.[21]

The Noetics' attempts to develop a new natural theology were not initially unacceptable to High Churchmen. John Keble had been a fellow of Oriel since 1811 without being too ill at ease in their company. Newman joined him there in 1822 and Hurrell Froude in 1826. Baden Powell, who also had High Church connections, was to be associated with the Oriel circle when he became Savilian Professor of Geometry in 1827.

The Oriel constellation broke up under the pressure of the events of the late 1820s and early 1830s, when—in the nation at large— campaigns for both reform and the preservation of the status quo troubled English society. What happened in Oxford was, in a sense, a microcosm of that macrocosm: even apparently academic arguments were directly part of the struggle.

Within Oxford and Oriel one obvious source of disagreement was precisely the question of the relationship between dogma and revelation. On the one hand, Baden Powell's developing ideas on science and religion made it impossible for him any longer to regard the 'facts' of revelation as of the same order as the 'facts' of science.[22] On the other hand, the future Tractarians found the liberal approach of even the central Noetics increasingly unacceptable. And as early as 1829 Newman was declaring that an Easter sermon preached by Baden Powell on religion and science confirmed his worst fears about the tendency of Noetic teaching.[23]

This was, in fact, a clash between two sharply contrasting views of theology and the role of the university, with the more conservative of the Noetics in the middle. Baden Powell and Thomas Arnold believed that science and theology were two independent spheres of enquiry and favoured free discussion and an openness to secular and lay culture. Keble and Newman advocated an integrated

---

[21] Balliol College: Jenkyns I: Bishop of Llandaff to Jenkyns, 9 June 1845.

[22] For the development of Baden Powell's ideas see M. Ruse, 'The Relationship between Science and Religion in Britain, 1830–1870', *Church History*, 44, pp. 505ff.

[23] Corsi, p. 132.

Anglican world-view in which the Church, the nation, and the university would all have their proper place.[24]

But it was not the High Churchmen alone who were disturbed by Baden Powell's ideas. By 1835 he had come to believe that Christianity, though reasonable, needed to be purged of superstitious elements surviving from the ignorance of earlier ages. This purification, he believed, could be undertaken by science, not by providing 'evidences' in support of the Christian revelation but by putting natural theology on a firm base. Arnold, who thought Baden Powell 'a very sensible and liberal man', was almost the only member of the Noetic circle who supported him.[25] Whately, for instance, was highly critical of this approach, believing that it gave science far too final an authority, and the controversy between the two men continued till Powell's death just before *Essays and Reviews* appeared in 1860.

Baden Powell's attempt to find a synthesis between science and religion was, in fact, too radical for the older liberals of Oriel. He accepted that there were discrepancies between the scientific discoveries and the Bible. God, he believed, had only revealed those truths which man, by his own unaided efforts, could *never* attain to. Those things, therefore, which human enquiry was capable of explaining were not, by definition, to be thought of as explained by divine revelation. There could be no conflict. In effect this meant that religious truths, such as the corporate fallenness of humanity, were to be accepted on divine authority even if the polygenetic origins of man could be proved, as Baden Powell supposed, from scientific evidence.[26]

For Newman and his friends the liberal understanding of the nature of academic study in a university, of the relationship between Church and society, and of divine authority in relation to religious belief, was all of a piece. And in a very real sense they were right to take this view. Admitting that the truths of religion were open to free enquiry was bound to call in question the authority of revelation and of the Church. Therefore it was also bound to raise questions

[24] Corsi, p. 170.
[25] Corsi, pp. 168ff. and 199f.
[26] Corsi, pp. 191ff.

about the position of the established Church within society and the right of the university to insist on doctrinal tests of orthodoxy. Mixing some liberal assumptions with some traditional dogmatic formulations, almost according to individual taste, was bound to lead to an ultimately indefensible position. As events were to demonstrate, the liberals needed to provide themselves with a rationale within which the cardinal truths of revealed religion could be preserved. Otherwise it would be difficult, if not impossible, for them to maintain that they stood within a genuinely Christian tradition at all.

The Tractarians set themselves to meet the liberal challenge on all fronts. J. R. Griffin's attempts to show that the early phase of the Tractarian movement was politically radical, and that Hurrell Froude played a more central part in it than he is usually credited with,[27] has not met with much favour from most scholars in the field. But even if he were right, the radicalism he seeks to attribute to the Tractarians was of a very romantic kind. And the two events which have been labelled as the beginnings of the Oxford Movement—the meeting at Hadleigh Rectory and Keble's Assize Sermon—are and were much easier to interpret as moves in defence of the establishment and, therefore, as embodying an essentially High Church and Tory view of society. As Geoffrey Rowell has said, 'A Tory High Churchman like Hurrell Froude saw the Reform Act as pouring into the House of Commons "the turbid waters of sheer mammonry, democracy and republicanism".'[28]

The repeal of the Test and Corporation Acts in 1828, the emancipation of Roman Catholics in 1829, the triumph of the Whigs, and the Reform Act of 1832 have long been recognised as constituting a sort of revolution in English society. They combined to create in the minds of many a sense of the established Church being under attack. This was inevitably intensified by the much publicised and often justifiable criticisms of the Church and the establishment on the grounds that its great wealth was unequally and inefficiently used for

[27] J. R. Griffin, 'The Radical Phase of the Oxford Movement', *Journal of Ecclesiastical History*, 27, pp. 47ff. and the same author's *The Oxford Movement: A Revision*, Front Royal, Virginia 1980, n. b. pp. 39ff.

[28] [G.] Rowell, [*The Vision Glorious: Themes and Personalities of the Catholic Revival in Anglicanism*, Oxford 1983,] p. 1.

the benefit of a privileged minority. To preserve the identity of Church and nation meant defending the establishment but the establishment itself was in some—or perhaps many—respects indefensible and in need of reform.

The Hadleigh meeting led to the signing of petitions in favour of the preservation of the establishment. Keble's attack on the proposal to suppress ten Irish bishoprics labelled the government's attempt to alter or limit the established Church as an act of national apostasy. On the surface, therefore, they had a conservative character. But Keble was not defending the establishment as, in practice, it functioned in the England of the eighteenth and early nineteenth centuries. His was an ideal view of the establishment, in which the church was not subjected to the state but, rather, accepted by the nation just because it embodied divine truth. Froude, Rowell's example of the Tory High Churchman, was also the doomed, radical charmer of the Tractarian movement. When his *Remains* were published his dislike of the Reformation under Henry VIII, with which the establishment was identified in the public mind, was to bring notoriety on the movement as a whole.

It is not possible, therefore, to generalise simply about the Tractarians' attitude to the status quo nor is there any real contradiction between their early attempts to defend the establishment and their later disillusionment with it. In some ways, it is true, they looked back to the establishment of the seventeenth century, just as they looked back to the teaching of the early Church, but it was an ideal Church, an ideal establishment and, for that matter, an ideal university for which they longed. For all their concern for tradition and for a return to a more 'catholic' understanding of the Church, the Tractarians were primarily neither conservative nor merely 'high'. They were concerned, as Owen Chadwick has pointed out, for holiness, to make the Church numinous,[29] and were therefore also concerned for reform. When Newman published the first of the Tracts in 1833, its subject was the apostolic authority—not merely to advance a high doctrine of the ministry for its own sake but to assert the innate, independent, spiritual authority of the Church. The ensuing controversy between liberals and Tractarians within the

[29] [O.] Chadwick, [*The Mind of the Oxford Movement*, London 1960,] p. 28.

university was not a gratuitous piece of academic politics but a confrontation between two very different understandings of religion and of the way in which both Church and university needed to be reformed. The one attempted an unsatisfactory, piecemeal compromise with new ways of thought, but unsystematically and without an agreed theoretical framework. The other—equally unsatisfactorily—attempted to ignore those realities of the contemporary world which conflicted with their vision of the ideal. But it was no accident that the controversy, which spread so far beyond its boundaries, was also a controversy about and within the university itself.

The controversy soon spread beyond Oriel. In other colleges, not least in Balliol, the same confrontation between liberals and Tractarians took place and Jowett could not escape being involved in it. But there is curiously little evidence of his having taken very much interest—beyond the immediately personal level—in the great upheaval of political, religious, and university affairs which had coincided with his arrival in Oxford. Preserving Oxford for the Church of England and the establishment for the country were the crucial issues. The year when Jowett came to Balliol—1836—was also the year of the Tractarian campaign against Hampden's appointment as Regius Professor and that party seemed to be establishing a triumphant supremacy in Oxford. But there was also enormous pressure for the admission of dissenters and the Whigs were threatening to reform the universities as they had reformed Parliament. Even the Duke of Wellington was urging the colleges to get rid of some of their more obsolete restrictions.

Amidst all this it is surprisingly difficult to demonstrate exactly how Jowett's own opinions were developing on these politico-religious issues. Nor is there evidence to enable one to trace in detail the gradual development of his views from his early background, which was Evangelical, to his emergence as a liberal. But it is clear that his ideas changed and became more radical during his time as an undergraduate and a young fellow. Since Balliol's future academic greatness was not an achievement of Jowett's alone but owed much to his predecessors, he must himself to a marked degree have been the product of *their* efforts to improve the college—efforts which he later appeared to disparage. By the time he became master a very great deal had already been achieved, however incomplete it may have seemed to him to be. And in a way he recognised that this was so. Clearly he had a different idea of what constituted truth from that held by Parsons and Jenkyns. He regarded received opinion as a kind of fetter and truth as something to be discovered rather than accepted. But, while the brilliant younger fellows of Oriel, who developed the tutorial relationship to a new level of intensity, might be sceptical of the value of examinations, Jowett's Balliol never lost its older respect for them as a test of intellectual ability. In this he was genuinely an inheritor of the older tradition.

The Balliol senior common room which he was to join was not, in any case, simply and sharply divided between liberals and conservatives. Even on the purely academic level, the lines were ill-defined which separated the reformers from those who, like the Blundell's fellows, represented the eighteenth-century view of a don's privileges and responsibilities (or absence of them). Those who would have agreed, for instance, that the college must be academically above reproach were divided between the supporters of the essentially conservative course adopted at the beginning of the century and the radicals who looked for a much more thoroughgoing reform. The older and more conservative ideas of what a reformed college should be like are clearly illustrated by the fact that Parsons became bishop of Peterborough and Jenkyns dean of Wells, without either of them thinking it necessary to relinquish the mastership or, indeed, to cease to regard the college as their principal residence and responsibility. Balliol was, after all, part of the established Church. For Jowett, however, that kind of view of what the college should be soon became untenable.

He was elected a fellow of the college in November 1838, before he had actually taken his degree. It was the year of the publication of the first part of Hurrell Froude's *Remains* and excitement about Tractarianism ran high. Froude's private, unguarded views about the Reformation aroused suspicions of Romanising and the fact that Newman had written a preface to the work created the impression that the leaders of the movement approved. Two of the tutors of Balliol, W. G. Ward (the mathematics lecturer) and Frederick

Oakeley (the chaplain), were ardent Tractarians. The other tutors, Robert Scott and Archibald Campbell Tait (the future Archbishop of Canterbury), were—but for very different reasons—as vigorously opposed. Jowett, who seems to have been put up for his fellowship by Scott, was drawn into this controversy, though he was never more than one of the peripheral figures.

When Newman's Tract 90 appeared at the beginning of 1841 there was an attempt to persuade the university to censure the leaders of the Tractarian movement. Tait was one of the four Oxford tutors who published a joint letter condemning the Tract: Ward and Oakeley were among the Tractarians under fire. Tait was genuinely outraged by what he regarded as Newman's hypocritical disloyalty to the protestant tradition. But he was uneasy about some of those with whom he found himself allied, particularly a former friend of Newman's called Golightly. This man, who was actually Tait's curate in the parish of Baldon, took upon himself the task of whipping up antagonism to the Tractarians by methods of which Tait did not always approve.[30] Newman was censured by the hebdomadal board. The publication of the Tracts ceased but the furore continued until 1845, by which time Tait had succeeded Thomas Arnold as headmaster of Rugby. In that year Ward was stripped of his degrees by convocation for the views expressed in his *Ideal of a Christian Church* and Newman's Tract only escaped being condemned by the same body by the interposition of the proctors' veto. Ward, like Newman, subsequently became a Roman Catholic.

The senior common room at Balliol was bound to be affected by a controversy in which so many of its relatively small membership were protagonists. The master and Robert Scott were both opposed equally to the 'liberalism' of Tait and the Tractarianism of Oakeley and Ward.[31] Feelings often ran high, yet sometimes personal friendships seem to have survived remarkably well considering the extremes to which public and official action was taken. Jowett, in

---

[30] Lambeth Palace Library: Tait Papers: Personal Letters, vol. 77, fo. 54—a very curt letter from Tait to Golightly on the impropriety of using anonymous letters to the press, and cf. R. W. Greaves, 'Golightly and Newman, 1824–1845', *Journal of Ecclesiastical History*, 9, pp. 222f.

[31] Jones in *Balliol Studies*, pp. 109ff.

The Early Jowett

fact, disapproved of Tait's action against Ward and the other Tractarians in 1841. He wrote to Scott, who had become the incumbent of one of the college livings, lamenting that '. . . about the same time a year before we were united together in a different manner.' He told Scott that there were other fellows who, while opposed to Tract 90, felt as he did about Tait's action.[32] What is, perhaps, most interesting about all this is that Jowett was able to remain friends with Scott, Tait, and Ward—in the thick of the controversy—in spite of their very different convictions.

Ward, the mathematics lecturer, was a compelling, dynamic figure, half clown, half tragic hero. A clever logician with a brilliant intellect, he was all too often carried, by the force of his own arguments and the cleverness of his own wit, far beyond the point at which more sensible men would have rested their case. But Ward was not a typical Tractarian. He came to his Tractarianism, as his son was to point out,[33] through an early flirtation with the 'radicalism' of Mill and Bentham which led him in turn to admire Arnold's attempt to meet this radicalism by developing a liberal theology. Ward was later to come to the conclusion that Arnold's compromise between rationalism and faith was inconsistent and untenable; and this, in turn, led him to become a 'Newmanite'.[34] He was, nevertheless, to remain an admirer of Arnold's realistic and sensible approach to the Bible and particularly of his intense feeling for morality.[35] It may have been their shared and continuing interest in Arnold that made it possible for the friendship between Ward and Jowett to survive.

Ward, moreover, was a trained philosopher with a sceptical and critical approach,[36] which made him very different from other Tractarians and it would have been difficult for Jowett to level at him the charge he customarily made against them, that they were 'hazy'

---

[32] The letter is quoted in full in [J. M.] Prest, *Robert Scott [and Benjamin Jowett*, supplement to Balliol College Record, 1966], pp. 6ff. and is in Pusey House: Scott Letters, Packet 1.

[33] [W. Ward, *William George*] *Ward and the Oxford Movement*, [London 1889,] pp. 46ff.

[34] *Ward and the Oxford Movement*, pp. 78f. and also D. Nicholls, 'Conscience and Authority in the Thought of W. G. Ward', *Heythrop Journal*, 26, pp. 416ff.

[35] *Ward and the Oxford Movement*, p. 69.

[36] Chadwick, pp. 30f. and 42.

thinkers. Certainly Jowett felt a great deal of affection for Ward and was to describe him as having influenced him as much as Tait had done when he was a young man.[37] And it is clear that their mutual affection did continue and that Ward was even able to take up his friendship with Tait again.[38] Much later, indeed, after Tait had become archbishop, Jowett conceived a plan to invite them both to a dinner at Balliol for a reunion of old friends.[39]

Tait was a much more solid, down-to-earth, even dour, character than Ward, yet quite as difficult to label neatly. He contributed greatly to the way academic work was done at Balliol, both in raising the standards and in introducing a more personal style of teaching, creating something much more like the close relationship between tutor and pupil which had been established at Oriel and which Jowett himself was to favour. His role in 1841, as prosecutor of unorthodoxy, was an unusual one for a Broad Churchman,[40] though the disciplining of ritualists was to be a major preoccupation of his archiepiscopate. Geoffrey Faber, Jowett's most recent biographer, maintains that Tait was really an Evangelical beneath his liberal veneer,[41] but this is a serious misunderstanding of Tait's personal religious position.

Tait is probably not really to be understood in terms of English and Anglican religious parties at all. He had been brought up in Scotland as a Presbyterian though he developed a sympathy for Episcopacy. He came to Balliol, in fact, on a Snell exhibition, a seventeenth-century foundation intended to foster Anglican and royalist interests in Scotland by encouraging Glaswegians to further their education in the episcopalian south. What made him a liberal were his tolerance, an awareness of the world, and an unwillingness to be controlled by any clique. The well-known story of the tragic

[37] [B. Jowett,] *Sermons: Biographical and Miscellaneous*, ed. W. H. Fremantle, London 1899, pp. 137f.

[38] W. Ward, *William George Ward and the Catholic Revival*, London 1893, pp. 74ff.

[39] Lambeth Palace Library: Tait Papers: Personal Letters, vol. 92 fo. 264, Jowett to Tait 6 Oct. 1873.

[40] Strictly speaking the term 'Broad Church' is an anachronism in this context since it appears not to have been used until the early 1850s: see A. M. G. Stephenson, *The Rise and Decline of English Modernism*, London 1984, pp. 24f.

[41] Faber, p. 253.

deaths of his children, after he had become dean of Carlisle, illustrates his spiritual strength and self-discipline.[42] The part he played in the restoration of Carlisle cathedral is evidence of both intelligence and shrewd, practical common sense. Probably his personal religion and piety did not change greatly from that of his Presbyterian youth. He was no Evangelical in either the English or the Scottish sense, but something more like an eighteenth-century Scottish Moderate. Jowett, looking back from very near the end of his own life, was to describe him as 'a gentleman ... and very Scotch'.[43] He was very much the proponent of common sense in religion; theologically acute but not outstanding intellectually; devout and basically orthodox; a firm believer in a national establishment and very much opposed to popery.

Jowett was only twenty-four at the time of the excitements of 1841. He was not, of course, at any stage himself a protagonist in the controversy over the Tracts: he was primarily one of the young men to be influenced one way or the other by the more powerful personalities around him. While other people, even his own friend and contemporary A. P. Stanley,[44] were making their views known publicly, Jowett kept comparatively quiet. He objected to Tait's attack on Tract 90 because it must seem that Tait, by virtue of his office, was speaking for the whole college. But he also feared that, if it succeeded, it would have surrendered to the hebdomadal board the power to determine the *sense* in which the articles were to be subscribed.[45] This latter objection was very like that of Stanley to the later attempt to strip Ward of his degrees. But Stanley's beliefs led him to conduct a public campaign against subscription: Jowett's were only privately expressed.

Jowett had been brought up in the Evangelical tradition and in some ways retained an essentially Evangelical way of looking at Christianity. However much he might modify or abandon Evangelical beliefs his religious attitudes, at a deeper level, continued to reflect his early assumptions about what belief was. But, at one

---

[42] R. T. Davidson, *Life of Archibald Campbell Tait*, 2 vols., London 1891, i, p. 24.
[43] Abbott and Campbell, ii, p. 394.
[44] Ward, p. 108.
[45] Prest, *Robert Scott*, p. 7 and cf. Ward, p. 121 on Stanley's views in 1845.

stage, he was strongly attracted towards the Tractarians, principally because of his great affection for Ward. He once, indeed, described himself as having virtually become a Puseyite;[46] a danger—if danger it was—that he himself took seriously. Long afterwards he wrote to Tait, 'Supposing that the Tutors of Balliol had been all like Ward, where should I have been? [I] remember with gratitude that at the time of my election to the fellowship you helped to keep up some light of common sense in me.'[47] It was probably Tait's down-to-earth protestantism that Jowett was referring to.

Since Faber regarded Tait's liberalism as a façade he had also to suggest that Jowett lacked the perceptiveness to see through it.[48] In fact, Jowett seems to have understood Tait's position very well and to have realised that he would always be reluctant to be pushed into a situation in which he would be compelled to defend liberal *conclusions* as well as liberal attitudes. In 1845, when Stanley had drafted a pamphlet which might have exposed him to charges of Latitudinarianism and wished to have Tait's opinion of it, Jowett wrote to him, 'Concerning your pamphlet, I have spoken to Tait, who thinks that he cannot possibly judge without reading it. I do not think his opinion of much value in such a matter.'[49] It was a curiously prophetic remark. Twenty years later, during the controversy over Colenso's biblical criticism, Tait was to use the same sort of excuse to get out of an awkward situation but was to use it in a form which was quite openly biased. It was not his business, he told his brother bishops, to condemn a book he had not read, adding 'when I do read, I wish to read good books.'[50]

The young Jowett was plainly fond of Tait, and they remained friendly even when Tait had become a bishop and it began to look as though he was going to accept all the constraints of received orthodox opinion. Even Jowett's more formal letters to his old tutor contain flashes of reminiscence which recall, in affectionate terms,

---

[46] Abbott and Campbell, i, p. 74 and cf. Ward p. 131.
[47] Lambeth Palace Library: Tait Papers: Personal Letters, vol. 78, fos. 268–71. Part of the letter is illegible because of the way in which it has been bound in the volume.
[48] Faber, p. 253.
[49] Abbott and Campbell, i, p. 115.
[50] P. Hinchliff, *John William Colenso: Bishop of Natal*, London 1964, p. 104.

their relationship of half a century before. When Tait was made Bishop of London in 1856, Jowett wrote to say that he believed that he would be a good bishop 'because you are tolerant and keep your eyes open to what is passing around you; because I believe you will not suffer yourself to be surrounded by unfair men'.[51] But he disapproved of some of the ways in which Tait sought to express his piety, particularly his attempts—as Bishop of London—to engage in direct pastoral evangelism. When the see of Canterbury was vacant in 1862, Jowett expressed the hope that Tait was not 'to be shelved' (i.e. made Archbishop of York). He also hinted that his former friend and tutor ought to busy himself with major matters of ecclesiastical administration which would be 'of more real use than preaching to cabmen'.[52]

Tait, like Jowett, is usually reckoned a Broad Churchman but it is difficult to define precisely what it was that, theologically speaking, they had in common. One of Jowett's letters to Tait contains an affectionate and humorous postscript asking the bishop to tell Mrs Tait 'that "Latitudinarian" is a tremendous long name to call a fellow . . .'[53] By that time, at any rate, it looks as though the Taits had come to think of Jowett as much more radical than themselves. However much, therefore, Tait was the person who most influenced the young Jowett, possibly rescuing him from the 'dangers' of Puseyism and inculcating in him a concern for open-mindedness and common sense, there was very little theological common ground between them. Tait would have seemed to Jowett too careful and too conventional. Jowett would have seemed to Tait to be moving too rapidly away from traditional orthodoxy.

At a personal level Jowett was always very shrewd. Even as a young man he seems to have perceived not only that there were limits to Tait's liberalism but also to have sensed the reality of his personal piety, for all that it lacked the open fervour of Evangelical religion. His earliest surviving letter to Tait reveals the degree to which Jowett actually understood his former tutor's religious convictions, as well as providing some evidence for his own. It was

[51] Tait Papers: Personal Letters, vol. 79, fos. 25ff.
[52] Tait Papers: Personal Letters, vol. 79, fos. 305–8.
[53] Tait Papers: Personal Letters, vol. 79, fos. 25ff.

written from Paris in the summer of 1842 and its chief purpose was to ask Tait to arrange for some money to be sent to a somewhat impoverished Jowett. But it contains a short, possibly significant, and highly critical paragraph on the state of French religion.

What a sad Deistical set they are here—there seems to be no religion except among the priests and women and I think the latter very seldom confess. The other day I saw a priest with a rosary in the pulpit repeating with the congregation the same prayer to the Virgin at least fifty times.[54]

This is the kind of thing a young man writes to a former tutor when he thinks it is what the tutor might himself have felt. Jowett knows very well that Tait will respond sympathetically to his criticisms of Roman Catholic devotional practices. He also knows that Tait will disapprove of deism. Neither of them would have found it satisfying to substitute for faith in a personal God, a belief in a divine being whose responsibility extended to little more than setting creation in motion.

Throughout this period Jowett, who was ordained a priest in the Church of England in 1845, was very anxious to combat the idea that God might be conceived of as a distant, impersonal, uninvolved being whose existence could be accepted without that acceptance making much difference to life. He had a great friend called Benjamin Brodie, a scientist who was to become the Aldrichian Professor of Chemistry at Oxford in 1855. In 1845 Jowett told him,

What appears to me to make the greatest gulph [sic] between us is not your taking a rationalistic or mythic view of the Bible, or difficulties about miracles, or even prayer, but that you do not leave any place for religion at all, so that although you may hold the being of God as the Author of the Universe, I do not see how you would be worse off morally if Atheism were proved to demonstration. What would you lose but a little poetry which is a very weak motive to holiness of Life? And having shut yourself out from any moral relation to God as an incentive to Duty does this moral Atheism satisfy human nature?[55]

In another letter to Brodie of about the same date he wrote, 'I feel very deeply that one cannot live without religion, and that in proportion as we believe less, that little, if it be only an awful feeling

[54] Tait Papers: Personal Letters, vol. 78, fo. 175.
[55] Faber, p. 140.

about existence, must be constantly with us; as faith loses in extent it must gain intensity . . .'[56]

These letters were written just at a time when the problems of reconciling religious belief and scientific discoveries were being widely discussed. In 1844 Robert Chambers, the Scottish bookseller and publisher, produced *Vestiges of the Natural History of Creation* which not only contained much information of a popular kind about geology, zoology, and physiology but also argued for an evolutionary explanation of human origins. He believed that the creator had imposed upon his creation a 'law' of spontaneous development or complexification so that new forms of life emerged from existing ones, adapting to changes in the environment. It was not a theory which aimed at destroying religious belief: Chambers was concerned, indeed, to demonstrate that the natural law which he detected in creation was an expression of God in the world. But it was a somewhat deist view of the creator and it was unsympathetically received by scientists as well as churchmen. Baden Powell was almost the only academic to give the book a sympathetic hearing.

Jowett's letters to Brodie are very revealing about the religious beliefs and opinions of his late twenties. He was already aware that the discoveries of science might raise intellectual difficulties for the theist; he was anxious not to be forced into a deist position; and at this stage he seems rather naively to have thought that the way to deal with the problem was to compensate for a reduction in the number of *things* one could believe by increasing the fervour with which one believed them. The phrase which is, perhaps, most significant for the way in which Jowett's ideas were to go is 'constantly with us'. Jowett was to develop—perhaps because of his interest in Hegel—a theological understanding of the constant presence of God in history and in the universe. But at this stage it seemed to him that the acceptance of natural explanations for things would all too easily become a naturalism in which there was no real place for God at all.

The other important hint in these letters is that, long before Darwin and the attempt in *Essays and Reviews* to work out a proper

[56] Abbott and Campbell, i, pp. 114f.

response to new knowledge, Jowett had already begun to defend belief by an appeal to morality. Unlike Baden Powell, Jowett showed no interest in the actual content of scientific hypotheses. This is not really surprising. Baden Powell was, after all, a professional scientist: Jowett was not. His interests were primarily philosophical. It is true that the dividing line between science and philosophy was not yet clearly drawn. Nor was everyone yet agreed that scientific knowledge should rest primarily on experimental evidence. But Jowett seems simply not to have taken any interest in the factual content of the new knowledge. Like many of those who took the other side in the debate, his ignorance was sometimes to betray him into incautious argument.

In fact his attitude to natural science was always ambivalent and reflected other contradictions in his opinions. When he had become master, he was always concerned to provide opportunities for clever but not very wealthy young men to receive the benefits of an education at Oxford. But he plainly thought that the principal advantage they would gain was an ability to improve their position. It was social mobility rather than a radical change in the nature of society which he wished to promote. But to encourage people to study science might mean an increase in the number of undergraduates who would come from the industrial towns or grammar schools.[57] And, if their education was wholly scientific, they might fail to acquire the polish and manners of their social betters.

Jowett believed, in short, that the natural sciences did not contribute much to the education of a gentlemen—did not, indeed, broaden the mind and, thus, could not really be said to contribute to genuine education at all. He even seems to have thought that an ability in mathematics, though it might be evidence of considerable intellectual brilliance, was not at all the same thing as 'scholarship'—which he would have defined primarily as the amassing of knowledge (and especially philological knowledge) of the literature and thought of civilised man.[58]

As Jowett grew older he may have become more sympathetic to

[57] By the late 1880s this seems to have been a widespread opinion, see Engel, pp. 223f.
[58] *Sermons: Biographical*, p. 198.

the study of the sciences since it was complained that his vice-chancellorship in the mid-1880s 'was principally directed to the advancement of the cause of scientific and technical education . . .'[59] It may be true that he realised the necessity of building laboratories and providing equipment but his basic attitude to the natural sciences remained unchanged. Not until towards the end of his life did he show any real personal interest in acquiring scientific *knowledge* and, even then, he was quite certain that it was not very significant compared with the beauty of Plato's metaphysics.[60] One suspects that the young Jowett thought of science as being something like cooking and, indeed, the first chemistry laboratory in Balliol, where Brodie worked, looked very like a kitchen.[61] But he took the *results* of scientific enquiry seriously—even if he was not quite sure what they were. They must not be denied: they were part of truth.

[59] Engel, p. 221.
[60] Abbott and Campbell, ii, p. 431.
[61] For an account of early scientific developments in the college and university see T. Smith, 'The Balliol Trinity Laboratory', in *Balliol Studies*, pp. 187ff.

2

Education and Reform

Jowett's serious interest in education developed in the 1840s and early 1850s. He became a tutor in the college and discovered an enthusiasm for teaching. But he also began to think about education in the widest sense, what universities were for, how people ought to be trained for a variety of purposes, and how to test their abilities. In the 1850s he was to assist the Aberdeen administration in the reform of methods of selection for both the Indian and the British Civil Service.[1] Above all he interested himself in the reform of the university and the improvement of provision for proper teaching within it. A royal commission (part of whose findings have been quoted above) was to consider ways in which Oxford might improve itself and institute perhaps the most radical changes to which the university has ever been subjected. Jowett's close friend, Arthur Stanley, was to be its secretary.

At this time his friendship with Stanley was one of the most important influences in Jowett's life. They were working together on a projected set of commentaries on the Pauline epistles and developing joint ideas about the nature of the university and what part religion and theology should play within it.

Part of Stanley's significance in Jowett's life is that he represented a point of contact with Thomas Arnold. If the later Broad Church tradition can be said to have a founder at all, it was probably Arnold. More important still Arnold's religious attitudes had found expression in the school of which he had become headmaster in 1828 at the age of thirty-five. The educational tradition which he established at Rugby was founded upon a religious training but a religious training which was wide and undogmatic. It was designed to attract the middle classes and to inculcate in their sons a sense of their duty to

---

[1] Abbott and Campbell, i, pp. 185ff. and Prest, *Robert Scott*, p. 4.

serve the nation. That they might be good servants of state and Church, Arnold was concerned to emphasise the importance of a high moral character. The school itself became inevitably the archetypal Broad Church institution, setting itself to encourage Christian virtues, but reflecting that impatience with attempts to impose precise definitions of doctrine which had been so marked a feature of Arnold's *Principles of Church Reform* of 1833.

Though Arnold himself had been a fellow of Oriel, there began in the 1840s a long tradition of links between Rugby and Balliol. Tait and Frederick Temple each in turn became headmaster of the school after having been a fellow of Balliol: a significant number of clever boys (including Stanley and T. H. Green) came to the college from Rugby. Rugby replaced Blundell's as the school which most interacted with Balliol in the creation of a common tradition. And though this link began to develop long before Jowett was in any position to encourage it, what Arnold was attempting at Rugby might, *mutatis mutandis*, have served as a description of what Jowett sought to do later as master of Balliol.

Stanley, son of the amiable and liberal Bishop of Norwich, had been powerfully influenced at Rugby by Arnold's ideas. He was probably regarded by Arnold himself as the almost perfect example of the kind of boy he hoped his school would produce—generous, chivalrous, open-minded, intelligent; an intensely moral, deeply committed but undogmatic Christian. He was charming, good-looking, and popular. He was to become the ideal champion for liberal causes because it was so difficult for his opponents to say anything bad of him and expect to be believed.

Jowett, who came from a very different and much less privileged background, was plainly deeply devoted to his friend. It has, indeed, been argued that Jowett's feeling for Stanley was a homosexual one, repressed and unacknowledged.[2] The evidence for this is unconvincing and capable of being understood differently.[3] But it is clear that Stanley sometimes found Jowett's devotion rather stifling to his own intellectual development and his personal independence. Jowett was the person from whom he had 'learned more than anybody else since

[2] In Faber, pp. 213ff.
[3] For a full discussion of this point see Hinchliff in *Balliol Studies*, pp. 134ff.

Arnold's removal'.[4] Arnold's influence upon Stanley had been that of a powerful headmaster upon a schoolboy—an 'almost filial relationship' Stanley called it.[5] For Stanley, therefore, to describe Jowett as the person who had taken Arnold's place in his life, implies that Jowett's was the dominant personality. The letters that passed between them throughout their lives tend to bear this out. They are full of Stanley's asking, and Jowett's giving, advice about the next preferment likely to come Stanley's way. They never discussed what was to happen to Jowett, who seems like a fatherly figure watching what Stanley got up to; hoping to see him in a position of influence; and trying to prepare him as fully as possible for that moment.

All this suggests that Jowett was more likely than Stanley to be the leader in anything the pair of them engaged in. Since he probably possessed the more powerful personality and the better intellect, Jowett had a marked influence upon Stanley. But he was always anxious to know what Stanley thought and it would hardly have been possible for him to ignore the part that Rugby had played in forming his friend's character and opinions. Through Stanley he could begin to understand what Arnold's Rugby stood for, as a liberal Christian institution, almost from the inside. And he could begin to perceive how important an institution could be in disseminating ideas and, in consequence, how important was an individual who created and dominated such an institution.

In the matter of the reform of the university, there were many schools of thought within Oxford itself, or many different aspects of unreformed Oxford to which reformers objected. There were those who found it offensive that the university was the preserve of the Church of England, requiring subscription to the Thirty-nine Articles from anyone who was matriculated and restricting many of its offices to clergymen. Others were—or claimed to be—appalled by the slothful luxury of fellows' lives in archaic colleges in which little education was to be had by the young. To these the university seemed to be a reactionary home of privilege.

Within the university, there were three broad schools of thought

---

[4] Faber, p. 215.
[5] See G. Howes, 'Dr Arnold and Bishop Stanley', G. J. Cuming (ed.), *Studies in Church History*, ii, London 1965, p. 322.

among those who wished to see some measure of reform. There were those who thought that the main business of the university was to educate the undergraduates and therefore concerned themselves with building up the role of college tutors. There were those who thought that the power of the colleges was, in any case, too great and that what was needed was a far greater degree of specialisation among the university's teachers. They desired something much more like what they imagined the German universities to be and put considerable emphasis upon the professoriate and upon learned academic lectures rather than on college teaching. There were also those who thought that the proper function of universities was to encourage and provide opportunities for research or pure learning, not necessarily related to what undergraduates needed. They wanted the endowments of the university to be made available to the scholar rather than the teacher. A. J. Engel, who identifies these three interests, regards the reform of the 1850s as essentially a triumph for the college tutors.[6]

But not everyone fell neatly into one of the three categories. Jowett himself, analysing the varieties of opinion from the standpoint of twenty years later, pointed out that they need not necessarily have conflicted with one another.[7] And surprising people sometimes supported one or other aspect of a particular reforming proposal. The very conservative Scott seems to have favoured professorial research.[8] Jowett (who first became publicly identifiable as a liberal over the question of university reform) was also concerned to strengthen the professoriate but was equally anxious to maintain a close connection between learning and teaching and to preserve college independence. Mark Pattison, often Jowett's friend and ally in liberal endeavours, led the party in favour of endowing research.[9]

Most of the 1830s and 1840s was a period of pressure for revision of the examination system and of attempts at improving the way teaching was done. It had also been a period of agitation for and

[6] Engel, p. 55.
[7] 'Suggestions for University Reform: Memorandum by Professor Jowett', in [L.] Campbell, [*On the Nationalisation of the Old English Universities*, London 1901,] pp. 183ff.
[8] Engel, p. 42 n. 84.
[9] Engel, p. 106.

against the abolition of religious tests. A wide variety of reforming proposals were put forward though very few changes had, in fact, been instituted. The grievances of dissenters and the defects of the examination system remained.

In the 1840s Jowett began to formulate his own views on what was desirable. He wanted religious tests to be abolished so far as matriculation and the taking of degrees was concerned, so that dissenters might become members of the university. But he did not wish them to become members of colleges (largely, perhaps, because he thought that potential dissenting undergraduates would not be gentlemen). He was anxious that there should be an improvement in the standing, usefulness, and stipend of professors and that fellowships should as far as possible be opened to competition so that the 'best' candidate might be elected. He was also beginning to support the view (since there was a demand that Oxford should provide education for those who were less than rich) that there should be halls attached to colleges where life would be cheaper.[10]

These views were worked out in collaboration with Stanley with whom, by 1848 and 1849, Jowett was writing a history of the university and a plan for its reform. They recruited help from other liberals like Frederick Temple and Goldwin Smith (whom Jowett never much liked) and thus formed the nucleus of a small, loose alliance. What they aimed at was the abolition of doctrinal tests and a broadening of the university's academic interests through the professoriate, without abandoning college control of teaching.

In March 1848 Jowett and Stanley published—but anonymously—a pamphlet entitled *Suggestions for an Improvement of the Examination Statute* which embodied some of their ideas, particularly on the broadening of the university's range of disciplines. The history on which they were working does not seem to have survived: at any rate there is no trace of it among Jowett's papers, though there are references to it in his correspondence with Stanley.[11] It was never published nor even completed since it was overtaken by the appointment of the commission to reform the

[10] Ward, p. 140.
[11] Balliol College: Jowett MSS: Box E, letters of 1848 and 1849.

university.[12] But it provided a solid foundation for their opinions, enabling them to argue effectively from an informed position.

Their concept of a reformed university was closely linked with another project in which they were engaged together, a series of commentaries on the Pauline epistles which will be discussed in the next chapter. In almost daily contact with each other (for Stanley was a fellow of University College until he was made a canon of Canterbury in 1851) Jowett and Stanley were engaged in nothing less than a reconstruction of theology. And, in this, the reconstruction of the university was an essential part.

Stanley inherited the idea of the Pauline commentaries from Dr Arnold.[13] He had written a life of Arnold, which had appeared in 1844 and was quickly reprinted in several further editions. That biography records the fact that Arnold, having begun work on a translation of the epistles to the Thessalonians in 1836, was actually planning a complete 'Rugby edition' of the Pauline writings in 1841, the year of his death.[14] The commentaries and the proposals for university reform both owed much to Arnold and were really part of a single, more comprehensive approach to theology. The evidence for this is to be found in the friends' *Suggestions*, which included a proposal for the introduction of a new school of theology in the university.

Jowett wrote the preface to the pamphlet. In it he argued for an open approach to theology, advancing some of the arguments which he was later to use at greater length in his contribution to *Essays and Reviews*. He even employed the phrase that was to become so notorious and so much misunderstood twelve years later—that the Bible should be interpreted *like any other book*. 'Can it be truly said', he asked, 'that much has been done in this place for Scriptural interpretation, which seems to be the most hopeful mine in theology, and strangely enough the least explored? It would hardly have been an unreasonable hope that the meaning of Scripture, like that of any

[12] Abbott and Campbell, i, p. 177.
[13] Abbott and Campbell, i, p. 100 and [H. F. G.] Swanston, [*Ideas of Order: Anglicans and the renewal of theological method in the middle years of the 19th century*, Assen 1974,] p. 141.
[14] [A. P.] Stanley, [*The Life and Correspondence of Thomas] Arnold*, [6th edn, London 1846,] pp. 163 and 169.

other book, might by this time have become fixed, and raised above the fancies of sects or individuals.'[15] And the unifying factor between the two projects became even more clear at a later point in the pamphlet, where—to give, as it were, an ostensive definition of the kind of theology school they were proposing—Jowett and Stanley asked for 'a study of the New Testament after the manner of Dr Arnold'.[16]

When it is claimed that Jowett and Stanley were engaged on a 'reconstruction of theology' it has to be remembered that they were not so much—at this stage—advancing radical doctrinal conclusions, as coming to realise that their understanding of what theology *was*, was entirely different from that upon which both the constitution and the teaching of the university was founded. For Stanley and Jowett religious truth was to be discovered and tested rather than accepted and learnt. It was part of—and partly to be derived from—what the human mind was able to explore in other fields, rather than the basis for that exploration. This is the real significance of their proposal for the creation of a new honour school of theology which would be purely academic in its approach and not simply concerned with teaching or maintaining orthodoxy.[17] Up to this point, indeed, undergraduates had had no access to a degree in theology. Elements of religion and the Articles had been part of the course, but this was instruction in the doctrines of the Church of England. Degrees in divinity could be taken afterwards, but these were largely vestigial and purely formal exercises. Encouraging people to do theology as they might do mathematics or history was the radical thing.

Meanwhile, at the last moment so to speak, there was some revision of the Greats syllabus. In 1850, the very year in which the government appointed a royal commission to consider the university's reform, the school was reorganised so that 'scholarship' (i.e. the Greek and Latin texts) was examined at honour mods and history and philosophy in the final examination. This was chiefly significant in that it allowed, in the years that followed, a considerable growth

[15] Abbott and Campbell, i, p. 175.
[16] Campbell, p. 74.
[17] Ward, p. 147.

in the importance of philosophy at the expense of philology. Jowett was interested in enlarging the place occupied by Plato in the curriculum and the sharply contrasting philosophies of Hegel and Mill were both championed in Oxford. No place, however, was found for a new theology school.[18]

The commission was appointed by Lord John Russell but continued to exist after his administration was succeeded by the weak Aberdeen coalition. It consisted of Tait, Jeune the reforming head of Pembroke, J. L. Dampier to advise on legal points, Baden Powell, H. G. Liddell (well known for his support of radical reforms), and G. H. S. Johnson. Bishop Hinds of Norwich was its chairman and Stanley the secretary. Since most of the members of the commission were identified in the public eye as being, in some sense or other, 'liberal' there were many who regarded it as biased from the start. There were also those who treated any intervention by government in the affairs of the university as an improper interference in the independence of the Church, an infringement of property rights and vested interests, or actually illegal. A large number of conservative members of the colleges and university refused to recognise the commission by giving evidence before it. It is not surprising, therefore, that it was liberals like H. H. Vaughan, the Regius Professor of Modern History, whose views most influenced the commission.[19]

Jowett. submitted evidence to the commission. He urged particularly that the professoriate should be improved and made more important. He did not want to see Oxford ruled by a democracy of tutors but he wanted a reconstructed hebdomadal body and a share in the government of the university for the professors. Without surrendering his belief that there might be something to be said for colleges establishing halls where life might be somewhat easier for the poorer student, he told the commission that he did not believe that *private* halls could offer terms that would be significantly cheaper than colleges unless they were endowed.[20] He can hardly be said to have been outrageously radical in the views he expressed.

[18] Ward, pp. 213f.
[19] [E. G. W.] Bill and [J. F. A.] Mason, [*Christ Church and Reform, 1850–1867*, Oxford 1970], p. 32 and see also E. G. W. Bill, *University Reform in Nineteenth Century Oxford: A Study of Henry Halford Vaughan, 1811–1885*, Oxford 1973.
[20] Ward, pp. 157f.

The aims of the commission have been fairly and succinctly described as follows:

They sought to raise academic standards and to associate the University more actively with the lay professions, and they proposed to achieve these ends chiefly by improving the quality of Fellows and by encouraging new studies. They therefore proposed to open Fellowships to general competition, to raise their stipends, abolish undergraduate Fellows, limit the number of Fellows, and so far as possible relieve them of the obligation to take Orders. The effect of these measures, it was anticipated, would be the improvement of teaching in the colleges.[21]

When the report of the commission was published in 1852 one unforeseen effect was that it tended to drive Anglo-Catholics and liberals together against those, particularly non-conformists, who wanted much more radical reform. What united them was a determination to preserve the independence of colleges together with its concomitants, college control of undergraduate teaching and the power of tutors.

In December 1853 Palmerston, as home secretary, asked through Lord Derby (chancellor of the university) for the reaction of heads of colleges to the proposals. Richard Jenkyns at Balliol was obstinately reactionary. His fellows, he said, were full of reforming schemes with which he personally was not prepared to have any truck.[22] Jowett was, no doubt, among those reforming fellows but his devotion to the college and his conception of the importance of a tutor meant that he was not one of the most radical in the university as a whole.

The actual task of framing legislation on the basis of the commission's report was entrusted to Gladstone, the obvious choice since he was the university's Member of Parliament and Chancellor of the Exchequer in the Aberdeen administration. The tutors' association had Gladstone's ear, among them Lake and Woollcombe, fellows of Balliol. The association was frankly concerned to advance the cause of the tutors and Jowett regarded it as chiefly representing those who were most opposed to reform. This was, perhaps, a little unfair. The association did not want all power to continue in the hands of

[21] Bill and Mason, p. 32.
[22] Ward, p. 169.

authoritarian heads of houses and to that extent, at least, desired that some changes should be made. But they were not interested in improving the status of professors and they were not even particularly anxious for the state to take the initiative in the matter of reform.[23]

One of the strangest and least predictable events of these months was that Jowett made contact with Gladstone. Relations between the two men were always somewhat odd. They disagreed about so many matters and each was capable of making very acid remarks about the other. On Sunday, 25 January 1852, the feast of the Conversion of St Paul, Gladstone recorded in his diary that he had been to hear the university sermon, 'Mr. Jowett, very remarkable, but unsettling'.[24]

Jowett seems to have moved towards Gladstone in a rather crabwise fashion and perhaps the chief link between them was Frederick Temple. Enormously hard/working and energetic, intellectually able and also very practical, Temple was rather younger than Jowett and had been his pupil. He had been a Blundell's scholar at Balliol, the very symbol of the old unredeemed Oxford. But Temple himself was as much a reformer as Jowett. He was to become a leading figure in the Balliol-Rugby circle of liberals. He was elected a fellow of the college in 1842 and was ordained soon afterwards. From 1848 to 1857 he was attached to the department of the Committee of the Privy Council on Education (precursor of the Department of Education). For most of this time he was principal of Kneller Hall Training College, a new institution for training schoolmasters to teach pauper children in workhouses. He was to succeed Tait at Rugby in 1857—presumably a very sharp contrast to Kneller Hall—and to become Bishop, first of Exeter then of London, and eventually Archbishop of Canterbury.

Temple was another of those whose friendship was important to Jowett and played an important part in the development of his thought. To him Jowett dedicated the two volumes of his Pauline commentaries 'in grateful acknowledgement of numberless

[23] Ward, p. 181.
[24] [M. R. D. Foot and H. C. G. Matthew, The] Gladstone Diaries, [iv Oxford 1974,] p. 390.

thoughts and suggestions and of the blessings of a long and never-failing friendship'. There were many things that these two shared: lower middle-class background, somewhat impoverished circumstances, an interest in the education of the underprivileged, an enthusiasm for the philosophy of Hegel and a willingness to explore new theological ideas.

Temple had been a member of Gladstone's Oxford committee at the election of 1847.[25] Perhaps because of their close friendship, Jowett had voted for Gladstone on that occasion but in 1852 and 1853, when other liberals had begun to move towards an alliance with Gladstone's supporters, he had remained hostile.[26] Jowett took little part in the arguments about the commission's report which were going on within the university but he wrote to Gladstone in July 1853 on the subject of the Indian Civil Service, from which he was anxious that university graduates should not be excluded. His involvement in the whole business of reforming Civil Service entrance procedures had possibly given him a taste for influencing government activities behind the scenes. He wrote to Gladstone again on 14 December 1853 about proposals for reconstructing the university. Significantly, he was staying with Temple at the time when he wrote the letter and throughout the negotiations with Gladstone which followed from it.

Jowett was chiefly concerned at this stage to urge that a general measure of reform should be enacted before the colleges should begin to apply for individual enabling acts to carry out their own ideas of reform piecemeal. But when Gladstone suggested that he should set out his ideas more fully, Jowett took the extraordinary step of drafting an actual bill covering every aspect of university reform. In it he adopted the tutors' association's ideas for a revised hebdomadal body; proposed that foundations should be opened as much as possible and that one-sixth of fellowships should be suppressed to endow professorships. But he was still anxious that legislation should reform the whole university and not be left to the initiatives of individual colleges. He did not, therefore, like the

[25] Ward, p. 142.
[26] Ward, p. 142.

suggestion that there should be an executive commission to implement reform in the colleges after the broad lines of university reform had been enacted by Parliament. He argued that it would be almost impossible to find suitably qualified members for such an executive commission because any member of the university would also be a member of a particular college (and might favour it): anyone who was not a member of the university would lack the specialist knowledge required. The commission, he said, 'will work unjustly or it will not work at all'.[27] He still had no faith in private halls but thought the problem of poor students might be solved by multiplying scholarships.

Gladstone circulated Jowett's draft bill, together with his own draft, to all members of the Privy Council committee on education. It was an extraordinarily frank and honest act and one which gave considerable importance to the opinions of a relatively young and obscure don who had not played a prominent part in the preliminaries nor commanded a powerful faction in Oxford. Together with the opportunity to tender advice on Civil Service reform, it was Jowett's first venture into the corridors of power and his first taste of what it could be to exert influence on government.[28]

The final bill was introduced into the Commons by Lord John Russell on 17 March 1853 and was, in a sense, a compromise between the views of Gladstone and Jowett who both nevertheless supported it warmly.[29] The entry in Gladstone's diary for the day reads 'H of C . . . on Oxford Bill and Ways and Means. A good start for the first-named: thank God.'[30] The bill was criticised from all sides, however. Dissenters could complain that it would do little or nothing for them. Jowett's more radical friends disliked it, too. A vigorous broadside arguing that it was worth less than nothing was signed by Brodie and Stanley.[31] Gladstone's more conservative Tractarian allies were equally critical. Pusey measured everything in

[27] Ward, p. 192.
[28] I am indebted to John Prest, who has very kindly shown me material he has himself assembled, for this information about Jowett's part in the events which led up to the framing of the legislation.
[29] Ward, p. 193.
[30] *Gladstone Diaries*, iv, p. 602.
[31] Ward, p. 195.

terms of whether it represented a departure from what he regarded as religious orthodoxy. He had disliked any suggestion that there might be a theology school; objecting to 'history of dogma' (because it seemed to contradict the belief that the faith had once for all been delivered to the saints) as well as to biblical criticism.[32] Keble, however, was in general much less worried by the whole reform proposal than Pusey was.[33]

The act of 1854 committed the government of the university to an elected hebdomadal council on which all three of the major elements of the university were represented; removed many of the restrictions upon fellowships and opened them to general competition; aimed at increasing student numbers and making it easier for poorer men to come to the university; and made provision for transferring endowments from fellowships to the support of professorships. An amendment introduced by James Heywood, who had been campaigning for years to open the university to dissenters, allowed anyone to matriculate or proceed to the Bachelor of Arts degree without having to subscribe the Articles. Gladstone thought that this amendment, which altered the whole character of the reform, had succeeded because the religious census of 1851 had seemed to show that the 'national' Church only commanded the support of a relatively small proportion of the population.[34] The detailed reform of individual colleges was left to an executive commission, which would negotiate with each governing body about the amendment of its statutes. It was to be possible for colleges to continue to insist on any religious requirement they wanted.[35]

The only member of the original royal commission also to be on the executive commission was its chairman, Johnson, who had succeeded Jenkyns as dean of Wells. The appointment of the secretaries led to an interesting correspondence between Gladstone and Lord John Russell. In May 1854 Gladstone suggested that Stanley would be a very appropriate appointment but thought that it would be regarded as a declaration of war by many, even by those who

[32] [I.] Ellis, ['Pusey and University Reform',] in [P. Butler(ed.)] *Pusey Rediscovered*, [London 1983], p. 300.

[33] Ellis in *Pusey Rediscovered*, p. 310.

[34] Ellis in *Pusey Rediscovered*, p. 308.

[35] Engel, p. 56.

would accept someone of just as strong opinions if he were not so publicly committed to reform. Jowett, he thought, must have occurred to Russell as a possible candidate.[36] A few days later Gladstone was writing to ask whether Russell would prefer Temple to Jowett, though he was doubtful whether Temple could do the job while remaining principal of Kneller Hall. Of Jowett and Temple he said that he thought they were as alike in opinion as two such powerful and independent personalities could possibly be. But he thought that the government was in Jowett's debt, in particular, because of the help he had given at the start—though it was possible that appointing Temple might cause less a little less of an outcry.[37]

Gladstone went on to mention also the name of Henry Wall, another fellow of Balliol, and Russell seems to have believed that it would be best to appoint a dull but safe man. None of the people suggested by Gladstone was appointed, though, in the end, one of the secretaries of the new body was Goldwin Smith who had been associated with Jowett and Stanley when they were working on the history of the university.

Perhaps the most significant aspect of this correspondence is the evidence it provides for assessing the relative reputations of Stanley, Jowett, and Temple in the public eye. However much, in his friendship with Stanley, Jowett may have been the dominant partner, it would seem that as late as 1854 Stanley was the more notorious liberal. Presumably Jowett's earlier reticence (while Stanley made his views about subscription, for instance, quite explicit) accounts for the fact that he was thought to be less extreme. And this, in turn, may hint at something in Jowett's own temperament. Though he was shortly deliberately to embrace the role of controversialist, he appears never to have enjoyed conducting the actual debate in public.

Jenkyns's death in 1854 meant that the mastership of Balliol had to be filled in the same year as the act for the reform of the university was passed by Parliament. Jowett was a candidate but failed to be elected: Robert Scott was his successful rival. It was in some ways a

[36] BM add. Ms 44,291, fos. 180f., Gladstone to Lord John Russell 20 May 1854. I am extremely grateful to John Prest for drawing my attention to these letters.
[37] BM add. Ms 44,291, fos. 186f., Gladstone to Russell 26 May 1854.

very curious episode. Jowett was only thirty-seven and, while it is true that many heads of houses were elected at an early age and held office for very long periods, he was not someone with wealth or important family connections or other powerful outside support. Yet he—and his admirers—behaved as if the mastership was, in some sense, his right. Perhaps he and they had been misled by what the commission had said about Balliol being 'peculiarly free from all restrictions which might prevent the election of the best candidates to its Headship . . .'[38] Not that Scott, with his great reputation as a lexicographer, was in any sense academically unsuitable.

The election, like many of the crucial events in Jowett's personal life, presents problems which are difficult to resolve. It is often suggested that it was Jowett's unorthodox theology which was responsible for his failure, a theory that derives some support from the fact that Scott was the supreme conservative. But 1854—before even the commentaries were published—would seem to be really too early for this to be a powerful factor. It is possible, however, that Jowett's colleagues found his views 'unsettling', just as Gladstone did with his sermon on the conversion of St Paul. Jowett's biographers are at pains to point out that there is some evidence for supposing that as early as 1846 he was sometimes thought to be heretical.[39]

Since Scott seems to have devoted a good deal of energy, as master, to blocking Jowett's proposals for reforming the college,[40] it may have been the latter's concern for academic as much as for theological novelty which really turned fellows against him. Indeed, since Jowett himself seems to have seen the two things as very closely connected, it is conceivable that it was a combination of the two that frightened them. Moreover, the election and its aftermath displayed very clearly just how determined Jowett was to gain control of the college and institute his own policies and how vindictive he could be when thwarted. It is possible that something of this spirit showed itself a little too clearly while negotiations were still in progress.

[38] Above p. 7.
[39] Abbott and Campbell, i, p. 210.
[40] Faber, pp. 206f.

The problem with any theory which suggests that Jowett was rejected on account of his radical views is that his opponents had originally planned to propose Temple as their candidate. This hardly seems like a conservatives' proposal, even if Gladstone's assessment of the relative notoriety of the two men was correct. And it is also curious that it was W. C. Lake, later dean of Durham, who was responsible for persuading one of Jowett's supporters to change sides and vote for Scott.[41] Lake denied that Jowett's theology had anything to do with his defeat and, as Lake himself was a product of Arnold's Rugby,[42] and had some sympathy with theological liberalism, there is no reason to doubt the truth of his statement. Lake had also been a signatory, in 1850, with Jowett, Stanley, and Goldwin Smith, of a letter to Lord John Russell thanking him for appointing the royal commission.[43] He was not, therefore, opposed to reform nor afraid of associating with liberals. With another fellow of Balliol, the much more conservative Woollcombe, he had also been a leading figure in the tutors' association in the days when it was attempting to influence Gladstone towards its own ideas of how the university should be organised. It simply is not very easy to cast Lake in the role of leader of a conservative attempt to block Jowett's advance.

But the greatest puzzle of all is that Jowett seems to have been so convinced that he was entitled to the mastership. Scott was not really an outsider brought back from the country to prevent the election of Jowett. Nine years earlier, when Peel was considering Jenkyns for the deanery of Wells, he had feared that a vacancy in the mastership might mean the election of a Tractarian like Ward.[44] Jenkyns had let him know that, not only would the college statutes probably permit him to hold the deanery along with the mastership, but Scott was the person most likely to be chosen if he were to resign.[45] In a sense, then, it would have been Scott and not Jowett who was the obvious

[41] Prest, *Robert Scott*, p. 4.
[42] Ward, p. 130.
[43] Abbott and Campbell, i, p. 178.
[44] BM add. Ms 32920, fo. 410.
[45] Balliol College: Jenkyns I: Correspondence between the Master of Balliol and the Right Hon Henry Hobhouse about the vacant Deanery of Wells, 4 and 7 May 1845.

candidate in 1854, particularly as—at that stage—his public reputation as a scholar must have been much greater than Jowett's. Jowett's expectations seem to have been largely based on the fact that almost half the fellows of the college had been his pupils.[46] That in itself is a significant fact indicating the kind of personal loyalty that he believed to be implicit in the relationship. And, indeed, it may be that, with a very small electorate of eleven fellows, the whole matter was determined by personal likes and dislikes. Jowett's very determination, quite apart from his radical opinions, may have been enough to turn the scales against him.

His behaviour was often petty and petulant, if once he got it into his head that he was being deprived of something to which he was entitled. He was to behave in the same sort of way both over the failure of any British university to confer an honorary degree upon him and over his omission from the committee appointed to produce the Revised Version. And when a Dutch university offered him a doctorate, his official acceptance actually said that 'differences of theological opinion have prevented me from obtaining any similar honours in my own country.'[47] It is unattractively small-minded to assume that one has a right to something which is in the gift of others especially when one does not hesitate to say so; it is even more unattractive if one vents one's spleen on the recipient of the gift, the person perhaps least of all to blame.

Over the lost mastership, Jowett seems to have sulked quite openly. He withdrew from high table, common room, and chapel; and the governing body seems to have become two quite distinct parties—Scott's and Jowett's. For a whole decade the two men opposed each other on issue after issue. It seems clear that, on the whole, Scott's behaviour was far better and more charitable than Jowett's who, after all, owed the master a great deal.[48] Even the official college history seems to recognise both the bitterness of the quarrel and Jowett's sense of possessing a right to rule the college. Having set out an account of the various controversies of the time it says:

[46] Abbott and Campbell, i, p. 229.
[47] I. Ellis, 'Jowett's Dutch Degree' in *Balliol College Annual Record*, 1979, pp. 40f.
[48] See Prest, *Robert Scott, passim*.

After 1864 the deadlock came to an end. A single fellowship election turned the scale in Jowett's favour. Thenceforth to the day of his death there was no question of his supremacy.[49]

Nevertheless, early in the following year Jowett was still complaining to Florence Nightingale that Balliol was treating him badly.[50] It looks very much as though he had set himself up as a permanent and almost official leader of the college opposition. No matter how great his disappointment and regardless of any provocation Scott may occasionally have offered him, this was hardly graceful behaviour. It is possible that, when it was suggested that he should be a candidate for the mastership (for he does not originally seem to have thought of it himself),[51] he had suddenly realised that he might have the opportunity to make the college the institution he hoped for and that the destruction of this vision was more than he could bear. At any rate, during Scott's mastership, he used his role as leader of the opposition to push for liberal ideals.

One of the matters over which Jowett and Scott divided the governing body was the issue of tests of doctrinal orthodoxy. In the 1840s, when Stanley had been among those who campaigned vigorously for the abolition of clerical subscription of the Thirty-nine Articles, Jowett seems not to have felt as strongly about the requirement as might have been expected. He told Stanley that he thought it encouraged hypocrisy,[52] but he does not seem to have felt any great difficulty about subscribing himself or that he ought to take a public stand on the matter. Presumably he felt much the same about the subscription which was also required of everyone matriculating at Oxford.

The Balliol controversy developed in 1854 out of a proposal by the new master to require scholars of the college to sign a declaration that they were members of the Church of England. On the face of it, it seems a curious proposal. The Oxford Act of 1854, as a result of Heywood's amendment, made it possible for undergraduates to

[49] Davis, p. 193.
[50] Balliol College: Jowett to Florence Nightingale probably Jan. 1865.
[51] Abbott and Campbell, i, pp. 228f.
[52] Faber, pp. 152f.

matriculate without subscribing the Articles. But fellows and scholars still had to be members of the Church of England and colleges were allowed to retain considerable latitude in imposing any religious tests they liked on their own members. This particular controversy was, no doubt, part of Balliol's attempt to react to the provisions of the new legislation and it has been suggested that Scott's declaration was intended to exclude the dissenters whom Heywood's amendment would have allowed in.[53] But this is not a wholly satisfactory explanation because Scott's proposal would have applied to scholars, who were already covered by the act and by existing college requirements. Jowett claimed that it was intended to keep out the Presbyterian Snell exhibitioners from Glasgow. But, as this suggestion was made in a letter to Tait—himself a former Snell exhibitioner—it ought, perhaps, not to be taken very seriously.[54] Scott's intention may have been to prevent a college equivalent of occasional conformity—or he may have thought that, if people like Jowett believed that subscription encouraged dishonesty, it was time that some other test was devised which would really bind the conscience. It is even possible that the whole thing was simply a bout between Scott and Jowett, since it appears that there were whispers that the latter might soon lose his tutorship which was in the master's gift.[55] Jowett was certainly very angry, though he was still not willing publicly to declare that he had conscientious objections to all tests of doctrinal orthodoxy. He was, at any rate, prepared to vote for an amendment, put forward on the ground that 'old chains are the best', which simply required scholars to subscribe the Articles.[56] Scott's proposal was carried only because the master's vote counted as two votes. The opposition then appealed to the visitor who disallowed the imposition of any additional test.

[53] Ward, p. 201.
[54] Lambeth Palace Library: Tait Papers: Personal Letters: vol. 78, fos. 266f., Jowett to Tait 10 November 1854. The letter is quoted in full in Prest, *Robert Scott*, p. 9.
[55] Davis, p. 192.
[56] Balliol College: Jowett Papers Box E, an undated letter from Jowett to Stanley giving the names of fellows voting on either side.

3
The Pauline Commentaries

In the years between 1847 and 1854, while the royal commission was sitting and the controversial election of the new master was taking place, Jowett and Stanley were working together on their Pauline commentaries. These finally appeared in 1855. Neither Stanley on I and II Corinthians nor Jowett on Thessalonians, Galatians, and Romans would now be regarded as significant contributions to the study of Pauline theology, but there is no question that the work was of some importance at the time. For one thing, they abandoned the *textus receptus*, substantially the text of Erasmus and Beza, which had been used by the translators of the Authorised Version and by almost every English commentator since. This was a courageous as well as a scholarly thing to do, since pious sentiment had given a kind of sanctity even to the errors and inaccuracies of the received English text. Jowett and Stanley preferred the version edited by the German philologist Lachmann, which had been published in the 1840s and had used the oldest known Greek manuscripts, aiming to restore the text as it had been in the fourth century when those manuscripts had been in use.

Jowett became Regius Professor of Greek at Oxford in the very year in which the commentaries were published and his approach to the New Testament was essentially that of the classicist. He was concerned, above all else, to get back to the original text. His interest in philology and his classical training plainly influenced what he wrote. On Galatians 1:6, for instance, there is the comment:

Prepositions, when applied to place, have a fixed and definite meaning, or rather are the fixed and definite symbols of the meaning of the case which they precede. When transferred to the notion of cause, effect, manner, instrument, &c, they become ambiguous, and still more so when used to denote divine and spiritual relations. Hence, in the decline of the Greek language, and especially in the New Testament, they are often transposed, frequently placed in false antithesis . . .¹

Jowett was, of course, interested in what the epistles might mean and, particularly what they might mean in contradistinction to the way in which they had been interpreted in the past. (He deliberately refrained from citing the views of earlier commentators, even those of whom he approved, preferring simply to say how he understood each section of the epistles himself.) But he showed surprisingly little interest in the historical context and had little real knowledge of it—even allowing for the fact that hardly anyone in the nineteenth century was concerned to understand Paul in terms of Rabbinic Judaism. Stanley, who had some claim to be an historian and was later to become the Regius Professor of Ecclesiastical History, displayed more interest in history than Jowett—though it was not a *critical* historical interest.

The most exciting thing about Jowett's commentaries was that they turned St Paul from a text into a real person. Instead of treating what the epistles said as authoritative pronouncements written in order to be imposed on future generations of believers, he made it possible to see the apostle as a man who himself believed and experienced. Jowett may, all too often, have read Paul's words as if they had been written by a nineteenth-century liberal. But he also treated them as the remarks of a man who *felt* what he was writing not as a man who was laying down in advance what would have to be believed two thousand years later. It was presumably this sense of being in touch with a real human personality which led F. J. A. Hort to say that, whatever Jowett's failings as a commentator, he fathomed St Paul's mind and related it to real life in a way that none of the more conservative commentators—even Lightfoot—managed to do.²

It is clear that, in part, it was the influence of Thomas Arnold which was responsible for the way in which Jowett and Stanley approached the epistles. Stanley's attempt to recapture the historical setting of Pauline Christianity no less than Jowett's account of the

¹ [*The*] *Epistles* [*of St Paul to the Thessalonians, Galatians and Romans*, 2 vols., London 1855], i pp. 211f.
² A. F. Hort, *Life and Letters of Fenton John Anthony Hort*, London 1896, ii, p. 79.

'mind' of the apostle owes a very great deal to the example set by the former headmaster of Rugby and Oriel Noetic. Stanley's life of Arnold had appeared in 1845. In it he had included an account of Arnold's method of interpreting the scriptures. It was not, indeed, written by Stanley himself but had been contributed by another friend and former pupil of the headmaster's. Since, however, Stanley had included it without demur, he must presumably have regarded it as a fair description.

This account maintained that Arnold proceeded from three fundamental principles. The first was that one should—and could—distinguish clearly between the devotional and the 'scientific' understanding of the Bible. There was no reason to doubt that God could speak to the reader through what was written but this was an entirely different thing from the process of discovering what had been intended by the author. This implied the second principle; that one could and should distinguish carefully between the human and divine elements in scripture. This meant primarily, in practice, treating the authors of the books as real human beings situated in a specific context. Thirdly, doctrine must be the end and not the beginning of one's study.

Having established these three points, the account of Arnold's methods continued by recounting Arnold's belief that the 'scientific' understanding must be arrived at by means of the same historical methods and rules as would be used in dealing with classical authors (Thucydides, for instance) in which philology would be of primary importance. One's next task would be to give an account, in the language and forms of one's own age, of the 'thinking, feeling and acting' of the era in which the texts had been written. And, while one might and should possess a conviction that the texts were immediately inspired by the Spirit, one ought not to have any preconceived theory of precisely what 'inspiration' meant.[3] What Arnold said about using the same historical methods as one would with

---

[3] Stanley, *Arnold*, pp. 164ff. Stanley's informant, B. Price, cited as his authority for this account of Arnold's methods, 'the Appendix to vol. ii of the Sermons, the Preface to the third, the Notes to the fourth and the Two sermons on Prophecy' and also the posthumous volume of 'Sermons, mostly on the Interpretation of Scripture' (p. 169).

Thucidydes might serve very well as a rough, abbreviated description of Stanley's technique in the commentaries; and what he said about giving an account of the author's thinking, feeling, and acting, might serve as a similar characterisation of Jowett's.

Arnold was probably also at least partly responsible for Jowett's throwing in his lot with the liberal approach to theology and, indeed, to learning as a whole. The great gulf between the conservatives and the liberals was in their understanding of truth. For conservatives truth was that which was guaranteed by authority: in education, the authority of tradition and the teacher; in religion, the authority—ultimately—of God himself. Statements about metaphysical truths, thus guaranteed, could be made with at least as much certainty and precision as statements about empirical truths. But for liberals the case was very different. All truth was the result of human enquiry. It was perceived, formulated, and expressed by human minds. Therefore it had a tentative, provisional quality. And metaphysical ideas were to be seen as speculative and uncertain in a way that matters of fact were not. Jowett, who had grown up in an Evangelical family and in the very conservative educational tradition, based on authority and the transmission of correct answers, of Jenkyns's Balliol, made the very radical transition to the liberal viewpoint at some time in the late 1830s or very early 1840s. There is little or no direct evidence as to why this happened but it is possible that Arnold's *Principles of Church Reform* was partly responsible.

In that work Arnold probably drawing on John Locke, had said:

Whoever is acquainted with Christianity must see that differences of opinion amongst Christians are absolutely unavoidable. First, because our religion being a thing of the deepest personal interest, we are keenly alive to all the great questions connected with it, which was not the case with heathenism. Secondly, these questions are exceedingly numerous, inasmuch as our religion affects our whole moral being, and must involve, therefore, a great variety of metaphysical, moral, and political points:—that is to say, *those very points which, lying out of the reach of demonstrative science, are through the constitution of man's nature, peculiarly apt to be regarded by different minds differently.* And thirdly, although all Christians allow the Scriptures to be of decisive authority, whenever their judgment is pronounced on any given case, yet the peculiar form of these Scriptures, which in the New Testament is rather that of a commentary than of a text;—the critical difficulties attending their interpretation, and the still greater difficulty as to their application:—it being a constant question whether such and such recorded facts or practices, were meant to be universally binding;—and it being a farther question, amidst the infinite variety of human affairs, whether any case, differing more or less in its circumstances, properly comes under the scope of any given Scripture rule;—all these things prevent the Scriptures from being in practice decisive on controverted points, because the contending parties, while alike acknowledging the judge's authority, persist in putting a different construction upon the words of his sentence.[4]

So many of these ideas—the very personal nature of belief, the uncertainty of ideas which cannot be empirically demonstrated, the futility of trying to 'prove' doctrines from the Bible—recur so frequently in Jowett's writings that it is difficult to escape the impression that he derived them from Arnold.

It is clear, however, that Arnold's was not the only influence contributing to Jowett's radical shift in perspective. At about this time he also discovered Kant and was captivated by his ideas. In the 1840s he was urging his friends to read Kant and take him seriously. He and Stanley together made a translation of some of Kant's writings.[5] And as Ieuan Ellis has pointed out, the first edition of the commentary on Romans contains a long extract from Kant.[6] Jowett incorporated, presumably from the translation which he and Stanley had made, about a page of what the philosopher had said about the possibility of developing a science of morality. It would be difficult to imagine anything more incongruous in a commentary on Paul.

Jowett's use of Kant is revealing, not simply because it is an indication of his interests at the time, but also because it shows how he made use of ideas taken from the writings of others. The passage reads:

There are two things of which it may be said, that the more we think of them, the more they fill the soul with awe and wonder—the starry heaven

[4] T. Arnold, *Principles of Church Reform, With an Introductory Essay by M. J. Jackson and J. Rogan*, London 1962, p. 99. The italics are not in the original.
[5] Abbott and Campbell, i, p. 90.
[6] [I.] Ellis, [*Seven Against Christ*, Leiden 1980,] pp. 298f. and cf. *Epistles*, ii, pp. 413ff. The passage is not, however, as Ellis supposes, from *The Critique of Pure Reason*. It is the opening section of Kant's conclusion to *The Critique of Practical Reason*.

above, and the moral law within. I may not regard either as shrouded in darkness, or look for, or guess at either in what is beyond, out of my sight. I see them right before me, and link them at once with the consciousness of my own existence. The former of the two begins with place, which I inhabit as a member of the outward world, and extends the connexion, in which I stand with it, into immeasurable space; in which are worlds upon worlds, and systems upon systems; and so on into the endless times of their revolutions, their beginning and continuance. The second begins with my invisible self; that is to say, my personality, and presents me in a world which has true infinity, but which the lower faculty of the soul can hardly scan; with which I know myself to be not only in the world of sight in an accidental connexion, but in a necessary and universal one. The first glance at the innumerable worlds annihilates any importance which I may attach to myself as an animal structure; while the matter out of which it is made must again return to the earth (itself a mere point in the universe), after it has been endued, one knows not how, with the power of life for a little season. The second glance exalts me infinitely as an intelligent being, whose personality involves a moral law, which reveals in me a life distinct from that of the animals, independent of the world of sense. So much at least I may infer from the regular determination of my being by this law, which is itself infinite, free from the limitations and conditions of this present life.[7]

[7] A clearer translation of the same passage, but near enough to Jowett's in time for it to have something of the same style, reads:

Two things fill the mind with ever new and increasing admiration and awe, the oftenener and the more steadily we reflect on them: *the starry heaven above, and the moral law within*. I have not to search for them and conjecture them as though they were veiled in darkness or were in the transcendent region beyond my horizon; I see them before me and connect them directly with the consciousness of my existence. The former begins from the place I occupy in the external world of sense, and enlarges my connexion therein to an unbounded extent with worlds upon worlds and systems of systems, and moreover into limitless times of their periodic motion, its beginning and continuance. The second begins from my invisible self, my personality, and exhibits me in a world which has true infinity, but which is traceable only by the understanding, and with which I discern that I am not merely contingent but in a universal and necessary connexion, as I am also thereby with all those visible worlds. The former view of a countless multitude of worlds annihilates, as it were, my importance as an *animal creature*, which after it has been for a short time provided with vital power, one knows not how, must again give back the matter of which it was formed to the planet it inhabits (a mere speck in the universe). The second, on the contrary, infinitely elevates my worth as an *intelligence* by my personality, in which the moral law reveals to me a life independent on animality and even on the whole sensible world—at least so far as may be inferred from the destination assigned to my existence by this law, a destination not restricted to conditions and limits of this life but reaching into the infinite.

(T. K. Abbott's translation, 4th edn., 1889: the italics are in the original).

In the original Kant was drawing his attempted analysis of practical reason to a conclusion. From the point at which Jowett's quotation stopped, Kant had gone on to argue that the awe evoked by these two different considerations were valuable only in stimulating one to a proper enquiry into the things which caused it. The awe itself was not, he maintained, a substitute for clear and critical thought. In the case of the world of nature, awe without intellectual rigour had led to such things as astrology: science led to a more careful and rational examination and more satisfactory results. Since, in the case of moral sense, mere awe led to fanaticism or superstition, critical enquiry alone could lead to a similarly satisfactory understanding of practical reason. Hence his critique.

But Jowett did something quite different with his extract from Kant. He proceeded to offer a 'paraphrase' of the passage which asserted that it meant that there were 'two witnesses of the being of God: the order of nature in the world, and the [moral] progress of the mind of man'. Neither of these things actally *is* God but both are evidences of his being. Both nature and morality are expressed in laws. What unites the two very different kinds of law is the fact that they both point to God and are expressions of his nature. And so Jowett was able, at least to his own satisfaction, to reverse Kant's division of awe-inspiring reality into the external and the internal. In doing so he laid the foundations for a concept of God's personality as 'clothed in laws' which was to become a very important part of his thought. But his so-called paraphrase was also plainly a distortion of Kant's original, not only as to its immediate context but also in Kant's system of thought as a whole. He had seized on a few phrases, taken them over and allowed them to suggest quite other thoughts in his own mind. He represented himself as developing Kant's ideas: he was really expressing opinions which had very little to do with either Kant or St Paul.

The incorporation of this long quotation in a commentary on Romans is, however, explicable if Kant's seminal ideas had contributed to the radical shift in Jowett's own theory of knowledge. The philosopher had, after all, insisted that the orderly structure of relationships constituting the patterns of external reality come, not from that reality itself, but from the fact that the consciousness of the observer inevitably interprets the data it receives in such a fashion. He had also insisted that there could be no knowledge without an ingredient derived from observation of external nature: one could not know things which wholly transcended observed reality. Traditional metaphysics was undermined. Therefore no one could be influenced by Kant and remain content with the conservative approach to knowledge and truth. Indeed, as Ellis has shown,[8] Kant's influence was crucial for all the early liberals. It was this influence which caused them to lay such emphasis upon morality and which led them to take the view they did about the nature of human knowledge and thus conditioned their understanding of revelation. It must have seemed important to Jowett, in the immediate aftermath of passing through this revolution himself, to allow his readers to follow the same course.

But Jowett was clearly not slavish in his admiration for Kant's thought. Indeed, it looks as though he had already begun to get over his first excitement about the philosopher's work by the time he came to write the commentaries. He was to omit the long Kantian quotation from the second edition of the commentary, perhaps because he had come to recognise its incongruity in that setting. And it is probable that, even before the first edition of the commentary appeared, he had begun to feel that Kant did not provide all the answers. In later years he was to argue that Kant's distinction between sensations and objects of sense, as Jowett described them, was far too sharp. He believed that it was possible to hold together religion and the external world by means of a belief in God as lawgiver, responsible for both the moral and the physical laws. And he also apparently believed that it was possible so to modify Kant's thought as to turn it into a justification for paradox.

In all the editions of his commentary there appeared an essay on free will and predestination which makes it plain that he had already begun to develop this line of thought even while he was still very much in the first flush of an enthusiasm for Kantian philosophy. It is worth setting out his argument in his own words as he attempted to deal with the question of how it is possible for human beings to be finite and at the same time experience a sense of being free. He made

[8] Ellis, pp. 294ff.

it very clear that he recognised that there was a great difference between empirical and metaphysical statements. He recognised the vulnerability of theological language. But he could not accept that there were no tests that could be applied to determine its truth:

A subject which claims to be raised above the rules and requirements of logic must give a reason for the exemption and must itself furnish some other test of truth. The reason is that logic is inapplicable to the discussion of a question which begins with a contradiction in terms [knowing oneself to be finite yet free] . . . We often speak of language as an imperfect instrument for the expression of thought. Logic is even more imperfect: it is contrary to the plastic and multiform character of language, yet deceives us by the appearance of a straight rule and necessary principle. . . . But if not logic, then some other test must be found for our theories or reasonings, on these and other like metaphysical subjects. These can only be their agreement with facts which we shall the more readily admit if the new form of expression or statement of them can be a real assistance to our powers of thought and action. . . .

The notion that no idea can be composed of two contradictory conceptions seems to arise out of the analogy of the sensible world. It would be an absurdity to suppose that an object should be white and black at the same time; that a captive should be in chains and not in chains at the same time, and so on. But there is no absurdity in supposing that the mental analysis even of a matter of fact or an outward object should involve us in contradictions. Objects, considered in their most abstract point of view, may be said to contain a positive and a negative element; everything is and is not; is in itself and is not, in relation to other things and our conception of motion, of becoming or of beginning, in like manner involve a contradiction. . . .

How a new substance can be formed by chemical combination of two other substances may seem also to involve a contradiction. [He cites, as an example, that water is and is not oxygen and hydrogen.] Life in like manner has been defined as a state in which every end is a means, and every means an end. . . .

It is at first sight strange that some of these contradictions should seem so trivial to us, while others assume the appearance of high mystery. In physics or mathematics we scarcely think of them. . . .

But in religion the difficulty appears of greater importance, partly from our being much more under the influence of language in theology than in subjects which we can at once bring to the test of fact and experiment, and partly also from our being more subject to our own natural constitution, which leads us to one or other horn of the dilemma, instead of placing us between or above both.⁹

This rather opaque argument reads as if it were a looking-glass rendering of Kant's criticism of natural theology. It is possible that Jowett had begun to read Hegel and to be influenced by ideas picked up from him. Whatever the cause, he seems to be inverting Kant's argument that proofs of God's existence were invalid because they attempted to transfer to the metaphysical realm what was appropriate only to the empirical, and reversing Kant's objection to a speculative theology because it drew opposing conclusions from the same evidence and thus infringed the law of contradiction.

Jowett's extensive use of Kant, particularly in the first edition of the commentary, is the more extraordinary in that he made so little overt use of critical scholarship which, on the face of it, would seem so much more appropriate to his task. Jowett is usually thought of as one of the first English scholars to take account of German criticism. Because that is true it is the more extraordinary that he should have displayed so little concern for history and almost none for the application of historical critical methods to the epistles. Though he acknowledged an indebtedness to some of the leading critical scholars, including Ewald and F. C. Baur,¹⁰ he made virtually no use of their work in what he actually wrote in the volumes. He quite specifically denied that there was any development of a kind that could be called historical (and would, therefore, be of use in critical comparison) between, say, Thessalonians and Romans. Any development in the epistles, he asserted, was the development of spiritual life and experience, not an intellectual development. He was not much concerned, even, with establishing the chronology of the Pauline writings,¹¹ although there is a brief 'dissertation' on the subject in the first volume. Though he pointed out that Paley's work must be regarded as defective because he had not known that Acts could be 'dismembered' into its sources,¹² Jowett himself assumed—in his attempt to sort out the events described in the early

⁹ *Epistles*, 2nd ed., ii, pp. 599ff.
¹⁰ *Epistles*, i, p. ix.
¹¹ See *Epistles*, i, p. 3.
¹² *Epistles*, i, p. 10.

part of Galatians—that the chronology of Acts was accurate.[13] When he came to discuss the parousia in Thessalonians in an essay 'On the Belief in the Coming of Christ in the Apostolical Age' he did not attempt any kind of critical analysis of the eschatology of the epistles, or ask whether the later epistles have a less immediate expectation than the earlier ones. He contented himself with looking at the problem created for faith by the fact that Paul and Christ could both be said to have been mistaken about the second coming. And, even though he appended to the essay a list of other passages in Paul which refer to the second coming, he made no attempt to compare or analyse them.[14] As an exercise in biblical criticism the commentaries were hardly significant.

It is not surprising then that, if his readers were upset by his work, it was something other than Jowett's performance as a Greek philologist, textual critic, or historical interpreter which caused the trouble. What drew his opponents' fire were his theological opinions, and chiefly those contained in essays within the commentaries. For the most part, his actual commentary, even when it was theological or devotional rather than philological, was mild and inoffensive. Sometimes, it is true, his more radical attitudes show through. On St Paul's conversion, for instance, he wrote:

It has often been remarked, that miracles are not appealed to singly in Scripture as evidences of religion, in the same way that they have been used by modern writers. Especially does this remark apply to the conversion of St Paul. Not a hint is found in his writings that he regarded 'the heavenly vision' as an objective evidence of Christianity. The evidence to him was the sudden change of heart . . . The last enquiry that he would have thought of making, would be that of the modern theologian—'How, without some outward sign, he could be assured of the reality of what he had seen or heard.' . . . But we may remember that the belief in some outward fact [defined in a footnote as 'seen by more persons than one' or 'by a single person in an unimpassioned state'] was not the essential point in St Paul's faith, and therefore we need not make it an essential point in our own.[15]

Moreover, where the Pauline text gave him an opportunity to set out the theological and religious ideas which informed his own faith,

[13] *Epistles*, i, p. 143 cf. pp. 217ff., 229ff., and 253.
[14] *Epistles*, i, p. 96.
[15] *Epistles*, i, pp. 230f.

he seized upon the opportunity. Dealing with Galatians 3: 27ff., for instance, he expounded an idea which was to be central to his theology of the atonement.

> The figure of putting on Christ has a reference, first, to the robe in which the newly baptized person was arrayed on coming up out of the water, and recalls also an idiomatic expression in later Greek, of 'putting on another' to signify close and intimate friendship with him. . . . In one sense the believer is regenerate; in another not. His whole life is anticipated in the beginning, and still he may be exhorted to believe. . . . The whole argument from ver. 26 turns upon the oneness of the believer with Christ. This it is which makes him the son of God. This it is which is given, not to the Jew only, but to all mankind. This it is which is the means whereby he is made the heir of the promises to Abraham, the coheir with Christ, who is in a special sense, the seed of promise.[16]

Though these comments, when made in passing, might not have attracted much adverse attention, it was otherwise with the essays on specific issues which Jowett included in the volumes, particularly five pieces in the commentary on Romans.[17] They hardly help to uncover the theology of St Paul: they are outspoken and radical comments on contemporary orthodoxy.

A fairly clear and coherent theological position is set out in the essays. In spite of Jowett's doubts about the value of a scientific education, his determination to take the results of scientific enquiry seriously emerges very clearly. What is known to be true must not be denied simply because dogma requires it. His essay 'On Natural Religion' pointed out that far too many people lived as if there were two different worlds—a religious world and the world of actual experience—each with its own kind of truth, which seem never to touch each other. Religion and the real life of common sense, he said, are treated with different sets of words and ideas, as if it would be bad taste to allow them to intermingle. And this clearly set him in the camp of those who accepted a scientific world-view.

Science, he believed, was not something to be feared even by the religious: it had brought many advantages as well as problems. The

---

[16] *Epistles*, i, pp. 272ff.

[17] *Epistles*, ii, particularly the essays 'On Natural Religion', 'On Righteousness by Faith', 'On Atonement and Satisfaction', and 'Predestination and Free-will'.

very things which it *explained*, were explained in terms of 'laws', so that the universe had become a stable and predictable place rather than a mysterious and frightening one. It might be that all things did not equally exhibit the marks of design but all things are equally subject to the operation of law. Now that man knows that nature operates in terms of laws, there is no need to fear nature. It would be immoral—as well as foolish and retrograde—to try and draw men to God by ignoring the scientific understanding of nature and reverting to the state of ignorance and fear 'when men cowered like animals before the storm'.

The implied rejection of 'evidences'—'marks of design'—must have been very disturbing to a generation for whom Paley's natural theology based on the argument from design was still the great rational defence of Christian faith. But, as Hamish Swanston has pointed out, Jowett had perceived the snag about Paley's argument. If one wishes to maintain that the universe is a single interacting system—like a watch, which was Paley's well-known analogy—then it becomes necessary to show that the parts work together in and for the whole. And this is precisely what it is so difficult to do.[18] Faith is left with the problem of trying to make barren deserts and venomous snakes a sensible part of a complete system.

But Paley's argument, which was required reading for almost every aspiring clergyman, attempted precisely that task. He tried to do two things which were not normally to be found in the classical 'proofs' of the existence of God. Not only did he purport, in an odd way, to use the very experimental methods being developed by science but he maintained that it was possible to demonstrate God's characteristics as well as his existence. So Paley maintained, for instance, that the precise amount of poison in a snake's bite was evidence of the divine goodness. More poison would have allowed it to kill animals too large for it to eat: less would have meant that it would eat its prey alive. And this Paley believed to have been shown in experiments conducted by a French priest on 'enraged vipers'.[19]

[18] Swanston, p. 138. and cf. D. Cupitt, 'Darwinism and English Religious Thought', *Theology*, 78 (1975), p. 128. Jowett was also directly critical of Paley's *Horae Paulinae* in his commentary on II Thessalonians, *Epistles*, i, pp. 108ff.

[19] W. Paley, *Works: Complete in One Volume, to which is Prefixed the Life of the Author*, London 1851, pp. 536f.

Jowett was not concerned to advocate this kind of intermingling of the scientific and the religious way of thinking. Instead he advocated an acceptance of a scientific understanding of a universe which operated regularly and predictably and which could, therefore, be understood in its own terms. But there remained the problem which he had raised with Brodie ten years earlier. If one accepted a natural explanation of the universe and its workings, how was one to avoid deism and assert the centrality of God and the importance of a religious understanding of reality?

And there remained, also, the problem that science seemed to challenge many things that Christians had been taught to believe. People who accepted the discoveries of science could not believe that creation happened as Genesis described it or that the sun stood still at Joshua's command. If faith was a matter of believing a number of *things*, and some of these 'things' conflicted with the demonstrable truths of science, what was one to do? One plainly could not continue to believe untruths, but what one was to substitute for them was less obvious.

Jowett had not yet found answers to these consequences of his new position. Indeed, it could be said that he never found the answers and spent surprisingly little time in thinking about them. One of the features of his reliance upon 'common sense' was that he used it as an excuse for not facing up to specific problems. Rigorous, systematic thinking did not appeal to him very much: he was happy to generalise in terms of what he thought was sensible. He had, however moved some way from the naivety of his letters to Brodie ten years earlier when he had assumed that faith was a matter of 'believing things'. He was as passionately convinced as ever that accepting natural explanations must not eliminate faith. He was still certain that the best way to defend faith was by showing that it was interdependent with morality. But he had abandoned the crude idea of faith as something that could be quantified.

All these themes are to be found in a sermon which Jowett preached during the time when he was writing the commentaries. It is always difficult to know where the dividing line comes between someone's theology and his personal beliefs. Whether at a conscious or an unconscious level there may be quite marked differences between the two. Theology, in the sense of what is worked out as an academically defensible system, may not be what its deviser actually believes. This may be because he continues—in his heart of hearts—to think and behave in terms of what he was accustomed to believe before attempting to work out a coherent theology; or because he really has no religious beliefs at all and is concerned only with the intellectual exercise; or because belief, since it is an interior state of mind, may vary from time to time without necessarily causing him to rethink the theological system. In any case, a man's faith is not something which can be determined, analysed, and assessed with any certainty. It is, in a real sense, inaccessible to the observer.

Sermons may reflect the preacher's theology or faith or both; and this will make them difficult to interpret. But they cannot be simply ignored. They may be an important indicator of the way in which their author's thought is moving just because they are likely to be a particularly honest and sincere statement of his beliefs. In Jowett's case, his sermons are crucial for the reconstruction of his theology because there is so little other evidence one can use, particularly in the later period. The significance of the sermon here referred to, is that it is possible to see how it mirrors the thought that is found in the commentaries and thus suggests that what Jowett said in sermons is legitimate evidence for his theology.

This particular sermon is a moving piece, preached on the text 'Lord, I believe; help thou mine unbelief.'[20] In it Jowett proclaimed his faith, in spite of the many difficulties it encountered; in the distance of two thousand years which separated him from the historical Christ; in the absence of miracles and mass conversions; and in the fact that 'science seems to close me in on every side and forbids me to pierce that veil of flesh with which I am encompassed, or to draw aside the curtain of the natural world that conceals me from the eye of the Almighty'. And there was a further problem for him. The low level of social, political, and even personal morality in the world around him made him doubt the power of Christianity.

But Jowett's answer was always to be found in morality itself. He divided unbelief into two categories: unbelief of the head and

[20] [B. Jowett,] *College Sermons,* [ed. W. H. Fremantle, London 1895,] p. 20.

unbelief of the heart. He did not think that argument would convince a sceptic but living the life of Christ might do so. One's own doubts might best be cured by remembering that they were often rooted in weaknesses of temperament or personality such as vanity, restlessness, or ambition. Intellectual doubt, in other words, is often a consequence of a morally feeble character. But Jowett thought unbelief of the heart more important. Reason is largely dependent upon will, he argued. Those who habitually lead a worldly life will almost inevitably cease to believe what they have so little interest in believing.

Then he turned from unbelief to belief and, once more, divided it into belief of the head and belief of the heart. It was the second, again, which he thought the more important. 'Belief then must radiate from life: what we are, in a certain sense, we shall believe.' The great changes in thought and opinion within the university which had happened during the previous twenty years were not, he thought, something to be afraid of: honest enquiry was always good, but fashions of thought were transient: what mattered was the quality of one's life.

He who, kneeling at the Lord's table to-morrow, can discharge his mind of all envy, malice, irritability, coldness, can raze from his memory all impurity, can pluck from his soul every disguise of untruth and self-deceit, can devote his life a sacrifice to the service of God and man, has that within him at which the clouds of unbelief fly away, which, as it is independent of the opinions of teachers and thinkers, will survive them in the hour of death and the day of judgement.[21]

The close connection between faith and morality, always so characteristic of Jowett and which was so prominent in this sermon, found its place again and again in the commentaries themselves. The opening chapters of Romans provided him with an opportunity to include one of his dissertations, this time on the theme of the links between idolatry and immorality. God is 'the ideal and perfection of all morality'. 'Morality has to do with an unseen world: it has no form or comeliness, when separated from the hope which the Gospel holds out; it is severe and stoical in its demands. It tells men to look within; it deepens the battle with self. It presents duty almost as

[21] *College Sermons*, p. 24f.

an abstraction which in the face of death they must pursue, though there be no reward here, though their name perish for evermore.'

At this level it is clear that there was very little difference between the tone of his sermons and that of his commentaries. And if the latter are to be regarded as theological writings, then the sermons reflect the same theology.

It was Jowett's new conception of faith which, curiously enough, was really responsible for the vigour with which the commentaries were attacked and which led to the first public accusations that his opinions were heretical. His critics, for the most part, simply ignored the essay 'On Natural Religion' and concentrated upon the essays on justification by faith, on predestination, and, above all, on the atonement. If Jowett's abandonment of the apologetic arguments beloved of eighteenth-century proponents of a rational Christianity, shocked the conventionally religious, what he had to say on the subject of justification and predestination aroused the fury of the Evangelicals. And in each case it was his understanding of faith which led him to adopt the views set out in the essays. His essay 'On Righteousness by Faith' bluntly put aside the whole tangled controversy about whether men are saved by faith or by works, which had been going on since the Reformation. Luther, he admitted, had an instinctive sympathy with Pauline ideas; an emphasis upon simplicity, true inward religion, faith, humility, and dependence upon God. But he believed that the reformer's theology had distorted the meaning of Paul's language, and this distortion had been made worse by subsequent generations. St Paul had not defined faith as faith in the blood or even the death of Christ; nor did he suggest that the person who is justified would have any sense of assurance or consciousness that this was so. But that, Jowett thought, was what the doctrine had come to mean.

The truth is that Jowett no longer thought of faith as believing a set number of 'things'. It would have been impossible for him any longer to talk about 'more' or 'less' faith, as if one were assessing the *amount* that it was possible to believe. Faith had become, for him, an attitude of mind, what he called 'a spirit', 'a return to God and nature', 'a living communion with God'. Such a conception of faith has little to do with how *much* one believes. To speak of having *more* faith, in the sense in which Jowett now used the term, would be to speak of intensity not quantity.

The essay 'On Atonement and Satisfaction' attracted most of the wrath of Jowett's critics because of the obvious and direct challenge the author was issuing. The essay on natural religion planted its barbs almost in passing. The essay on righteousness, though plainly taking a line very different from Evangelical orthodoxy, did not actually deny that orthodoxy in so many words. The essay on the atonement quite clearly and specifically pronounced the conventional belief of the day to be wrong. And it did so in terms which not only attacked the penal substitutionary theology of the Evangelicals but also the satisfaction language of the medieval theologians beloved by High Churchmen. There was no possibility that Jowett's purpose might be overlooked. He described the conventional explanation of the atonement as revolting to men's moral feelings. God, he said, is represented as angry with us for what we never did; he is believed to be willing to inflict a disproportionate punishment on us for what we are; he is said to be placated by the vicarious offering of his own son. In place of this Jowett offered an alternative view, hesitantly and with a repeated insistence that any theological formulation must fail to capture the essential religious mystery. He thought that communion with Christ, in part a mystical sense of his presence, in part a more down-to-earth determination to identify with his moral standards, was the way to understand atonement.

The weakness of Jowett's view was that it was almost all negative. He attacked conventional beliefs but devoted very little space to advancing or defending his own positive views. Nor was he at all systematic. He contented himself with expressing sentiments whose implications he did not examine. And he tended to take refuge in the necessity of 'mystery' which, because it must be impenetrable, he did not attempt to explain.

Even those critics like J. B. Lightfoot,[22] who were not entirely unsympathetic, found Jowett's attempt to formulate an alternative

---

[22] In a review in *Journal of Classical and Sacred Philology*, 2 (1856), pp. 104ff. For a discussion of the philological point at issue between Jowett and Lightfoot see Swanston, p. 170 and J. Barr, 'Jowett and the Reading of the Bible "Like Any Other Book"', *Horizons in Biblical Theology*, 4 (1982), pp. 21ff.

theology less convincing than his attack on the conventional view. In a sense they were justified in doing so. Jowett had, in effect, advanced a purely subjective and exemplarist theory of the atonement and had thus laid himself open to the charge that he was embracing a theological position which Christian orthodoxy had always declared to be inadequate. He had, indeed, come very close to admitting this himself, saying in the closing section of the essay, 'We know nothing of the objective act on God's part by which He reconciled the world to Himself.'[23]

But most of Jowett's critics were far more radically opposed to his theology than Lightfoot was. To them it seemed not simply too subjectivist but utterly and entirely heretical, if not an outright denial of Christian truth. He was denounced to the university authorities for holding views contrary to the teaching of the Thirty-nine Articles. Golightly, who had embarrassed Tait by the fervour of his attacks on Newman in 1841, now became one of the prime movers in this campaign against Jowett. The Vice-Chancellor summoned Jowett and required him to subscribe the Articles again, undoubtedly a degrading experience. Jowett signed. It was 'the meaner part', as he told Stanley, 'I could not do otherwise without giving up my position as a Clergyman.'[24]

It is possible, of course, that this last remark is evidence that Jowett signed, somewhat dishonestly, merely to retain his position at Balliol. But it need not necessarily mean that. He took his clerical duties seriously till the end of his life: theology, religion, personal devotion, and his preaching remained important to him. He was a believer. But he always stressed the impossibility of treating theological statements as if they were precise and exhaustive definitions. And he seems to have believed—with some reason—that the Articles were originally intended to be inclusive rather than exclusive. He regarded the requirement that one should take the formularies in the 'plain and literal sense' as an innovation.[25] And to be asked to subscribe so complex a statement without reservation, seemed altogether unreasonable. In any case, as a good Arnoldite he

---

[23] *Epistles*, ii, p. 422.
[24] Faber, p. 226.
[25] Faber, pp. 152f.

would think it absurd to assume that everyone could agree on the precise meaning of a theological statement.

It seems likely, in fact, that he still felt as he had done in the 1840s, at the time of his ordination. No doubt he thought that subscription was undesirable. It asked for the impossible and therefore encouraged hypocrisy. He would clearly have liked to get rid of it if he could. If it was to be retained, then it ought to be required in the general rather than the literal sense of the Articles. But he felt as able to sign them in 1855 as he had done in 1845, and in the same sense and spirit in which he had done so then. To describe Jowett as 'an implacable foe of subscription' or, worse still, as someone who would sign anything, whether he believed it or not,[26] is to fail to understand his real position.

But the very fact that he honestly felt himself able to subscribe the Articles made his critics the more furious. 'How after writing such sentences [in the commentaries] Jowett could again deliberately sign the articles is beyond my comprehension . . .', wrote one former fellow of Balliol to Robert Scott, urging him to remove Jowett from his tutorship.[27] Golightly was also enraged by Jowett's willingness to sign the Articles. He, too, demanded that Scott remove Jowett from office.[28] The Vice-Chancellor, who was Pusey's brother-in-law, invited Scott to preach in the university church on the subject of the atonement. This, he thought, would provide an opportunity to vindicate Balliol as well as to controvert antichristian views. Scott, to his eternal credit, refused to do any of these things. He forwarded Golightly's letter to Jowett who did not think it necessary to read it—or at least claimed not to do so.

Though Jowett refused—as was to become typical of him—to be drawn into public debate about his theological opinions, he attempted to meet the attacks of his critics by revising the essay on the atonement in subsequent editions. Not that he was willing in any way to modify his opinion, but he attempted to make his argument clearer and more watertight. The only effect of this was to make his

---

[26] Ward, p. 131: A. M. Ramsey, *From Gore to Temple*, London 1960, p. 60; and cf. also above pp. 43f. for Jowett's view that 'old chains are the best'.

[27] Quoted in Prest, *Robert Scott*, p. 10.

[28] Ibid. p. 12.

onslaught on conventional theology seem the fiercer. The revised essay opened with what was almost a caricature of the penal substitutionary theory which he then bluntly rejected. Moreover, Jowett abandoned his attempt to remain agnostic about the objective aspect of the atonement. Instead he surveyed the alternative theories of German philosophers and theologians from Kant to Hegel. But these, he said, Englishmen would find too remote and theoretical since they substituted the metaphysical for the practical, and thus placed 'at too great a distance what ought to be very near us'.[29]

The subjectivism of his own view was made even more obvious. Jowett argued that Christ's death is to be understood primarily as the greatest moral act ever performed which, for that reason, set the seal upon everything his life had represented. That death, he maintained, moved men and women to perceive their own imperfection and their need for greater closeness to God while at the same time assuring them of God's love. They are then able to use the knowledge of that love, real as the love of an earthly friend but with the power of the divine, to become like Christ, to be reconciled to God and pass into the relationship of sons of God. This was, and remained, the heart of all Jowett's theology. He believed that the essence of being a Christian was to use knowledge of God's love to experience what it was to be God's son. It was unashamedly subjective, individualistic, and emotional. It was also very real to him.

Years before, when they had hardly begun the work on the commentaries, Stanley had asked him:

What is the moral to be advanced for the Undergraduate World from 'A man shall be justified by faith without the deeds of the Law'—Is it the entire freedom of religion from all outward circumstances, and therefore the possibility of serving God, however far removed from church, clergy, sacraments, or the like—or is it the substitution of the motives of love and gratitude for those of law and fear—or is it (after the manner of Hare's Victory of Faith) the power of trust in things unseen and future over things seen and present—? I am inclined to think the former—but if either of the latter, in what form is it to be brought home to the youthful mind?[30]

The essay on the atonement almost reads as if Jowett was trying to

[29] *Epistles*, 2nd edn., London 1859, ii p. 585.
[30] Balliol College: MS 410, Stanley to Jowett, 29 Sept. (probably 1846).

provide an answer which would incorporate all three of Stanley's suggestions.

Whether or not he had brought it all home to the youthful mind, there were many who feared that he might have done so. It was the very subjectivism of Jowett's theology which had seemed to Golightly to contradict most blatantly the tenor of the Thirty-nine Articles and to make him unfit to teach undergraduates. The new edition did nothing to soften it.

Jowett sent a copy of the revised version of the commentary to the long-suffering Scott. Scott was evidently not much comforted by what it now contained. He wrote Jowett a letter, the original of which does not survive and which incensed its recipient for reasons which are not entirely clear. Jowett told Scott that he resented being prayed for and treated as 'a thing to thank God upon'. Scott later maintained that what he had said was that he would be '*very, very* thankful, if I find that it is so far modified as in any way to diminish the pains which some things in the first edn. gave me'.[31] Whatever the truth of the matter, it is clear that Jowett resented the thought that Scott was hoping he would abandon what he had come to believe to be the truth. Characteristically he declined to argue about what was actually contained in his book. He had said his piece. He was not going to retract. He and Scott remained unreconciled.

In Pusey's view also the second edition was theologically more offensive than the first. Writing to Gladstone about the endowment of the regius chairs of civil law and Greek, he complained that Jowett (as the occupant of the latter) was a great embarrassment to churchmen. His views on the atonement, Pusey said, were hardly different from those of Joseph Priestley, the Presbyterian minister who had come to hold unitarian beliefs. Since Priestley was equally famous as the scientist who had discovered oxygen and notorious as a champion of the revolution in France, the use of his name appears to be a way of suggesting that Jowett was on the slippery slope towards radical opinions of all kinds. Pusey complained bitterly that Jowett denied that the death of Christ was in any sense vicarious and that he was unsound on the subject of Christ's divinity.[32]

[31] Prest, *Robert Scott*, pp. 14f.
[32] BM add. MS 44,281, fos. 218f. I am grateful to John Prest for drawing my

Continuing complaints that his essays conflicted with the Thirty-nine Articles meant that, while Jowett was trying to develop his theology of the subjective, he also had to give more serious thought to the whole question of doctrinal tests. It was all very well for him to maintain that a strict, literal, and exclusive interpretation of the Articles was unreasonable. But it was not unreasonable to require a clergyman (and especially one engaged in training prospective clergymen) to make a public declaration that he held to the teachings of the Church. Jowett was an academic and an educator at a time when traditional orthodoxy and the traditional relationship between Church and university were coming under attack from new academic scholarship. He found himself caught between opposing pressures. It is not surprising that he came to believe that 'really great men were never clergymen' because they disliked the constraint of the received creeds. It would be better, he thought, 'for a great man in high Ecclesiastical station . . . to drop all dogmatic theology—and to fill his mind with great schemes for the regeneration of mankind . . .'[33]

But there was also the more fundamental problem of determining the precise character of the constraint imposed by the Thirty-nine Articles. Since the Articles asserted that all doctrine ought to be founded upon the scriptures, the way in which the Bible was to be interpreted was obviously inextricably bound up with the question of what the Articles actually meant. German professors of theology were already in the habit of arguing that, if confessions of faith were required to be subscribed *in so far as they were in accordance with scripture*, they could not exclude radical interpretations of scripture itself. For, if the radical interpretation were true, it revealed the real meaning of scripture. Jowett faced a similar issue in relation to the Thirty-nine Articles. He believed, as he was later to argue, that any doctrine of inspiration must take account of all well-ascertained facts of history and science. If such a doctrine of inspiration led to a new way of intereperting the Bible, and if this led one to a new and different understanding of the text, then the force of the Article's

attention to this letter.
[33] [P.] Hinchliff, ['Benjamin Jowett and the Church of England: Or Why really great men are never Clergymen'] in *Balliol Studies*, pp. 127ff. and cf. Faber, p. 136.

own claim that doctrine must proceed from scripture, might be very different from what was generally supposed.

It is not surprising, then, that Jowett should have felt compelled to tackle seriously the whole matter of the interpretation of scripture. He had, indeed, first begun to draft an essay on the subject in 1847, intending to include it in the Pauline commentaries. It was still incomplete when the manuscript went to the publishers and it had to be left out. He had hoped that it would be ready for the second edition of 1859 but again failed to complete it. It finally became his contribution to *Essays and Reviews*.

4
Essays and Reviews

It is far from clear whether all the contributors to *Essays and Reviews* shared the same motives or even how that particular group came to be constituted. Broad Churchmen were not a 'party' like the High Churchmen or the Evangelicals. They believed in tolerance and in making the national Church as comprehensive as possible. They believed, like Dr Arnold, that religion had a role in unifying the nation—and this was another reason for regarding doctrinal formularies with suspicion. The establishment, most of them were convinced, enabled the common sense and fairness of English law to be the judge of what was permissible. This naive trust in the unprejudiced good sense of the lawyers made them prefer secular courts to potentially partisan ecclesiastical tribunals. Jowett, at a time when he had begun to be disturbed by Tait's apparent willingness to act against those who did not conform, nevertheless told him that he approved of the Public Worship Regulation Act because it would provide 'a judge who is impartial in place of a partizan'.[1] This was the kind of thing that other liberals also said. F. D. Maurice, for instance,—speaking, perhaps, from bitter experience—once wrote to *The Spectator*, 'Every Churchman about to undergo any trial himself, owns how much rather he would be in the hands of lay judges than of Presbyters and Bishops . . .'[2]

Above all, Broad Churchmen were rather self-consciously liberal, in the sense that they would passionately defend a man's right to speak his mind even when they did not agree with him. This, together with their suspicion of doctrinal tests, meant that they were individuals and individualists. They could not be a 'party'. They

[1] Lambeth Palace Library: Tait Papers: Personal Letters, vol. 93, fo. 290.
[2] Rhodes House, Oxford: Archives of the United Society for the Propagation of the Gospel: Macrorie Papers: Press cuttings—the date on Maurice's letter has not been preserved.

disagreed among themselves with a vehemence that is surprising in view of their conscientious liberalism, yet was almost a facet of it. Jowett himself, though he had been strongly opposed to the campaign against Hampden, privately described him to Stanley as 'a Janus' about whom 'I could not say anything in his favour.' Because Hampden had accepted the idea that the Articles should be subscribed in a literal sense, Jowett suspected that he was about to swallow 'all the ins and outs of S. Oxon [Samuel Wilberforce]'s Theology'. 'He has', Jowett wrote, 'made ambiguity so ambiguous.'[3]

Ieuan Ellis, in his authoritative study of *Essays and Reviews*, suggests that the contributors are best thought of as 'Stanleyites'.[4] Attractive though this suggestion is, it is actually very difficult to think of Stanley as *leader* of a group or movement. The only way in which he might have linked the liberals together was as the focal point of a network of friendships—a possibility Ellis himself seems to recognise. Stanley was certainly the friend to whom, perhaps above all others, Jowett was most deeply attached. If Tait was the person who most influenced him in the 1840s, Stanley—in a very different way—did so in the 1850s. But, devoted as Jowett was to Stanley, there does not seem to be much doubt that he was the stronger personality of the two, the leader in their joint enterprises. Stanley was—in one sense—the archetype of the individualistic liberal, courageously willing to defend the persecuted, while insisting on his own right to disagree as much with them as with their persecutors. But, however attractive so much broadmindedness may seem at first sight, it is not the most desirable characteristic in a leader of a group. Stanley was to defend *Essays and Reviews* with a typically Broad Church appeal to the role of the state as the defender of religious liberty but with a lack of vigour which hurt his friends.[5] And he seems also to have had a knack for dissociating himself, often in advance, from dangerous opinions and enterprises. His refusal to contribute to *Essays and Reviews* on the ground that it was an ill-

[3] Balliol College: Jowett Papers: Box E, an undated and incomplete letter from Jowett to Stanley.

[4] Ellis, pp. 11f. and cf. Swanston, p. 182 for a different argument in favour of regarding the essayists as a single, coherent group.

[5] *Edinburgh Review*, Apr. 1861, pp. 461ff.

advised venture was not the only example of this. As dean of Westminster he was to refuse to allow the first Lambeth Conference to use the Abbey because he was afraid that there might be an attempt to condemn Bishop Colenso. But at the same time he let it be known very publicly that he disapproved vigorously of much that Colenso had written. In fact it almost looks as if in the 1850s Jowett and Stanley were exchanging roles. Whereas in the earlier period Jowett had been something of a background figure, while the young Stanley's strong opinions were making the headlines, it was now Jowett who was in the forefront of things.

Even as the focal point for a group of friends, it would seem that Stanley was not always staunch and predictable. A few years after the publication of *Essays and Reviews*, Jowett was to tell Florence Nightingale that Stanley 'has behaved strangely to me at times and I have always imagined there to be explanations'. The 'explanations', Jowett thought, were that Stanley's sister tried to influence him against his friends,[6] and that he was not, for this reason, someone who could be counted on. If, therefore, Stanley really was the nucleus for the Oxford group of liberals, it is less likely to have been in his own right than in his role as the favourite pupil—almost as the symbol—of Thomas Arnold. There certainly was, as W. R. Ward, has argued, a Rugby and Balliol circle, to which most of the liberals in some degree belonged.[7] And Stanley was undoubtedly somewhere near the centre of it. But if one is to believe a sarcastic and unsympathetic article published in *Blackwood's* after Jowett's death, Stanley was always a 'light horseman' whose 'type of mind was so palpably shallow' that he took 'an active part in many a hot battle' without exciting permanent animosity. (Even Stanley's most savage critics seem to have found it difficult to describe him except in metaphors drawn from chivalry.) The same writer thought that Jowett 'after his failure to attain the Mastership . . . came to be looked upon as a ringleader of the Oxford Liberals'.[8] At all events, since Stanley was characteristically unwilling to become involved in

[6] Balliol College: Jowett to Florence Nightingale, 28 Nov. 1865.

[7] Ward, p. 130.

[8] 'Mr Jowett and Oxford Liberalism', [*Blackwood's Edinburgh Magazine*, 161 (1897),] p. 723: *The Wellesley Index to Victorian Periodicals* attributes the article, on the basis of the publishers' accounts, to J. H. Millar.

the project, the only other Balliol contributor to the volume was Frederick Temple.

Jowett's contribution to *Essays and Reviews* was solicited—according to his quasi-official biography—by H. B. Wilson. It was intended that 'theological subjects should be freely handled in a becoming spirit'.[9] Wilson had been, with Tait, a signatory of the tutors' letter attacking Tract 90. But, while Tait's less radical spirit was becoming more obvious, Wilson—the champion of orthodoxy of 1841—was on the path to becoming the heretic of 1861.

Essays and Reviews appeared in 1860 and was rapidly reissued in several new editions in the next few years. The essays were varied and uneven. Temple revised and extended a sermon, 'The Education of the World', in an attempt to expound a theory of the development or progress of revelation and the knowledge of God. It was neither very radical nor very rigorous. Rowland Williams wrote on the critical biblical scholarship of Baron von Bunsen. Baden Powell's essay on the 'evidences' of Christianity and Charles Goodwin's 'On the Mosaic Cosmogony' also dealt with matters in which natural science and Christian faith were thought to be in conflict. Mark Pattison wrote on 'Tendencies of Religious Thought in England, 1688–1750' and H. B. Wilson himself contributed an essay on the national Church.

There was neither plan nor editorial policy. Nor was there an agreed theological perspective. It was a typical Broad Church production. Every man spoke for himself: outraged conservative opinion—if not the devil—tried to take the hindermost.

Jowett's essay, the last in the book, was a long one, almost double the length of the other contributions. For the modern reader it is also rather tedious, not just because of its somewhat verbose style but also because Jowett uses so much space to argue a case which would now be readily conceded. For Jowett's own day, no doubt, it needed to be set out step by step. There was little in the argument that the author had not already adumbrated, touched on, or hinted at elsewhere, but it was now expounded fully and in order.

Jowett insisted that it was essential that the results of scientific

---

[9] Abbott and Campbell, i, p. 273.

enquiry and critical scholarship be taken seriously. The Bible ought to be treated as any other book would be treated, in its context and as expressing the mind of a particular author, an era, and a cultural setting. He wanted to get rid of the complex patterns of symbolic, traditional, and allegorical interpretation which, he maintained, had been read into, rather than out of, the actual text. He thought that trying to 'prove' doctrinal positions from scripture was an ill-conceived and impossible task. Above all, he seems to have felt that getting back to the meaning of the New Testament itself was essentially a process of simplification and that the benefits accruing from the process would be those which resulted from simplicity. It would be easier, for instance, for Christians to agree and to engage in mission together, if they could get back to the original meaning of the Gospels. The whole of this has a very Arnoldian ring to it.

John Rogerson, pointing out that Jowett's essay was chiefly concerned, like Temple's, to stress progressive education and progressive revelation, argues that its chief strength lay in his analysis and description of contemporary attitudes. In other words, as with the commentaries, Jowett was better at writing critically about received opinion than in offering a positive substitute. Rogerson also believes that Jowett's principal contribution lay in his attempt to define inspiration as 'That idea of Scripture which we gather from the knowledge of it'—in other words, that scripture itself is to define scriptural inspiration. This belief that a proper concept of the inspiration of scripture must be derived from scripture itself, Jowett almost certainly derived from Arnold through Stanley.[10] And, in fact, Jowett was really concerned to make a very simple point; that the way to interpret scripture is to discover the meaning which it had to those who first wrote or read it. But Rogerson is right in asserting that Jowett did not limit the meaning of the Bible solely to what the authors initially intended: he recognised that its meaning is, in a sense, inexhaustible. But the only way to avoid fanciful or idiosyncratic exegesis was to place each writer in the context of the continuum that makes up the Bible as a whole. And this is where the

[10] Above p. 47.

idea of a progressive revelation was important to Jowett. The controlling sense of continuity lay in the unfolding knowledge of God, reaching its climax in Christ.[11]

Jowett's summary of his own argument, with the point about the continuum made very clearly in the final sentence, was succinct and accurate:

> That Scripture, like other books, has one meaning, which is to be gathered from itself without reference to the adaptations of Fathers and Divines; and without regard to *a priori* notions about its nature and origins. It is to be interpreted like other books with attention to the character of its authors, and the prevailing state of civilization and knowledge, with allowance for peculiarities of style and language, and modes of thought and figures of speech. Yet not without a sense that as we read there grows upon us the witness of God in the world, anticipating in a rude and primitive age the truth that was to be, shining more and more unto the perfect day in the life of Jesus Christ, which again is reflected from different points of view in the teaching of His Apostles.[12]

This summary comes about two-thirds of the way through the essay. The last third is taken up with various *obiter dicta* and includes, significantly, a warning that the intending clergyman may not be the best person to tackle problems of critical theology unless he has 'clearness of mind to see things as they are, and a faith strong enough to rest in that degree of knowledge which God has really given . . .'. This touch of the patronising does not altogether disguise the fact that Jowett still partly shared with his critics the feeling that religion and an open mind do not go together.

Jowett's attitude to scripture, as expounded in his essay, has often been misunderstood. It was, as James Barr has argued, a remarkably biblicist one.[13] Jowett's essay reveals no greater interest in the technicalities of biblical criticism, than his commentaries had done, so that Rogerson suggests that he may even have been largely ignorant

---

[11] [J.] Rogerson, [*Old Testament Criticism in the Nineteenth Century: England and Germany*, London 1984,] p. 216.

[12] [B. Jowett, 'On the Interpretation of Scripture',] *Essays and Reviews*, [London 1860,] p. 404.

[13] [J.] Barr, ['Jowett and the "Original Meaning" of Scripture', *Journal of Religious Studies*, 18 (1982),] p. 435. This article and another by the same writer already cited above are of very great importance for understanding Jowett's essay.

of the work of biblical critics in Germany.[14] He was still supremely the classical scholar whose primary interest lay in establishing the *text*. Nor was he much concerned to advocate an historical approach to the critical study of the Bible. For Jowett history was a way back to the text: it was not a tool for the internal analysis of it. Historical enquiry, he believed, could play an important part in arriving at the text itself, behind the centuries of comment and interpretation which had come to be inextricably associated with it. But once one had gone back to the text itself, historical enquiry had done its work. One simply then read what the authors had written.

Jowett seems hardly to have been aware how easy it would be, with such an approach, to *misread* the original. There is an implicit inconsistency in his approach which he does not seem to have recognised and which he was to build into his whole Christology. He complained of the way in which earlier generations had imposed interpretations upon the text: he does not seem to have feared that he might himself be doing the same thing. Moreover, he believed that understanding the scriptures required 'a vision and faculty divine'.[15] What this meant is not quite clear. If it meant something like an inspired intuition, then this, also, might only too easily have led him to read into, rather than out of, the text. He had, in fact, fallen into precisely the error of which he complained so bitterly when he encountered it in others—the temptation to find what one wanted to find in the text of the Bible.

In some ways the supposed radical was, in fact, very conservative in his attitude. Like the most thoroughgoing literalist he believed that what the authors of the New Testament books had written ought simply to be taken at face value and that one would be 'guided' into an understanding of it. He differed from the literalists in two particulars. He did not believe that the text had been directly dictated by God: nor did it always mean what it had been traditionally understood to mean. The phrase which he had already used in the proposals for a theology school and which appears several times in the essay, that the scriptures should be read 'like other books', has to be understood in this light. He did *not* mean that its value was no

[14] Rogerson, p. 217.
[15] *Essays and Reviews*, p. 337.

greater than that of other books nor that what one derived from it or the way in which it was derived, was the same as with other books. He meant that, in order to understand what the author intended, one had to read a book as one would read anything else, and a classical text in particular: one ought to concentrate on what was actually being said on the page. In biblical contexts this would mean more or less confining one's attentions to one particular author at a time. One could not understand Paul by cross-reference to verses taken out of context from some other part of the Bible, as though the scriptures had sprung—whole and entire—from a single mind. Nor ought one to rely on, for instance, patristic or Reformation interpreters. It was essentially a plea for a common-sense approach. And in relation to tests of doctrinal orthodoxy, which may originally have provoked the ideas set out in the essay, the implications seem clear. If the Articles insisted upon the primacy of scripture in determining doctrine, and if it could be shown that the teaching of the Bible was different from what had hitherto been thought, then one was positively *required* to change one's doctrine.

Once one perceives what Jowett's principal concern was, the meaning of his own summary of his essay becomes very clear. He was chiefly asking for a return to the sources and a willingness to read them with a mind entirely open to what he would have called the plain sense intended by the original authors. This was the approach to the Bible which he had originally derived from Arnold. It was also the approach which he and Stanley had tried to persuade the university to adopt as the basis for a new school of theology. In this respect, at least, Jowett's ideas had not significantly changed.

The question inevitably arises, however, as to what other sources he had drawn upon in developing his theology. So far as English thinkers were concerned, and in spite of their common interest in Platonism, Jowett seems never to have been very interested in the thought of Coleridge and his disciples like Maurice and Colenso.[16] Though they were sometimes allies, they seem to have shared few ideas. But it is just possible that Jowett picked up themes from John Locke. In the 1870s, when he was at odds with T. H. Green on the

---

[16] See [D.] Newsome, [*Two Classes of Men: Platonism and English Romantic Thought*, London 1972,] pp. 76f.

subject of Idealism, he was to assert that Locke was a more important philosopher than Hegel or Kant. And some of the ideas expressed in the latter part of his contribution to *Essays and Reviews*—on the potential importance of simplicity in achieving greater unity among Christians, for instance—suggest the possible influence of Locke's concept of a reasonable Christianity whose universal essence was to be distilled from the particularities of its historical manifestations.

The truth is that Jowett was an incorrigible eclectic and this is why it is so difficult to locate him with any precision in the history of nineteenth-century religious thought. He simply will not fit neatly into any school. In a sense it was always the weakness of the liberals, exemplified in the Noetics, for instance, that they lacked a theoretical framework which would enable them to develop a *system* of dogmatics. In a liberal like Jowett, who positively disliked systems, the temptation to eclecticism was irresistible.

One of his greatest admirers, attempting to describe the development of his ideas during the first fifteen years after his election as a fellow of Balliol, admirably captured the way Jowett's mind worked. In spite of the fact that the passage is intended to counter a charge of eclecticism, it shows very clearly just how and why he picked up ideas from all sorts of sources:

... his mind wandered from Plato to St John, from Hegel to Comte. He read widely and encouraged his pupils to do the same; but eclecticism was the last result at which he aimed. He learned something from every philosopher, but he was never a mere borrower. Experience, he said in effect, is our one clue to the nature of man, the world and God. But in the interpretation of personal experience we must call to our aid the great minds of the past; they will help us to analyse what we have thought and felt. As our experience is ever growing wider, so must we always be adding to our knowledge. For that reason a final system can never be constructed; at the best a system is but a synthesis of what we know in the present state of our experience. He who adopts a system closes the eyes of the mind; he becomes blind to the facts which controvert his theory.[17]

One may doubt whether Jowett ever paid any very serious attention to Comte. The young man who had disliked the scepticism of

[17] Davis, pp. 189f.

Paris in the 1840s was unlikely to be attracted by early French positivism. Nor was a philosophical system that set itself to dispense with theology and metaphysics, as outworn modes of thought, likely to be temperamentally agreeable to a person of Jowett's interests and sympathies. And those very aspects of Comtism—religious rather than philosophical—which repelled people like J. S. Mill, George Eliot, and T. H. Huxley,[18] would certainly have been equally distasteful to the Jowett who so admired common sense. Indeed, he once described a candidate for a fellowship as a person 'of no great intellectual pretensions who is believed to be a Comtist',[19] as though he thought that the two things went together. He need say no more and could say no worse.

Jowett was much more sympathetic to the ideas of a variety of German scholars and it is possible to make some guesses as to which of them he was reading in this period. The Balliol library possesses a manuscript catalogue of Jowett's own collection, which eventually passed to the college. There is also a printed catalogue of books which dates from about the time when Jowett became master, as well as the register for the period of the late 1830s, the 1840s, and the early 1850s in which fellows of the college recorded the books which they borrowed. Discovering which books Jowett took out is therefore possible in principle though it is not entirely easy. Fellows recorded in the borrowers' register the shelf mark rather than the author and title of a book. Though the library catalogue gives the shelf mark of each book, the books themselves are naturally listed in alphabetical order of author. Finding which book is represented in the register by a particular shelf mark therefore involves searching through the whole catalogue until one comes to it. It is nevertheless possible to make some generalisations about Jowett's interests. Most of his own books and most of those which he borrowed were the writings of the standard classical authors, though he also borrowed some biblical commentaries and some contemporary philosophical works. On 6 December 1853, for instance, he borrowed Griesbach's 'New Testament' and Tisschendorf's edition of the *Codex Ephraimi*

[18] W. M. Simon, 'Auguste Comte's English Disciples', *Victorian Studies*, 7 (1964), p. 162.
[19] Lambeth Palace Library: Tait Papers: Personal Letters, vol. 88, fo. 167.

of 1843–5 and in January 1858 he took out Mill's essays 'On some unsettled questions of political economy' of 1844.

Both the library and his own collection contained a considerable number of works of German theology, most of it issued in the early 1840s. Jowett possessed twenty-three volumes of the collected works of Schleiermacher published in 1838 and one or two individual books by the same author including *Christliche Glaube*, in addition. He also owned ten volumes of the Hartenstein edition of Kant of 1838 and six of Hegel's works published in Germany between 1840 and 1848, including *Phänomenologie des Geistes* in the edition of 1841. Also among his own books were Schelling's *Von der Weltseele* and eight volumes of the 1845/6 edition of Fichte's works. The library, too, owned books by most of these writers and also—significantly, in view of the fact that Jowett had included his ideas in one of the essays in his commentaries—seven volumes of Daub's *Philosophische und theologische Vorlesungen* and his *Die dogmatische Theologie jetziger Zeit*.

That Jowett had access to so much German theology is not, of course, evidence that he read it. He was probably not as thoroughly acquainted with German thought as was, for instance, Mark Pattison,[20] whose contribution to *Essays and Reviews* attracted so much less attention than Jowett's. But there seems to be little doubt that he made a genuine attempt to discover what was being written.

The books which he possessed and those in the college library were in the original (though Jowett may have have had English versions of one or two of Fichte's works). For most of the books, indeed, English translations did not exist until later in the century and this, presumably, is why Jowett was engaged with Stanley and Temple in translating Kant and Hegel. It is difficult to determine just how good his German was. He had visited Germany in 1842 and again, with Stanley, in 1844. At the end of the decade his parents actually lived in Bonn for a time. His biographers assert that his 'familiarity with German is clearly shown by his writing more than once in that language at some length to Arthur Stanley, out of mere

---

[20] D. Nimmo, 'Learning against religion, learning as religion: Mark Pattison and the Victorian crisis of Faith', K. Robbins (ed.) in *Studies in Church History*, xvii, Oxford 1981, pp. 317ff.

playfulness, in 1844–6'.[21] One such letter still survives at Balliol. Its tone might be described almost as 'arch' rather than playful; only the first short page and a bit is in German (which could hardly be described as 'writing . . . at some length') and it is very 'English' German at that.[22] One might hazard a guess that Jowett was competent rather than fluent; that he would read German rather slowly; and that his natural tendency to eclecticism would be reinforced by encountering new and difficult theological ideas through the medium of a foreign language.

Jowett's interest in Hegel is well known: his biographers assert that he was the first person to give any real currency in England to Hegelian philosophy,[23] and Anthony Quinton, perhaps the most recent scholar to examine this claim, accepts its validity. It may be significant that Quinton attributes the popularity of Hegel among Jowett's disciples in large part to the fact that his Idealism 'succeeded in steering religion clear of a head-on collision with science . . . by reinterpreting those elements of the faith to which the new scientific developments were most destructive as poetic images of the abstract metaphysical principle of the spirituality of the world'.[24]

Jowett and Temple had set out—in the 1840s—to translate some of Hegel (probably the *Wissenschaft der Logik*) into English, though the enterprise was abandoned when Temple moved from Balliol in 1848. As is the case with that other abandoned project—the joint history with Stanley of the university of Oxford—no trace of any manuscript for this work appears to survive. But Hegel's influence can be detected in Jowett's commentaries on Plato as well as Paul. Indeed Jowett seems to have believed that Hegel had enabled him to develop a proper method for the critical understanding of Greek philosophy. One would, therefore, expect Jowett to exhibit—in general terms—the same broad approach as the German Idealists, who have been neatly described as transforming 'the Kantian theory of knowledge into a metaphysics of reality'—a vision of the

---

[21] Abbott and Campbell, i, p. 90.
[22] Balliol College: Jowett MSS: Box E, letter dated 1 Jan. 1849.
[23] Faber, pp. 178ff. and Abbott and Campbell, i pp. 129f.
[24] A. M. Quinton, 'Absolute Idealism', *Proceedings of the British Academy*, 57 (1971), pp. 320 and 308.

world and human history as the objective expression of creative reason.[25]

Yet this was not quite Jowett's approach and it is, in fact, not easy to decide, precisely and in detail, just how far his own thought was directly influenced by Hegelianism. He was later to be extremely critical of some of his younger colleagues for being 'Hegelian'. There are very few overt references to Hegel in his writings on Plato, even where one might have thought to find the two kinds of idealism contrasted. Yet his introduction to the *Republic*, for instance, contains a very illuminating passage where he seeks to explain how justice is related to the nature of the state. He uses a very Hegelian phrasing about idea and reality and, at the same time, relates what he is trying to say to the Christian concept of the kingdom of God, which is 'within' one and yet is identified with the Church or external realm.[26] It is as though, Hegel—like Plato and the Gospels—had become a natural and unselfconscious part of the way in which Jowett's mind worked. It would seem, in fact, that Hegel affected his thought in much the way in which it had already been affected by Kant's ideas. When he first encountered them, they seemed revolutionary, altering the entire perspective from which he looked at everything. But once they had become part of his thought he moved on, not abandoning the new point of view but not allowing it to dominate everything else either. The first excitement generated by the new ideas subsided, but his thinking could never again entirely ignore what he had learnt.

Probably what attracted Jowett most in Hegel's philosophy was that it was a serious and systematic attempt to give an account of providence—the way God acts in history—perhaps the last serious attempt to do so. It may have seemed to be part of the answer to deism (which sought to remove God from the events of history) as well as to the challenge of science (which excluded miracles and other supposed instances of divine intervention). Certainly Jowett's later sermons and other notes and jottings contain both possible echoes of Hegel and frequent references to the need to trust history

[25] F. Copleston, *History of Philosophy*, New York 1965, vii. i, p. 22.
[26] *The Republic of Plato; translated into English with an analysis and introduction by B. Jowett*, Oxford 1881, p. iv.

when traditional dogma is challenged. If he had taken from Hegel the thought that truth reveals itself in the processes of history and had constructed from it the concept of a process of revelation in a continuum, advanced in his essay on the interpretation of scripture, then the argument that history is an alternative to dogma would make sense. It would also fit with the problem he had taken over from the Noetics: of how to define the relationship between revelation and doctrine.

The earliest reference to Hegel in his biography contains a strange but revealing comment taken from a letter written to Stanley in 1846.

Hegel is untrue, I sometimes fancy, not in the sense of being erroneous, but practically, because it is a consciousness of truth, becoming thereby error. ... The problem of ... Truth idealized and yet in action, he does not seem to me to have solved; the Gospel of St. John does. Hegel seems to me, not the perfect philosophy, but the perfect self-consciousness of philosophy.[27]

And one of his favourite sayings seems to date from the same period—that Hegel's philosophy was splendid 'if you can only get it out of its dialectical form'.[28]

While it seems, on the face of it, absurd even to try and imagine an undialectical Hegelianism, part of the meaning of both these comments seems to be that Jowett was offended by the systematic tidiness of Hegel. But the reference to ideal Truth actualised in the Johannine Christ may hint at another reason for his unease. He was, perhaps, unhappy with a God who needed to actualise himself in history in order to arrive at completeness: he wanted a God whose eternal moral perfection could be conceived of as already actualised at a specific point in history. And so he would be happier with a concept of God's revealing of himself in a continuum rather than in a dialetical process. He often used to say that the philosophical movement in Greece was far more important than German metaphysics. And it would be wholly characteristic of Jowett if, having worked through Hegel and gleaned from him the things he found most useful, he decided that there were other ideas which he must take

[27] Abbott and Campbell, i, p. 92.
[28] Abbott and Campbell, i, p. 130.

account of as well, without feeling any obligation to explain exactly how he fitted them together.

After Hegel, the other German whom Jowett took most seriously was Schleiermacher. There are a great many echoes of his key themes in Jowett's writings. Like Schleiermacher he believed that doctrine was of little value unless it could be preached in a form that was of use for faith. Like Schleiermacher he was convinced that there was a sense of the infinite for every soul that looks within itself. Like Schleiermacher he took seriously the existence and beliefs of other religions. Like Schleiermacher he continually emphasised the powerful attractiveness of Christ, which—like Schleiermacher—he believed was derived from the unique strength of Christ's own awareness of God.

It was probably Schleiermacher's conception of Christ's God-consciousness which appealed most of all to Jowett. Again and again in his writings there appears the theme of man's awareness of and communion with God, available to everyone but found so perfectly in Christ as to constitute the divine life itself. Jowett was anxious always to assert that the life and death of Christ was of immediate relevance to the life of the individual and his relationship with God. This, as Ieuan Ellis has argued, was very like Schleiermacher, except that he insisted even more than Schleiermacher did upon the direct subjective relationship between the Christian and Christ himself, to the exclusion of almost any role for the Church.[29] In this, as in what James Barr calls his 'biblicism',[30] Jowett showed himself to be as ineluctably protestant as Tait could ever have wished him to be. Perhaps, even, the very eclecticism of his approach was partly an expression of an essentially protestant individualism.

At all events, what Ellis calls Jowett's 'mind of his own'[31] meant that, wherever he may have derived this or that specific idea, he used it as it suited himself and to that extent was no *mere* borrower. He did not hesitate to take over a thought, when he came across it, which seemed to him to be useful in bolstering up a position which he wished to advocate or defend. Often this meant that the idea was

[29] Ellis, p. 16.
[30] Barr, p. 435.
[31] Ellis, p. 16.

taken out of its original context in the theoretical framework of the thinker from whom Jowett was borrowing it. It might, therefore, come to have a completely different significance or be used in a completely different way. This does not seem to have worried him at all. He was not, as we have seen, an admirer of systems. If an idea seemed to him to be good common sense he incorporated it into his mental vocabulary.

In many ways Jowett's closest affinity was not with any philosophical thinker but with a rather old fashioned kind of German scholarship and, in particular, with the work of the pre-Hegelian rationalist Johann Salomo Semler, who had died in 1791.[32] He had little, admittedly, of Semler's interest in the technicalities of the critical approach to the New Testament. He admired the work of F. C. Baur, whose approach Semler had, in a sense, anticipated and it may have been Baur's Hegelianism that attracted him. But it was only very occasionally that Jowett was willing even to discuss the theories of the critics. His commentary on Thessalonians contains a dissertation entitled 'Genuineness of the First Epistle' which is an answer to Baur's own view that I Thessalonians was not authentically Pauline. But Jowett's reply is really an argument from common sense rather than an essay in biblical criticism.

One of the things, indeed, which makes Jowett's approach so similar to Semler's is the fact that he was less concerned with formal logic than with reasonableness, that broadly sensible, naturally comprehensible approach which appeals to what most people will regard as likely. And one of Semler's principal concerns was to maintain that each book of the Bible had its own individual and specific context, which was the main point of Jowett's repeated insistence that the Bible was to be treated like other books. Even Jowett's assertion in *Essays and Reviews*, that it would be better for aspiring clergymen not to engage in the study of difficult questions of theology—though approached from the other end, as it were—is not unlike Semler. For the latter had maintained that Christian ministers should be required to make full and formal profession of traditional orthodoxy but claimed the right for theologians to pursue what he called '*liberalis theologia*'.

[32] I am indebted for this idea to Professor Hans Frei of Yale.

But, above all, Jowett shared with Semler an insistence on the centrality of morality. Semler had held that it was the moral law which was the core and kernel of the Old Testament and the moral teaching of Christ which constituted what was authentic in the New. He was not, of course, the only liberal scholar to substitute morality for dogma at the heart of Christianity. Nor is it actually possible to prove that Jowett had read Semler, though the college library contained some fifteen volumes of his works. Among these was a commentary on Galatians, which it would be reasonable to suppose that Jowett might have consulted before writing his own commentary on that epistle. There is, however, no actual record of Jowett having withdrawn this or any other of Semler's works.[33] Nor does Jowett list Semler among the German scholars to whom he acknowledges an indebtedness in his commentaries.[34]

The best clue to placing Jowett in relation to German theology is, of course, his review of various German thinkers in the revised essay on the atonement in the second edition of the commentaries. Those whose thought he examined were Kant, Fichte, Schelling, Hegel, Schleiermacher, and Daub. The inclusion of Daub in this list is one of the reasons for supposing that Jowett had actually read at least parts of the German works in the college library and in his own collection. For Daub would hardly now be regarded as belonging in the same category of influential thinkers as the others listed. At the time, however, it would not have been so easy to tell which of these men were going to leave a mark on the history of thought. It looks as if Jowett simply took as his examples the authors of the works coming from German publishers in the late 1830s or early 1840s. And it is also worth bearing in mind that, although the summaries of their ideas which he gives could now be duplicated by any undergraduate who took the trouble to consult any one of a dozen general accounts of the development of theology in the period, Jowett would have had to make these summaries for himself and would have had to have done so from the German originals.

---

[33] I am grateful to a former pupil of mine, James Nye, for undertaking the very boring job of checking the registers on this point.

[34] See *Epistles*, i, p. ix.

These 'great thinkers', he maintained, though they used the language of orthodoxy, really followed neither the simplicity of the biblical view of the atonement nor the classical orthodoxies of the patristic, medieval, or Reformation periods. He regarded them as valuable because they gave new meaning and prominence to scriptural ideas which had been lost sight of but they all encountered two almost insuperable difficulties: 'first, how to give a moral meaning to the idea of atonement; secondly, how to connect the idea with the historical fact'.[35] The truth of an idea, he used to say, does not prove the truth of a fact.

Jowett thought Kant had done little more than attempt to rationalise conventional Lutheran teaching on justification. He had set out to banish the mystical only to smuggle it back in again. And to rely on one's *sense* of being justified, Jowett thought, was to rely on nothing more than a projection of one's own feelings. Schleiermacher's failing was that while he could give a satisfactory account of the subjective element in atonement—a consciousness of union with God—the only objective element he could point to was the existence of the Church which was, in turn, no more than the corporate product, as it were, of that individual consciousness. But one suspects that his real objection was not Schleiermacher's subjectivism (for Jowett's own theory of the atonement was itself a subjective one) but that Schleiermacher seemed to have abandoned the good protestant belief in the immediacy of the believer's relationship with Christ.

The other Germans all fell, in Jowett's estimation, into the error of treating the atonement as 'a reconciliation of God with Himself'. What he disliked about this approach was that, however attractive it might be as metaphysics, it was concerned solely with the eternal and not with history or the life of the Christian. Fichte, he asserted, believed that the individual, by degrees, laid aside isolation and selfishness to return to the realm of the divine absolute, a blend of Christianity and Platonism impossible to locate in either subjective feeling or objective fact. For Daub the unity of man with God is also the unity of God with himself, pure abstraction returning to itself and remaining pure abstraction remote from the reality of Christ. In

[35] *Epistles*, 2nd edn., ii, p. 582.

Schelling's view God is active energy, man the child of God, and Christ the highest expression of that truth. The same struggle between good and evil which, in Christ, ended in the triumph of good, manifesting the infinite in the finite and promising the final triumph, is repeated in every individual and every age. Hegel perceived the atonement as the eternal reconciliation of the finite and the infinite in God himself: Christ goes forth from the Father as world and finite being to exist in a difference which is done away in the absoluteness of God. But the Hegelians have failed to locate this metaphysical concept in the facts of history or to make it something which has a bearing upon life.

The factual aspect which Jowett was so anxious to preserve in any theology of the atonement was plainly the historical fact of Jesus of Nazareth. He found the Germans too metaphysical and remote, insufficiently practical in their concerns. It was this impatience, perhaps, which earned for Jowett the reputation of being a man who disliked metaphysics.[36] In reality, however, he only objected to certain *kinds* of metaphysics. His concern that the death of Christ should possess an immediate relevance for the believer meant that he tended to dismiss any abstract account of theological concepts which could not easily be related to the events recounted in the Gospels or the practicalities of a moral life. It was all part of his appeal to experience and is clear evidence that at this stage a vivid personal devotion to Christ still played an important part in his religious thought.

The ideas, whether borrowed or not, which reappear again and again in Jowett's writings, sermons, and notes, add up to a kind of scheme without being a system. Like Semler, he treated morality as the touchstone for the authentically religious: religion manifested itself in the individual as morality and everything moral was attributable to God. Indeed, Jowett might have said that *everything*—except, presumably, evil though this point is not explicitly dealt with—is attributable to God. All reality, he often maintained and even more often implied, is spiritual in nature. This thought, no doubt, was a consequence of his early enthusiasm for Hegel and it is

---

[36] Abbott and Campbell, ii pp. 109f. It is clear from the passages cited by Abbott and Campbell that it was T. H. Green's idealism, in particular, that Jowett disliked.

why he so often argued that the true and demonstrable facts of history and science (a favourite phrase) are neither to be feared nor ignored. The laws by which the world of nature operates are the workings of the divine mind. And God is to be recognised in history, though as a continuum or process rather than, as Hegel had maintained, as a dialectic of self-realisation.

God is to be found most immediately in Jesus, with whom it is possible—because he is human—to have something which could be described as friendship; but a friendship which is also a relationship with divine power. The God-consciousness of Christ, which Schleiermacher thought central to Christology, thus finds its place in Jowett's thought. He could not, however, conceive of the Church as the medium through which Christ was communicated to the believer. Therefore he had to propose an alternative locus for discovering the Jesus Christ in whom God is manifest and through whose friendship the moral life becomes possible for the believer. For Jowett, of course, this locus was the Bible—understood, as Arnold had wished to understand it, in a common-sense, straightforward way. And what one would arrive at then would be, not an ecclesiastically preserved set of doctrines, but a rationally justifiable belief distilled out of the historical form taken by revealed truth. That revelation had its climax, its fullest moment in Christ. What went before him, led up to him: what followed, looked back to him. And that Christ, he believed, was available to everyone.

If this is a fair account of Jowett's theology, it was in many ways obviously naive. Edward Caird, who was to be Jowett's successor as master of Balliol and who could be very perceptive in his judgements on his predecessor, wrote of Jowett that 'his treatment of great questions never took the form of an attempt to think them out conscientiously but of a series of glances at truth from various points of view somewhat inconsistent with each other.'[37] In such an eclectic composite of ideas there were bound to be inconsistencies and incoherencies. But if it seems absurd to suppose that anyone could possibly hold together ideas garnered from such very different and sometimes conflicting sources, Jowett himself would have had an answer to such a charge. In his commentaries he had, after all,

---

[37] In *International Journal of Ethics*, Oct. 1897, p. 44.

advanced the view that the law of contradiction applied only in the sensible world: in the realm of thought, he believed, it did not. His defence of paradox may not be a convincing one but it is clear that Jowett believed himself to be free to accept any idea, from whatever source, which seemed true to experience. No doubt he seriously underestimated the difficulties involved in achieving the kind of eclectic amalgam he desired. Perhaps he never even really perceived that those difficulties existed. But, whether he thought them through seriously or not, his religious beliefs—in the 1860s and for at least some time thereafter—do seem to have added up to a scheme like the one set out above.

In a letter written to Florence Nightingale more than a decade after the publication of *Essays and Reviews* he defined his position against the idealists in language which seems to reflect the same scheme of ideas. He wrote:

Kant's idealism is too abstract and vague, and rests on his untenable hypothesis about space and time. I want to see a metaphysical philosophy which (1) deifies ideas or ideals (without any nonsense about time and space or confusions of sensation with objects of sense) (2) which shows them to be the universal or common sense of mankind.[38]

Jowett probably meant that the eternal moral verities were ideas in a quasi-Platonic sense, located somehow in the being or mind of God. (He can hardly have meant that they were literally to be deified or 'made God'.) But he also saw them as moral values innate in the human mind and, though he did not say so to Miss Nightingale, embodied in Christ. There are many passages in his sermons which would make good sense on the assumption that it was something like this which lay behind what he said.

By the time of this letter, Jowett plainly did not any longer regard himself as in any sense a disciple of Kant (as both the German and the British Idealists did) and he relished an English common sense which he contrasted with the abstract and speculative nature of much

[38] Balliol College: Jowett to Florence Nightingale, 25 June 1873. Two of my colleagues, John Prest and Vincent Quinn, are currently editing this correspondence. I am indebted to John Prest for deciphering Jowett's handwriting which is almost illegible at this point. Though 'deifies' is a difficult reading, it makes more sense than any of the alternative possibilities.

German thought. He honestly thought that that common sense could discover in the New Testament a Jesus Christ with whom a close personal 'friendship' was possible.[39] His early Evangelical upbringing doubtless played a large part in his determination to retain this warmly personal element in his liberal theology. The same assessment of his thought by his successor which has already been quoted also said of Jowett that 'born in a circle which was deeply influenced by the methodistic pietism of the last century, he retained throughout his life much of its religious spirit, even when he had ceased to hold by many of the doctrines of its creeds.'[40] This was, indeed, a very important factor in Jowett's thought. Whenever he wrote or spoke of Christ, he conceived himself to be dealing with an actual historical person whom he loved rather than a metaphysical abstraction.

The theological debate which resulted from the publication of *Essays and Reviews* has been meticulously analysed by Ieuan Ellis.[41] It was, of course, of considerable importance in the development of theology in England in the nineteenth century. In the course of it a wide range of scholars and churchmen stated, argued about, and sometimes even modified their opinions and beliefs on the authority of scripture, the nature of revelation, and the meaning of traditional orthodox doctrine. The debate, no doubt, influenced and affected the beliefs of many others. What is curious, however, is that it had very little apparent effect on the way in which Jowett developed his own thinking. He was, of course, very conscious of being the object of criticism and even hatred. He believed that he and the other contributors were (rather heroically) paying the price of defending truth and honesty. But he took little or no part in the theological debate.

This was already characteristic of his attitude to theological controversy and was to become more obvious in the future. After the publication of the first edition of the commentaries he had refused to argue doctrinal points with Scott and had ignored Golightly's attack. He seems simply to have continued to hold to his beliefs,

---

[39] For a discussion of 'friendship' in Jowett's Christology see below pp. 34–7.
[40] E. Caird, 'Professor Jowett', *International Journal of Ethics*, Oct. 1897, p. 43.
[41] Ellis, pp. 112ff.

clarified them further, looked for new arguments in support of them, and eventually to have restated them without reference to what other people had said. He had shown no desire to argue about them in the arena of either public or private debate. It was the same after 1860. *Essays and Reviews* continued to come out in one new edition after another. The debate went on all about him. But Jowett took little apparent interest. It was left to Stanley to make public defence of the essayists. Mansel's Bampton lectures of 1858 had attacked the English rationalists, including Jowett, for adopting fashionable German ideas. In 1861 Mansel contributed an essay to a volume called *Aids to Faith* which was a reply to and attack on *Essays and Reviews*. He was regarded as one of the most effective of the protagonists of orthodoxy. Yet Jowett does not seem to have owned a single copy of any of Mansel's works.

Jowett's obvious dislike of theological controversy, which led him to adopt different tactics for progagating his beliefs, is somewhat puzzling. In the college he was almost a professional controversialist, fighting battle after battle with Scott in the governing body and exerting every effort to gain control. In that context he showed no fear of personal odium, official displeasure, or disciplinary action. Simple cowardice, therefore, does not explain the fact that *Essays and Reviews* was his final venture into public theology.

It was not long, in fact, before *Essays and Reviews* came under official attack. Samuel Wilberforce urged his fellow bishops to take concerted action against it. After a meeting at Lambeth, the archbishops and twenty-four bishops issued a letter expressing their disapproval of the views contained in the essays. In what seemed to Jowett—and even more to Temple—to be an act of near-treachery, Tait was one of the signatories. The convocation of Canterbury formally debated whether to pass synodical judgement upon the book. The lower house voted to proceed to judgement but the upper house took no immediate action because Williams and Wilson were about to be prosecuted for heresy before the ecclesiastical courts. The book was, however, eventually to be condemned by convocation in 1864.

Meanwhile the prosecution of the two essayists proceeded. Williams and Wilson were the most vulnerable of the essayists because their views seemed clearly unorthodox and they were also without doubt subject to the authority of the Church courts. The Court of Arches found them guilty but the Judicial Committee of the Privy Council, acting as court of appeal in ecclesiastical causes, reversed the judgement. The whole process took nearly three years.

Jowett himself came under attack in the university. He could not be tried in the ecclesiastical courts, for he held no benefice, but he was delated to the vice-chancellor's court for teaching doctrines contrary to and inconsistent with the doctrines of the Church of England. The attempt to have him censured was led by Dr Pusey of whom Jowett said, 'he is very shrewd for a saint and has more than any man I ever came across the gift of concealing his thoughts and intentions'.[42] The vice-chancellor's assessor (effectively judge in the case) decided that his jurisdiction was, at best, doubtful and refused to proceed in the matter.

Pusey and Jowett must have been evenly matched and formidable opponents. Pusey was always a dogged and determined controversialist whose courage in battle was sustained by his absolute conviction that he was fighting—like a modern Athanasius—for the truth of the divine revelation. Jowett, in spite of his dislike of religious dispute, had become an accomplished academic politician. His constant campaigning against Scott in Balliol had given him practice in, if no taste for, the art of controversy. Against the Tractarians in the university, too, he showed no sign of being afraid to fight for what he believed to be right. The truth probably is that he had come to realise that he could much more effectively propagate his beliefs through the institutional structure of the college and the university than by publishing his theological writings. In order to gain and retain the freedom to do so he was willing to engage any opponent. The battles with Pusey must have been awesome affairs for it was said of Dr Bandinel, Bodley's librarian from 1813 to 1860 and himself a fierce and formidable character, 'that there were only two men of whom [he] was afraid, Dr Pusey and Benjamin Jowett.'[43]

The 1860s were years in which the liberals lost ground in the

[42] Lambeth Palace Library: Tait Papers: Personal Letters, vol. 78, fo. 268.

[43] Quoted in A. Livesley, 'Regius Professor of Hebrew', in P. Butler (ed.), *Pusey Rediscovered*, London 1983, p. 108.

university and the Tractarians seemed once more to be gaining the ascendancy. The new state of the parties was so significant that in 1865 both Pusey and Jowett changed sides on the matter of an honour school of theology. Pusey, confident that the supremacy of the conservatives would ensure that teaching and examining would be in the hands of orthodox dons, began to support the introduction of such a school. And it was Jowett's turn to argue that theology was too sacred a subject for examination.[44]

Pusey was also a protagonist in another, more complicated wrangle over Jowett's stipend as Professor of Greek. Jowett's appointment to the chair may have been due to efforts made on his behalf by H. G. Liddell, who became dean of Christ Church in 1855.[45] Liddell, though Scott's collaborator in the famous lexicon, was an ally of Jowett's in the sense that they were both counted as liberals in the university. But it is also possible that Palmerston offered Jowett the post in recognition of the help he had given in the reform of the Indian Civil Service in the preceding two years.[46] If this latter is the real explanation then it was a very modest recognition, for the professor's salary was £40 a year.

It is sometimes suggested that, as Regius Professor of Greek, Jowett ought to have had a canonry at Christ Church.[47] That would have been, in financial terms, a splendid reward—though one cannot help wondering whether Jowett would have accepted it if it had meant moving from Balliol. It is also tempting to speculate how different his own history and that of the college would have been in that case. In fact canonries were actually *attached* only to the regius chairs of Divinity and Hebrew[48] and the Greek chair might be held with a fellowship at another college. Though the house, the chairs, and the canonries were all funded out of the same sixteenth-century endowment, the sum paid to the Professor of Greek still stood at the amount fixed at that date. The reforms of 1854 had included provision for increasing the stipends of professors and it was supposed that Jowett's salary should have been increased to a sum more

[44] Ward, pp. 250ff.
[45] Ward, p. 212.
[46] Prest, *Robert Scott*, p. 4.
[47] Engel, p. 75.
[48] Bill and Mason, p. 5.

appropriate to nineteenth-century prices. But Jowett's opponents felt very strongly that what was essentially a *religious* endowment should not be used to pay a man of heterodox beliefs. The affair dragged on for six years and was only finally settled in 1865, again largely through the efforts of Liddell—though it has to be said that Pusey also was willing to help devise a formula that would not offend the orthodox. Jowett's stipend was eventually increased and for all that he used to talk—typically—of the persecutions he had suffered on account of *Essays and Reviews*, he had really escaped very lightly.

5
Master

Jowett was finally elected master of Balliol in September 1870, just ten years after the publication of *Essays and Reviews* and apparently as a result of the direct and deliberate intervention of Mr Gladstone. The two had met a year earlier when they were both staying with the Earl of Camperdown. They had talked, apparently, about the Irish question, on which Jowett thought Gladstone 'so unsound'.[1] At the end of the year Robert Lowe, who had been a close friend since the 1850s when he had been a private coach in Oxford, told Jowett that Gladstone was anxious to 'do' something for him. 'I told him that I did not intend to leave Oxford, and therefore the only thing that could be done for me would be to make Scott a Dean or a Bishop. Mr Lowe thought that this would be done, and set about the matter with great zeal.'[2]

There was a false alarm when it was rumoured that Scott was to be offered a bishopric. Jowett had the grace to recognise that Gladstone could hardly be expected to make a man a bishop in order to do someone else a favour but Lowe encouraged him, in a hearty rather than sympathetic fashion, to wait a bit longer. It is plain—even from the letters which his biographers thought it safe to publish—that, though he pretended otherwise, the defeat of fifteen years earlier still rankled with him. He wanted desperately to be master and to be free to rule the college without the necessity for perpetual controversy. At last, in June 1870, Robert Scott was appointed to the deanery of Rochester. Jowett was elected to the vacancy thus created, as he and everyone else had confidently expected.

Gladstone's action was, on the face of it, odd. He disapproved

---

[1] Abbott and Campbell, i, p. 406, where Jowett's earlier contacts with Gladstone are ignored except to mention the fact that they had once breakfasted together.
[2] Abbott and Campbell, i, pp. 408f.

vigorously of Jowett's theology. The pencilled comments he wrote in the margins of his copy of Jowett's essay—Gladstone was in the habit of annotating the books he read—were the comments of an orthodox Tractarian and very critical of Jowett's theological position. They were also, in some cases, virulent in the extreme and *ad hominem*, if not *ad personam*. Where Jowett had written 'Everyone . . . has need to make war against his prejudices . . .', Gladstone remarked, 'None more need than the writer of this essay.' And his final comment on the essay as a whole was, 'A cold, vain, barren Philosophy, ending with the Grave here. The sport and Triumph of devils hereafter.' None of the other essays was annotated except Temple's and, in that case, there were as many approving underlinings or ticks as there were disapproving 'ma's. The only articulate note was 'Homer! Dante!' written against Temple's assertion that a modern child of twelve stood at the intellectual level once occupied by a full grown man.

No other book he read seems to have provoked Gladstone as Jowett's essay did. Even Colenso (of whom Gladstone disapproved very severely) did not receive such savage treatment. The bishop's *Pentateuch and the Book of Joshua, critically examined* (or rather the first part of it, for Gladstone seems to have become less and less interested in the later, more technical—and positive—volumes) was favoured with the usual onomatopoeic noises but no real comment.[3]

One would not have expected someone who disliked Jowett's theology so much to have wanted to 'do' something for him. But Gladstone was a sufficiently fair man not to allow personal antipathy or theological differences to outweigh all other considerations. More immediately to the point, he sent Temple to be Bishop of Exeter in 1869, the very year in which Lowe was acting as go-between with Jowett. On the flyleaf at the back of Gladstone's copy of *Essays and Reviews* there is a pencilled list of names which include those of Jowett, Stanley, Maurice, Temple, Pattison, and even Colenso, along with others of a less radical reputation. One is tempted to wonder whether, in the early 1860s, he had been making

---

[3] Gladstone's copies of *Essays and Reviews* and of Colenso's works are now in St Deiniol's Library, Hawarden. I am indebted to John Prest for drawing my attention to the comments on the last few pages of Jowett's essay.

a list of liberal names for Palmerston to consider for preferment, perhaps as a counterweight to the Evangelicals whom Shaftesbury usually suggested to him.

If Gladstone could be savage about Jowett, Jowett was more than able to return the compliment. In the early 1860s he had made the acquaintance of Florence Nightingale, who had returned from the Crimea in 1856 and was more or less an invalid thereafter. The two became close friends and she was the recipient of many of his confidences and, perhaps, the person with whom Jowett was as nearly completely honest about his thoughts and feelings as it was possible for him to be. In 1865 he told her that Gladstone was 'a great deal more mad than he is supposed to be. Everyone who wishes to understand him should read his Homer. I am afraid he is always in the hands of some confessor. Is he a Roman Catholic? I don't feel certain.'[4] The joke about the insanity revealed in Gladstone's translation of Homer, on which Jowett was supposed to be advising him, was a favourite one and seems to have been borrowed from Lowe.

Even after he became master Jowett was still often sarcastic at Gladstone's expense. 'Mr Gladstone . . . makes no secret of his conversion to disestablishment. Neither did he when I met him about six years ago. But then it became a secret again which no friend of the Ministry was allowed to question.'[5] To Lord John Russell, and therefore presumably with some deliberation, he ventured to say that he thought Gladstone 'the most impressible of human beings, notwithstanding, or perhaps as the result of his wonderful gifts. And he is apt to get the wrong sort of persons about him.'[6] One of these wrong sort of persons was Pusey, whom Jowett loved to refer to as 'the Hebrew Conservative'.

The problem is to know how seriously one ought to take Jowett's gadfly comments about any of his acquaintances. Sometimes he seems to make them merely for the pleasure of turning a neat and witty phrase. He was only too easily inclined to complain about his allies and even his close friends and he found it difficult to allow an

---

[4] Balliol College: Jowett to Florence Nightingale, 21 Oct. 1865.

[5] Jowett to Florence Nightingale, 16 Nov. 1874.

[6] Quoted in [J. M.] Prest, *Jowett['s Correspondence] on Education [with Earl Russell in 1867*, supplement to the Balliol College Record, 1965], p. 13.

opportunity for an apt but back-handed compliment to go unused. One of the least attractive features of his personality was his willingness to give way to this kind of emotional disloyalty, so that he only too frequently said unkind but funny things about people he was fond of. And about people he disliked or was opposed to, he could be very nasty indeed. Once, with a rare but honest insight into his own failing, he told Miss Nightingale, 'Some day I will make another compact with you not to speak evil of any one which I am always doing and which I always feel to be a great weakness and can often trace in myself to a personal motive . . .'[7]

When he made this particular confession he was thinking, he said, of the way he had spoken of, among others, Tait and Goldwin Smith, both of whom had been allies of his in earlier campaigns. Tait had been more than an ally and Jowett owed him, as he acknowledged at other times, a very great deal. But he also irritated him into incautious unkindnesses and so Jowett could sometimes say very cruel things and sometimes very kind and affectionate things about Tait. One can never be sure which really represented his considered opinion. In a final judgement on Tait—written not much more than a year before his own death—Jowett said that he 'was always a very kind friend to me' 'He was an excellent man and a gentleman, very good and very Scotch; but . . . I used to miss in his conversation, any interest about truth in the higher sense. He did not seem to think that it was of the least importance compared with "keeping the Church together." If he had possessed this element he would have been a great man.'[8]

It is not easy, then, to know whether Jowett's malicious comments on his friends and acquaintances are to be taken seriously. But even if one discounts the most waspish comments it is difficult to see why Gladstone should want to do something for Jowett. Not only was liberal theology distasteful to the Tractarian politician: Gladstone's 'secret' unease about anything remotely resembling Erastianism would have been a further barrier between the two men. Jowett, like most Broad Churchmen, regarded the state connection as a protection for theological freedom. But, perhaps, it is just worth

[7] Jowett to Florence Nightingale, 16 Mar. 1869.
[8] Abbott and Campbell, ii, pp. 394f.

remembering that the end of the 1860s was a period when there was a brief conjunction between Gladstone and Tait to reform some aspects of the administration and worship of the established Church.[9] Since Gladstone was willing to be allied with Tait, whose attitude was much more thoroughly Erastian, he may also have been willing to help Tait's friends.

Jowett was, of course, in some sense, a liberal in politics as he was a liberal in theology. In fact an unpleasantly unsympathetic reviewer of his biography was to assume that it was not necessary to distinguish between the two kinds of liberalism, as though no self-respecting Tory would ever have held a heterodox religious opinion.[10] But it is easiest, perhaps, to define Jowett's political views as Liberal, in the sense that they were most decidedly not Tory. Faber has argued that he would not have accepted any political label,[11] but his interest in the reform of the university, quite apart from anything else, put him firmly in the anti-Tory camp. All his closest associations, in theological and religious circles, were with the 'Arnoldites', who favoured a broad and inclusive national Church. And that would put him in the traditionally Whig rather than the Tory camp.

But, just as there is very little available evidence for reconstructing the development of his early ideas about theology or university reform, so there is almost none about his early political opinions. And there is a further parallel between his theological and political opinions. In politics as in theology he was far too idiosyncratic to be fitted neatly into any particular school or party. He had some knowledge of political theory and was not entirely happy about pure Benthamite economics.[12] He thought that Utilitarians might, with some justice, be suspected of 'vulgarity of mind'.[13] He favoured Turkey against Russia and Napoleon III against Prussia. He was sympathetic towards Italian nationalism, met Mazzini in 1871 and

---

[9] P. T. Marsh, 'The Primate and the Prime Minister: Archbishop Tait, Gladstone and the National Church', *Victorian Studies*, 9 (1965), pp. 113ff.

[10] 'Mr Jowett and Oxford Liberalism', [*Blackwood's Edinburgh Magazine*, 161], pp. 721–732.

[11] Faber, p. 24.

[12] Abbott and Campbell, i, p. 131.

[13] *Sermons on Faith*, p. 233.

was very impressed by his ideas—chiefly perhaps because Mazzini laid such stress on a moral rather than a materialistic society.[14] He never took kindly to the movement for the higher education of women.[15] (But there were other leading political and theological liberals of whom that would have been true.) He voted Liberal till Gladstone brought in his Home Rule Bill for Ireland and was probably a supporter of the Liberal Unionists after that. But he was sometimes critical of the Liberals, complaining that they were becoming un-English. He was, indeed, always somewhat self-consciously patriotic and rather proud of being English.

It is probable that in political affairs Jowett's interest, when he was not motivated simply by idiosyncratic prejudices, sprang from his passionate concern for morality. We have already seen that he sometimes felt that social and political morality had sunk so low as to be almost a cause for doubting the truth of Christianity. He seems also to have hankered for an earlier age when, as he believed, politicians had been nobler and more moral. Towards the end of his life he praised Peel, for whom he seems to have had a particular regard, as a representative of what he called 'the old pre-Reform Bill days . . . when statesmen seem to me to have been more loyal and faithful to one another than they are now'.[16]

But those words reveal that, when he spoke of political morality, he was chiefly thinking of the personal behaviour of politicians rather than of the moral effects or consequences of policies. Though he recognised the need for some reform of society, he found it difficult to relate this to a specific system of political philosophy as both T. H. Green and Edward Caird were to do. Consequently he believed that morality in politics was best served by having the right men in the right places. And he thought of his own task as grooming them and getting them there.

It is probable that, in any case, Jowett lacked the imagination to be thoroughly radical in politics, though his instincts would always have been against anything which put inherited privilege above personal ability. He and friends of his like Temple tended, in a

[14] Abbott and Campbell, ii, pp. 10f.
[15] 'Mr Jowett and Oxford Liberalism', p. 727.
[16] Abbott and Campbell, ii, p. 395.

general way, to favour attempts to improve the fairness of society. But he was, in many ways, a snob, though he would himself have argued that the reason why he devoted so much time to the successful and aristocratic was that they had many opportunities for doing good and noble things. And he would have said that exercising an influence upon them was the most important part of his work as master. Balliol, his enemies asserted, 'was the chosen haunt of the prig, and many was the prig of promise who passed through his hands. While not really a prig himself, he got the credit of being the cause of priggishness in others, though perhaps he was only to blame in not warning them off a very obvious and well-marked shoal.'[17]

But if his job was to create prigs (people, that is to say, who would deliberately and self-consciously strive to behave morally) and place them in important positions, then perhaps it was important for him not to be enmeshed too openly in the machinery of any particular party. Influential Tory prigs would be just as much grist to his mill as Liberal ones. And, in any case, he preferred to influence affairs—as he had already done in 1854—from behind the scenes. He once told Miss Nightingale, 'The only way is to work through the press— newspapers, Magazines, Books;—especially through private and carefully written letters to distinguished persons. There is no means more efficacious than this.'[18]

Robert Lowe had been Jowett's closest contact in politics for some time before 1870. Jowett thought he had 'a mind whereas Gladstone has only a sort of madness akin to genius'.[19] But this had not prevented his being a great admirer of Lord John Russell in whom Lowe could see no good. No doubt Russell's membership of one of the great Whig families played some part in Jowett's respect for him. But this need not have been mere snobbery. Intellectually as well as temperamentally he would have had a great deal in common with the man who had been in the vanguard of Whig reformers in Jowett's favourite 'old pre-Reform Bill days'. Aligning himself with the radicalism of one generation previous to his own is somehow very characteristic of Jowett.

[17] 'Mr Jowett and Oxford Liberalism', pp. 726f.
[18] Balliol College: Jowett to Florence Nightingale, 6 July 1883.
[19] Jowett to Florence Nightingale, Oct. 1866.

At all events he had greeted the Russell/Gladstone administration of 1865 with enthusiasm. 'I am pleased with the Election; the new Parliament will certainly be a great improvement on the old one.' But, in spite of this enthusiasm, he could not resist a dig at Gladstone who, having lost the university seat, had been elected to represent the textile manufacturing constituency of South Lancashire. 'I hardly know whether to rejoice or not at Gladstone's departure. I see the Hebrew Conservative is at him, trying to fling his toils round him declaring "that he is faithful to his Church and his God". I suppose a great conflict of Romanism and Radicalism, Aristocracy and Plutocracy, Manchester and Oxford is going on in the mind of that distinguished man.'[20]

Most of Russell's policies, particularly on university and electoral reform, he supported wholeheartedly and was therefore very distressed when Lowe viciously attacked the proposal to extend the franchise.[21] Lowe, who by the end of the year was dismissing Gladstone 'as knowing nothing but Homer',[22] was one of the promoters of the so-called 'Cave of Adullam' which brought down Russell's short-lived administration in 1866. Once again, in spite of the disappointment he must have felt, Jowett indulged in a jab at Gladstone when the government fell. He commented with enjoyment to Miss Nightingale that 'being only half a Liberal [he] is not thought worthy (by Providence I mean) to pass a Reform Bill just as David was not thought worthy to build the Temple'.[23]

Meanwhile Jowett had not abandoned his desire to see further reforms carried out in the university. One of his chief objectives was to remove the remaining doctrinal tests. As early as 1864 he had been at a meeting in London, also attended by T. H. Huxley and Bishop Colenso among others, in support of a bill to abolish all tests for Oxford degrees.[24] At the meeting he seems—characteristically—to have sat with two of his lay Balliol friends rather than with any of the leading liberal churchmen or theologians.[25] That presumably

---

[20] Jowett to Florence Nightingale, 23 July 1865.
[21] Prest, *Jowett on Education*, p. 3.
[22] Jowett to Florence Nightingale, 15 Nov. 1865.
[23] Jowett to Florence Nightingale, Mar. 1867.
[24] Ward, p. 245.
[25] A list of those present at the meeting is printed in an appendix to [L.] Campbell,

unselfconscious choice of companions symbolised his whole attitude to religion in the university and explains why he thought subscription undesirable. He aimed to create an approach to Christianity which would meet the needs of the intelligent layman and undergraduate, rather than those of the clergymen of the established church.

In this period just before he became master, Jowett had begun to take an interest in a wide range of social issues—the care of the incurably sick, the insane, destitute children, sanitation, and rates on property. A conviction that 'moral improvement could not be effected without material changes'[26] began to be characteristic of his thought. While this conviction probably figured more in what he said and wrote than in what he actually did, it meant that his concern for political morality was sometimes expressed in terms of policies and institutions, not merely of men. And his pupils took over and expanded this concern.

Towards the end of the decade Jowett took up the whole question of the English educational system—or lack of it. By 1867, the Russell administration having been replaced by Derby's, there was widespread support for educational reform. Since proposals for electoral reform were in the air, a great many people were saying that something had better be done to educate those who were going to be given political rights and responsibilities. Jowett urged Lowe actively to take up the cause of primary education as well as to be conciliatory towards Russell. Sheer chance then gave him the kind of opportunity he loved. The Russells had a son whom they wished to send to Oxford and Lady Russell asked Jowett for advice. Russell himself was planning to move a series of resolutions on education in the Lords and and on this, too, he canvassed Jowett's opinion. Jowett feared that the new administration's extension of the suffrage would provoke hasty and ill-considered attempts to provide educational facilities for future generations of voters. He thought it worth sending Russell a lengthy memorandum which contained fairly

---

[*On the Nationalisation of the Old English Universities*, London 1901]. Since the names are not in alphabetical (or any other obvious) order, I am assuming that people signed the lists in the order in which they were sitting.

[26] Abbott and Campbell, i, pp. 392f.

detailed and practical proposals for reforming grammar schools and primary schools as well as the universities.[27]

The memorandum is a remarkable piece of work. It is not, as Jowett's paper for Gladstone was in 1854, an actual draft of proposed legislation and is not, therefore, as detailed. But it shows a considerable knowledge of the current situation and makes practical proposals for reforming the whole system. So far as the universities were concerned (though the suggestions were really only applicable to Oxford) Jowett wanted admission to the MA degree without religious tests; the admission of dissenters to fellowships in colleges willing to have them; permission for students not to be members of colleges so that an Oxford education might be cheaper; changes in the government of the university in order to reduce the power of resident clergymen who were not engaged in education; provision for colleges to change their own statutes, which he thought the most important matter of all; and the appointment of a commission to redistribute endowments so as to abolish sinecures and increase the number of positions for married men. His views on primary and grammar school education followed from his proposals on university reform because he believed 'that the development of the Universities depends upon the Improvement of the Schools. Every part of this subject hangs together.'[28]

Perhaps the only surprising feature of the memorandum is Jowett's suggestion that 'The Monopoly of the Colleges should be abolished' by allowing students to be members of the university without being members of a college. This was a subject on which, from time to time, he changed his mind. But it may be that in 1867 he believed all other considerations were outweighed by the necessity of making universities 'economical places of learning' so that they could be truly national without restrictions of 'class or denomination';[29] or he may simply have thought that this might be another stick with which to beat the unfortunate Scott. It is even possible that he was so confident in Balliol's superiority and its

---

[27] The memorandum and related correspondence are printed in Prest, *Jowett on Education*, pp. 4ff.

[28] Quoted in Prest, *Jowett on Education*, p. 7.

[29] Prest, ibid. p. 7.

ability to attract students that he was willing to make the concession. He added to his proposal the comment that 'when the better Colleges are full [the student] is compelled to resort to the inferior ones. The Class Lists show that there are not more than 3 or 4 Colleges at which a good education is given.'[30]

The memorandum contains a good many clues about Jowett's political and religious attitudes at the time. Indeed the whole correspondence with Russell is very revealing. It would seem, for instance, that by 1867 Balliol was giving some encouragement to those interested in science. Jowett told Russell that it would be possible for his son to matriculate at the college on the basis of a knowledge of the physical sciences, provided he knew enough Greek and Latin to be likely to pass the university examinations.[31] It is, of course, possible that Jowett's apparent sympathy for the sciences was tailored to his knowledge that the young Russell wished to pursue such subjects. But by this date there was, as his own partisans insisted, 'no question of his supremacy' in the college.[32] It must, therefore, be assumed that the admission of scientists with an inferior knowledge of the classical languages had, at the least, Jowett's tacit approval.

For an understanding of his theology perhaps the most important point of all is contained in 'a few more notes about Education' which he sent to Russell in November 1867. In the seventh of these notes he said:

Is there not as much danger of making education depend upon the shifting views of popular religion as upon those of any particular denomination? The reading of the Bible in schools is apt to become a mere form. The difficulty of reconciling the Protestant faith with the knowledge and spirit of the latter half of the 19th century is almost if not quite as great as that of reconciling the Church and the World or the Church and Science among Catholics. A large proportion, some say the greater number of our Artisan Class are the enemies of religious belief. If they are to be regained and restored to religious influences at all, this must be accomplished not by repeating the letter of Scripture or by insisting on their belief in miracles or on Genesis versus Science and History but by presenting to them Christianity unawares or the

[30] Ibid. p. 7.
[31] Ibid. p. 4.
[32] Davis, p. 193.

moral aspect of the Christian faith. This, although not to be obtruded in public discussions about education has to be seriously considered by the Statesmen who would provide for the wants of the next generation.[33]

This is so like what he had said particularly in the last part of his contribution to *Essays and Reviews*, and so typical of the younger Jowett in its insistence upon a 'real' Christian faith (and especially morality) as opposed to a dogmatic and literalist orthodoxy, that it is difficult to believe that his theological opinions had changed in any essential particular.

Russell moved his resolutions, most of which were clearly influenced by Jowett's memorandum, in December 1867. 'Every child', he argued, 'has a moral Right to the Blessings of Education.' At about the same time Jowett was telling Miss Nightingale that Lowe and others were 'trying to screw Gladstone up to the point about the Universities and Education'[34] But soon afterwards he reported Lowe as saying that 'Lord Russell has done one good thing by his resolutions: he has discredited himself. This is his savage reckless way of talking which will leave him without a political friend.'[35]

In fact, Lowe did himself no great harm. By 1868 he was in office as Gladstone's Chancellor of the Exchequer. In 1870 Jowett was once again in touch with him about the abolition of religious tests in universities even for heads of houses. And in the same year, of course, Lowe and Gladstone between them organised Scott's departure from Balliol, making room for Jowett's election. By that time Jowett had many contacts in political circles. His views as a liberal and a reformer—though somewhat old-fashioned—would have been known. And even if he and Gladstone were not temperamentally sympathetic to one another, he had some friends in high places.

One may suppose that Robert Scott was glad to be given a graceful way out of the impossible situation which Jowett had created in the college and to be delivered from the continual pressure for reform. He had had nearly a decade of being forced to accept responsibility for changes which he did not approve but had no power to prevent once Jowett controlled the governing body. Scott

[33] Prest, *Jowett on Education*, p. 12.
[34] Balliol College: Jowett to Florence Nightingale, 4 Dec. 1867.
[35] Balliol College: Jowett to Florence Nightingale, Dec. 1867.

was the last master of the college to go on to an important office in the established Church. The very fact that one simply cannot imagine that Jowett would regard such a thing as promotion, reveals that he stood for a completely new and different idea of what the college should be. He was where he wanted to be at last. Certainly no ecclesiastical preferment would have tempted *him* away from Balliol—even if anyone could have been induced to offer it. A. J. Engel has argued that by the 1890s 'The traditional clerical Oxford had been destroyed to make way for a new secular profession.'[36] That transformation—'from clergyman to don' as the title of Engel's book describes it—Jowett *almost* epitomised. Not that, for reasons to be advanced below, he was ever a wholly secular person, yet he would certainly have thought of himself as a professional educator, unlike those of his contemporaries who became college fellows as a stepping-stone to ecclesiastical preferment. He represented a transitional phase between the two.

It is very unlikely that Jowett had ever wanted the older kind of career. In a letter, probably written in January 1865, he had said that no mitre had ever been made that would fit his head. Deaneries were better, but even they were not what he really wanted.[37] One simply cannot imagine his being lured away from Balliol as Scott had been. In reply to a letter from Tait congratulating him on his election he wrote, 'I am where I wish to be. My desire here is not to be leader of a party but to educate the young men or get them educated.'[38] It was the height of his ambition and one suspects that he would not have regarded a bishopric as a step up from the mastership.

Ecclesiastical preferment would also have required a degree of submission to conventional orthodoxy which he would have found it difficult to accept. In spite of the fact that the Judicial Committee of the Privy Council had found for Williams and Wilson in the *Essays and Reviews* case and also for Colenso in his appeal against the attempt to excommunicate him, Jowett had retained his horror of subscription. When, in 1865, Stanley tried to persuade him of the joys of marriage, Jowett replied, 'I could not marry without giving

---

[36] Engel, p. 1f.
[37] Balliol College: an undated letter from Jowett to Florence Nightingale.
[38] Lambeth Palace Library: Tait Papers: Personal Letters, vol. 88, fo. 163.

up Balliol, on which my life has been spent, and probably signing the XXXIX Articles over again, or having to make a statement of opinions to a Bishop, if I took a living or could get a Deanery or Canonry.'[39] Once he became master he was, in any case, in a position to use the college for the purpose for which he had intended it for more than fifteen years, as a home for a genuinely religious, genuinely liberal thought.

In the years that followed his election, Jowett was to concentrate, academically speaking, on the Greek philosophers and particularly on Plato rather than on theology. The college, of course, occupied more and more of his time and thought. He continued courageously, in typical Broad Church fashion, to defend theological freedom. Bishop Colenso's pentateuchal criticism had succeeded *Essays and Reviews* as the theological storm centre. When Colenso, having been excommunicated by Robert Gray of Cape Town, came on a visit to England Samuel Wilberforce refused to allow him to function in the diocese of Oxford. Jowett, who had become master by this time, invited him to preach in Balliol chapel which was not under the bishop's jurisdiction.[40] He continued, therefore, to be quite open about his own sympathies and his theological silence was not merely due to cowardice nor the discretion that might have been thought proper in a head of house.

There had, indeed, been a proposal to produce a second volume of *Essays and Reviews*. In January 1870 Jowett had written to Edward Caird, a former Balliol man who had become Professor of Moral Philosophy at Glasgow, to solicit his help:

Wilson and I have determined to have a second volume of *Essays and Reviews*, to appear on or about January 1, 1871. We mean to take every possible pains that this volume should be adequate to the subjects of which it treats and should be written in a religious spirit. Wilson proposes to write on the progressive principle of Protestantism, showing the element of progress in the Reformation, and the element of fixedness. I am intending to write (perhaps) two essays. The first, on the Reign of Law, showing (1) the relation of the laws of Nature to Morality, and (2) the impossibility of basing religion on miracles. The second essay would be on the present and future

[39] Abbott and Campbell, i, p. 374.
[40] Abbott and Campbell, ii, p. 64.

position of the Church of England, discussing its present state and possibilities of establishment and disestablishment. . . . Of course no one can write on these subjects without incurring a certain amount of odium, and the adversaries will be bitter, because they think that they have extinguished us, and will find that they have not. The old name [i.e. *Essays and Reviews*] is likely both to command attention and bring odium. The position we are likely to take up is the most hateful to them, that of religious men who care about the truth.[41]

Though it is not clear why the volume never appeared, this letter is evidence that Jowett's theology had not changed. He was still concerned to maintain a position which would be in accordance with new scientific knowledge and not rest upon the supposed authority of miracles; that would accord with a belief in development or progress in religion without ceasing to be protestant; and that would tackle the relationship between morality and the new understanding of the world (which was to become an overriding concern in later years). He certainly had not become in any sense an unbeliever. After reading Seeley's *Ecce Homo* he said, 'His book has the advantage of considering the subject in some way, whereas most people are contented with words and formulas. But it is wholly uncritical in not examining the documents—and unspiritual in regarding Christ as the founder of a Church rather than as a sacred individual—and unphilosophical in imagining that moral defects are reached by the Church in the same way that legal offences are reached by the law.'[42] That Christ was a 'sacred individual' rather than a purely human figure was clearly of the utmost importance to him.

Moreover, he seems to have been both sincere and quite serious when he assured Tait that he had no desire to found or lead a party. He might have fostered a whole generation of Balliol bishops and divines. But though the college did produce some eminent ecclesiastics in the nineteenth century, very few of them could be described as in any sense Jowett's protégés. This is the more surprising because in other fields Jowett is remembered as someone who devoted a great deal of time and energy to picking, training, and placing able young men who became leading establishment figures. He was, in other

[41] Abbott and Campbell, i, pp. 441f.
[42] Abbott and Campbell, i, pp. 425f.

words, a respected and influential figure, except in his own profession where he was something of a maverick without obvious heirs.

One might think to explain this by saying that Jowett tried his hand at theology, got into trouble, and then turned to more secular activities. His biographers suggest that the reason why the projected second volume of *Essays and Reviews* failed to appear was that Jowett 'may well have hesitated, after his appointment to the Mastership, to risk another storm'.[43] But that is hardly fair to Jowett: he made no attempt to disguise his beliefs. And to suggest that he turned to more secular affairs would be to misunderstand late nineteenth-century Oxford which, even after 1871, was not a wholly secular place. Religion still occupied a good deal of the time—and the minds—of heads of colleges and Jowett was not, in any case, really a secular person. Nor did he regard his clerical role as an empty formality.

He wrote to Gladstone in 1871 about the bill to abolish religious tests in the university, drawing attention to the fact that the clause which retained these tests for heads of houses might become an absurdity if there were to be in the future, Methodist or Roman Catholic colleges, which Jowett thought very likely indeed. The greater part of the letter, however, was taken up by a plea for a change in the proposed clause which dealt with services in college chapels. He argued that the clause which permitted only an abridgement of morning and evening prayer was too strict and would prevent varied and carefully planned forms of service. He asked that the bill be revised so as to permit adaptations as well as abridgements, provided that the material was taken exclusively from the Prayer Book or the Bible. It would, he said, be very important for the proper religious training of the undergraduates that there should be varied forms of service and an appropriate selection of readings from scripture for a year which consisted, in practice, of twenty-four weeks. Attractive services, he insisted, mattered a great deal to those—like himself—who were anxious to bring the young men to chapel without compulsion.[44]

These are not the words of a secular man and, in fact, Jowett produced his set of weekday services which incorporated a wide

---

[43] Abbott and Campbell, i, p. 405.
[44] BM add MS 44, 430, fo. 226, Jowett to Gladstone, 20 May (1871).

variety of extracts from the Book of Common Prayer and continued to be used in the college chapel until well into the present century. Jowett thought that an ideal liturgy would be 'ancient' but not at variance with modern scientific opinion, variable within certain limits and adapted to private as well as public use. It should contain no creeds—'for these almost at once pass into mere words'; should correspond to what is highest in thought and to the fears, hopes, and sorrows of mankind, and should *elevate* ordinary religion.[45] It cannot be said that his proposed forms of service met all these criteria but they met the most obvious ones. He was very proud of the fact that undergraduates would come to chapel quite voluntarily to these services.[46]

In turning from academic theology to the business of running the college, then, Jowett was not abandoning religion for a secular career. But neither did he moderate his radical theological opinions nor try to hide them. Right up to the end of his life he had plans for writing theological works. But his close *theological* friendships with Balliol men of the 1840s were fading. He remained on good but not intimate terms with Tait till the latter's death. He continued to count Stanley as a close friend (even Florence Nightingale was not allowed to denigrate him) and preached regularly for him in the Abbey. But Stanley had this knack of never being quite in the front line and had 'behaved strangely' at times.[47]

Perhaps the greatest betrayal was Temple's. Although Temple's nomination to Exeter provoked an outcry, he had already dissociated himself from the other contributors to *Essays and Reviews*—ironically in view of Temple's anger with Tait for signing the bishops' letter. Even in the rather muffled account given in his biography, which tried very hard to present Temple in the best possible light, his action hardly appears very creditable.[48] He seems to have done three things—asked the boys not to read the book,

[45] Abbott and Campbell, ii, p. 87.
[46] Abbott and Campbell, ii, p. 31.
[47] Above p. 71.
[48] [E. G.] Sandford [(ed.), *Memoirs of Archbishop Temple*, 2 vols., London 1906,] i pp. 219ff. and cf. A. O. J. Cockshut, *Anglican Attitudes: A Study of Victorian Religious Controversies*, London 1959, pp. 68ff. for another attempt to put Temple's action in a more favourable light.

asserted that as headmaster of Rugby he would not have contributed to it, and stressed that he had had no idea what was in the other essays. Subsequently, after he had become a bishop, he 'withdrew his essay from further publication'.[49] The dedication in Jowett's commentaries must have acquired an ironic overtone. The 'long and never failing friendship' had come to an end.[50] Yet Jowett seems not to have been as bitter about Temple as about some others who, at one time or another, he thought had betrayed him. He came to a fairer judgement about him—in which, nevertheless, the bitterness is still clear enough—more quickly than was his usual habit. By 1869 he was able to say to Florence Nightingale that Temple 'is a good man and he has great powers, but he has neither caution nor courage. I got a great deal of good from him in early life but I am always disappointed when I come back to him now.'[51]

In Jowett's opinion Tait and Temple both lacked what he thought of as a concern for truth—by which he meant that they were not willing to say publicly and categorically that they no longer held to a belief in the literal truth of the Bible or to all the old orthodoxies. A good many of the bishops were by no means simple literalists. It was one of Colenso's great complaints against Samuel Wilberforce that he was prepared to say privately that he did not believe that everything in the Old Testament was literally true but, nevertheless, behaved in public as if it were unquestionable.[52]

What had happened, in fact, was that Jowett no longer had any close friend near at hand who could be trusted absolutely yet with whom he could strike the old theological sparks. His close friends of later years were not theologians or clergymen. Even in the religious field, he was primarily concerned to expound a faith which would capture the interest of intelligent laymen and to exert a moral influence on those who occupied high places in society. After he became master he was chiefly interested not in theologians and clergymen but in the men who figured in public affairs.

[49] Sandford, i, pp. 301ff.
[50] Curiously the rather ornate phrasing had already been omitted from the dedication to Temple in the 2nd edn., published in 1859 before *Essays and Reviews* appeared.
[51] Balliol College: Jowett to Florence Nightingale, 1 Aug. 1869.
[52] G. W. Cox, *Life of John William Colenso DD, Bishop of Natal*, 2 vols., London 1888, i, p. 470.

Perhaps his closest confidante was Florence Nightingale. Whether he ever actually proposed marriage to her or not is doubtful.[53] Miss Nightingale herself contributed to the mysterious aura which surrounds their friendship by refusing to allow her name to be used by Abbott and Campbell who simply refer to her as 'a friend'. Though there is absolutely nothing in the letters which could possibly have caused her any embarrassment, the mere fact that she was not named was bound to provoke speculation. She was not the only close woman friend whom Jowett possessed. He was particularly fond of George Eliot, in spite of the fact that he did not care much for the ideas of G. H. Lewes: presumably a common interest in Strauss and German theology was the principal bond between them. Many of his letters are addressed to women but with none of them was he as frank and at ease as with Florence Nightingale. She seems to have been a woman friend in almost exactly the sense in which he once defined the 'ideal of female friendship'—'strictly regulated—never allowed to pass into love or excitement—of a noble, manly sort, with something of protecting care in it'.[54]

Since Florence Nightingale was a highly intelligent woman of powerful personality but without any formal higher education, he could treat her in some sense like a very able pupil, leading her into new ideas and at the same time trying out his own thoughts on her. She was the ideal person on whom to test his ideas of what the layman would find sensible and credible. Like George Eliot she was interested in religion and yet not at all conventional in her beliefs. Because, in her own field of nursing, she was regarded as an expert on organisation and training, she would understand his plans and experiments for running the college. She was also right outside the world Jowett normally moved in and he could, therefore, tell her things without fear that they would reach the wrong ears. Finally, her powerful personality meant that she was not afraid to lecture him for his own good in a way that he might not have accepted from a man. And there was in the relationship an element of protecting care. This is shown in letters from Jowett to Tait (when he was Bishop of London where Florence Nightingale lived). Jowett sought

---

[53] Faber, pp. 306ff. for a discussion of the relationship and n.b. p. 312.
[54] Abbott and Campbell, ii, p. 108.

permission to give her communion during her long period of ill-health after her return from the Crimea, frankly explaining to Tait that she was 'not what some persons would call orthodox'.[55]

The fact that there was to be no more public theology and that he did not wish to be the leader of a party certainly did not mean that Jowett had lost interest in religious ideas. He was, after all, where he wanted to be, getting young men educated. And education, for Jowett, included education in religion—though not, indeed, in the way it had conventionally been done. He thought it was 'not a useful lesson for the young student to apply to Scriptures, principles which he would hesitate to apply to other books: to make formal reconcilements of discrepancies . . . to divide simple words into double meanings . . . to adopt the fancies or conjectures of Fathers or Commentators as real knowledge'.[56]

But he had also asserted in *Essays and Reviews* that the study of scripture, properly undertaken, ought to be part of a *liberal* education because there is 'a sense of things into which we must grow as well as reason ourselves, without which human nature is but a truncated, half-educated sort of being'.[57] He became a preacher.

This appears to have been a quite deliberate decision and its genesis can be traced quite clearly. As early as 1865 he had told Florence Nightingale that he would concentrate on preaching, 'putting off the more heterodox aspect of things until I have gained (if I can) some hold'.[58] At that stage, then, he was chiefly concerned to arouse no more opposition to himself. But in several of the letters that he wrote in the years immediately before he became master, there are expressions of a growing delight in preaching for its own sake.[59]

Sermons in college chapel were a relatively recent innovation. Earlier there had been a system of catechetical lectures at which the undergraduates, who attended chapel compulsorily, were informed in advance of the questions they would have to answer at the end of the lecture. Jowett had been unwilling to undertake these universally

[55] Tait Papers: Personal Letters, vol. 79, fos. 305–8.
[56] *Essays and Reviews*, pp. 428f.
[57] Ibid.
[58] Jowett to Florence Nightingale, 31 Aug. 1865.
[59] e.g. in Abbott and Campbell, i, pp. 428 and 430.

unpopular exercises though he, like other tutors, regularly gave religious addresses to his pupils gathered once a term in his own rooms. In 1869 he was appointed college preacher, which presumably would not have happened if he had not desired both that the office should exist and that he should fill it. Scott would not have wanted him to be preaching regularly to the undergraduates. The novelty of college sermons took a little getting used to apparently, because there was one Sunday when the catechetical lecturer forgot that Jowett was due to deliver a sermon and got in first.[60]

By this time there was no question of the sermons being a way of disguising his rather radical theology: his views were forthrightly expressed. After he became master in the following year he preached regularly twice each term in the college chapel.[61] He had already set down in print somewhat ambitious views on the subject of the preacher's function in relation to the Bible. 'If we would only be natural,' he had written, 'and speak of things as they truly are, with a real interest and not merely a conventional one!' The preacher should 'avoid the form of argument from Scripture, and catch the feeling and spirit. Scripture is itself a kind of poetry, when not overlaid with rhetoric.' One ought not to deal with 'questions of Jewish law, or controversies about the sacraments, or exaggerated statements of doctrine which seem to be at variance with morality'.

The life of Christ, regarded quite naturally as of one 'who was in all points tempted like as we are, yet without sin', is also the life and centre of Christian teaching. There is no higher aim which the preacher can propose to himself than to awaken what may be termed the feeling of the presence of God and the mind of Christ in Scripture . . .[62]

How far Jowett managed to live up to his own very high standards was, of course, largely a matter of opinion. Some of the undergraduates seem to have regarded his preaching as honest and courageous, dealing with real life and practical things. 'Real' is a word that recurs in many comments,[63] and to that extent, at least, Jowett succeeded in what he set out to achieve. But not everyone found his sermons

[60] Abbott and Campbell, i, p. 430.
[61] *College Sermons*, p. vi.
[62] *Essays and Reviews*, p. 429.
[63] W. H. Fremantle in *College Sermons*, p. ix.

helpful, and some dismissed him as lacking in passion, whether for good or evil. One young man thought his sermons useful only for ordinary people in making 'their decent commonplace money-making life a little higher if possible'.[64]

The young Henry Scott Holland recorded his impressions of what may be Jowett's first appearance as the official college preacher. It is a splendid vignette in which the undergraduate gently mocks the don's mannerisms and captures both the strengths and weaknesses of Jowett's pulpit style.

[Jowett] preached yesterday in Chapel amidst intense excitement, 110 people in Chapel. He looked so fatherly and beautiful and brought out the best bell-like silvern voice with quite rich tones that he had hitherto hidden in the depth of his stomach and preached the most lovely little practical sermon in a quite perfect style with the most wonderful grace. I have only said all this laud in anticipation of having to confess that though I felt how beautiful it was in its way, it was most unsatisfying to me. It was just Platonism flavoured with a little Christian charity: Christianity is gutted by him: it becomes perfectly meaningless, if it is only an attempt to take some useful moral hints from just what happens to strike you in a very good, 'perhaps I may be excused in saying' a Divine life. He is perfectly self-sufficient; self-dependent, without any consciousness of anything beyond a certain human weakness in carrying out his ideal; there is not an atom of the feeling of prayer, of communication with God, of reliance on anyone but self. He even begs pardon for using as vague an expression as 'sharing in the Spirit of God'. I admire the Symposium with all my heart and soul; but I must have something more to have brought God down to death to procure for me.[65]

In fact Jowett was in many ways at his best as a preacher and it has to be said that that particular medium was probably also very well suited to his temperamental dislike of systems. Preaching enabled him to adopt a more occasional approach, tackling one issue at a time and not being forced to relate each to everything else he might want to say. His published sermons are in a much more direct and simple style than most of his other writings, though we do not know precisely how far the printed version corresponds to the original for it would seem, from what survives among his papers at Balliol, that

[64] R. L. Nettleship quoted in [S.] Paget, [*Henry Scott Holland: Memoir and Letters*, London 1921,] p. 27 and cf. Sandford, i, p. 91.
[65] Paget, pp. 33f.

he often preached from very brief notes. The published volumes of sermons may, therefore, consist of specially rewritten pieces. But the very fact that their style is different from his other work suggests that—consciously or unconsciously—he wrote them up in something like the language he actually used in the pulpit.

What comes across is not the Jowett represented in most of the history books, arid and rather cold, without faith or fervour. The theological eye is able to detect echoes of Hegel, Schleiermacher, and others but it is unlikely, of course, that the undergraduates were aware of these. The sermons are full of obvious personal devotion to the Christ of the Gospels and of affection for the young men in his charge. But it could equally truly be said that what he preached was a religion of endeavour, of moral integrity, and of fulfilling one's obligations in life. Almost all his sermons end on that note.

It was a curious failing in someone who was acutely aware of the dangers of moralising. He liked to quote the butler whose employers' son had been ordained. When Jowett asked how the young man was getting on, the butler replied, 'He offends the people by reproving them for drunkenness. 'E should 'a stuck to the doctrine, sir, that could do no 'arm.' And Jowett, recounting this story, used to say 'there must be more to your discourse than mere morality. If you give them a moral essay, not a poor woman in the congregation but will feel there is something wrong.'[66] But he also believed that a sermon should demonstrate the connection between religion and real life and perhaps it was his determination to do this that brought him back, again and again, to questions of morality. His successor as master was to say of him that 'His so-called worldliness was . . . in the main due to a persistent effort to bring ideal aims into the practical life of the world.'[67] His preaching on morality may have been part of the same concern. Moreover, he used the moral demands of Christianity as a kind of apologetic, saying that there may be problems in theology that cannot be solved but there is no doubt about how to live a Christian life. So, when he came to deal with the application of doctrine to life, he was inclined simply to urge his congregation to be moral. There was much less of hope, of

[66] Abbott and Campbell, ii, p. 272.
[67] E. Caird, 'Professor Jowett', *International Journal of Ethics*, Oct. 1897, p. 47.

forgiveness, or of redemption in what he said. And it was this that Scott Holland and his friends detected—and found passionless. It suggested to them that Jowett thought it was easy to rise above human weakness: why, then, as Scott Holland agonisingly asked, should God need to die for man?

It seems clear that one of the favourite themes of Jowett's sermons was that one ought to *achieve* something with one's life. He was always careful to insist that by 'achievement' he did not mean worldly success. As in a sermon on the text 'It is finished', which Tait always remembered as helpful and striking,[68] he meant to convey to his hearers that their lives were given them that they might create with them something valuable and beautiful. But even if Jowett's admiration for greatness and successs found no expression in his preaching, it would have been well known among his pupils and, coupled with his stress upon the demands of morality, may sometimes even have had a crushing effect upon those who did not find life easy. An irate clergyman wrote to Tait (after he had become archbishop) saying that the laity needed to be protected from clergymen like Jowett. To support his charge he retailed gossip he had heard from the younger generation about Balliol sermons. Miracles were sneered at, he said, the literal truth of the scriptures questioned and—after the suicide of an undergraduate—it had been said that when a man found himself beaten in the battle of life it might be better that he should give it up. All this offensive talk, said Tait's correspondent, was a consequence of the judgement in the *Essays and Reviews* case.[69]

The event referred to in this letter was probably also the basis of a story told by W. H. Mallock to discredit Jowett and his theology. Mallock was an undergraduate at Balliol in Jowett's early days as master. Jowett seems not to have thought much of Mallock: Mallock actively disliked Jowett and seized every opportunity to be cruel at his expense.[70] There seems to have been no good reason for

[68] The sermon is no. XIX in *College Sermons* and see Abbott and Campbell, ii, p. 237.
[69] Tait Papers: Personal Letters, vol. 90, fos. 199f.; the Reverend G. R. Portal to Tait, 13 Oct. 1872.
[70] M. Jarrett-Kerr, 'W. H. Mallock: Radical Tory, Romantic Classicist', *P. N. Review*, 43 (1984), pp. 46f. attempts to make the best possible case for Mallock; Faber also deals with Mallock and Jowett, pp. 376ff.

this hatred, except that Mallock disagreed with the master's political and religious views. He admitted that Jowett treated him with 'much sympathetic good nature' and that what he felt was really no more than an instinctive antipathy.[71] Mallock's own religion was a rather romantic Anglo-Catholic orthodoxy and his political views are hinted at in the title of one of his many books, *Aristocracy and Evolution*, published in 1898. He was a social Darwinist, admiring wealth and lineage with a passionate intensity which makes Jowett's snobbery seem mild and inoffensive, and believing that the upper classes justified—and were justified by—the theory of the survival of the fittest.

Mallock's best-known work is *The New Republic*, which ran into many editions and is a clever satire demonstrating the author's ability to produce pastiche after pastiche in imitation of those he wished to ridicule. Jowett figures in the work as 'Dr Jenkinson' and there is a very brilliant parody of a Jowett sermon put into that character's mouth. But, for all the cleverness of the style of the parody, which captures the same tentative, self-deprecating manner that Scott Holland made more gentle fun of, the theology of 'Dr Jenkinson' is not Jowett's. Mallock makes the preacher say, for instance, that a theory of 'moral evolution' was 'alike the Christian and the scientific theory; and I thus wish you to see that the very points in which science seems most opposed to Christianity are really those in which it most fundamentally agrees with it.'[72] In fact one of the points Jowett was most anxious to make, throughout his life, whenever he spoke about Darwinism was that the term evolution could not mean the same thing when applied to moral and to biological development.

It is not, however, the 'Jenkinson' sermon which is at issue in the matter of the undergraduate's suicide. Mallock purports in his biographical jottings to give an account of a real sermon preached by Jowett which may be a description of the same occasion as that referred to by Tait's correspondent.

The most sensational event which occurred during my first term at Balliol was the suicide of one of the undergraduates. He was a poor Scotch student

[71] [W. H. Mallock], *Memoirs [of Life and Literature*, London 1920,] p. 30.
[72] W. H. Mallock, *The New Republic*, London 1877, i, pp. 135ff.

of a deeply religious character who had found, so his friends reported, that the faith of his childhood had been taken from him by Jowett's sceptical teachings, and who had ended by cutting his throat with a razor in Port Meadow. Jowett preached his funeral sermon—the only sermon which I ever, so far as my recollection serves me, heard preached in Balliol chapel by himself or anyone else. Jowett, who on this occasion was obviously much moved, chose for his text the story of the woman taken in adultery and of Christ's challenge to her judges, 'Which of you will dare to assault with the first stone?' The course of his argument was curious. He began with examining the passage from the standpoint of verbal [sic] scholarship, the gist of his criticism being that its authority was at least doubtful. From this argument he diverged into one of wider scope, insisting on how much is doubtful in what the Gospels record as the sayings of our Lord generally, from which illuminating reflection he advanced to one wider still. It was as follows. Since we know so little of what Christ really said about God, how much less can we really know of the nature of God himself; of what He loves, condemns, or, in His infinite mercy, pardons?—the moral being that we ought to cast stones at nobody and should in especial refrain from condemning our dead brother . . .[73]

It is worth noting that Mallock wrote this account some fifty years after the event. It is clear that his memory was far from reliable since he claims that this was the only sermon he ever heard in college chapel, whereas Jowett was preaching regularly twice a term and, indeed, Mallock could hardly have captured his pulpit style so accurately in *The New Republic* unless he had been very familiar with it. What he claimed that Jowett said bears very much the same sort of superficial resemblance to what Jowett is known to have said in some of his sermons as the Jenkinson sermon does, and is, at the same time, just as significantly different. It is difficult to escape the impression that Mallock had told this story a great many times, embroidering it maliciously in the process, and that it is no less a parody than the openly fictitious satire in *The New Republic*. In any case it is clear, even in Mallock's account, that Jowett was, however clumsily, trying to bring comfort or to defend the man's action in an age when suicide was regarded not only as a crime but as an unforgivable sin.

[73] *Memoir*, p. 59: parts of this passage are quoted—but inaccurately—in Jarrett-Kerr, 'W. H. Mallock'.

6

A Liberal Gospel

One of the effects of Jowett's decision to give up writing theology and take to preaching instead was that it moved him, as it were, out of the mainstream of theological debate. This may even have been one of his reasons for making the decision. He had never enjoyed public controversy on religion and had always ignored his critics' attacks on his theological position. He was convinced, in any case, that a quiet and subtle influence behind the scenes was always the way to shape opinion and to get things done.[1] Using Balliol as the vehicle for his theology was, in a sense, a version of this same technique: he was able to put his views across to clever young men who would be influential later. But it also had the effect of further isolating him from the general theological debate. He had never, perhaps, been a theologian's theologian: he was now almost in the proverbial position of being a man among boys and a boy among men. Because his religious ideas were very largely expressed through his occasional preaching to undergraduates, he did not have to define them over against what other theologians were saying. And equally, of course, that meant that he could be ignored by other theologians.

This partly explains why Jowett usually figures in general accounts of nineteenth-century English religion as a man who wrote one significant essay and then played no further part in the development of thought. His influence on a wide range of other younger thinkers, whether through his sermons or his academic teaching, is almost entirely ignored. Nor is this an entirely false picture. In the theological world of the 1870s and 1880s Jowett seems to have gone his own way—or, rather, seems almost to have stood still—paying very little attention to what was happening around him. He was no

[1] Above p. 101.

longer reading all the latest theology, as he had done in the 1840s and 1850s. This may simply have been because he was older and much more busy with administrative matters. He was, in any case, concentrating on Greek philosophy. But both his biographies convey the impression that, compared with the period before he became master, the later part of his life was much less eventful. The story of the years from 1870 onwards is a story of a man who had arrived and who was concerned with influence rather than action. His ideas, perhaps, became rather fixed and, just as he was to become somewhat conservative in the matter of university reform, so in other areas as well he tended to live as though it were still the 1850s and 1860s.

Moreover, his famous essay had been largely negative in its approach, concerning itself with what could *not* any longer, in his opinion, be believed. And the same might be said of his theological pieces attached to the Pauline commentaries. What he had said on the atonement had been almost entirely an attack on the conventional belief. As time passed, fewer people cared about the old orthodoxies. What Jowett had attacked began to seem very out of date. That he should be remembered as a man who did nothing theological after 1860 and as the worst kind of liberal protestant—negative, reductionist, not really a believer at all—was in a sense inevitable. And it has to be admitted that in many ways he *was* a typical liberal protestant. He clearly believed that humanity was always progressing in knowledge and civilisation. He also regarded the Jesus of the Gospels as the pattern of the divine/human relationship to which all men could aspire.

Moreover, the very thing that made sermons such a suitable vehicle for Jowett's views—their occasional character—makes it particularly difficult to derive from them a succinct account of his theology. The editor of the sermons, W. H. Fremantle, remembered Jowett's saying to him, 'I think we have been too afraid of systems.'[2] And, in a sense, it is doing a disservice to someone as afraid of systems as Jowett was, to force his thoughts into systematic form.

[2] [B. Jowett,] *Sermons on Faith* [*and Doctrine*, ed. W. H. Fremantle, London 1901], p. ix.

Fremantle tried, with reasonable success, to do so in an introduction to one of the volumes:

> Metaphysically, [the readers of the sermons] will find that he shrank neither from the assertion of the divine personality, though conscious of the limitations attendant upon the transfer of that expression from man to God, nor from speaking of Christ as 'our Saviour', and as the expression of the divine nature in a human form; and that God and immortality were all in all to him. Morally they will find the image of Christ is dominant in the preacher's thoughts.[3]

This is a useful and even a fair summary, though it was plainly written in order to present Jowett in the best possible light. It also ignores the opacity of some of his teaching.

There seem to be three main points, which Jowett was particularly anxious to stress in his sermons generally. First, there is the point raised by Fremantle—the personality of God. This is a crucial but difficult aspect of Jowett's thought and it turns upon the question of whether God is to be regarded as 'abstract'. There were times when Jowett was very insistent that God was not abstract in the sense of remote. But he seems also to have believed, nevertheless, that there was a good or proper sense in which God must be conceived as abstract, that is to say as universal, absolute, or transcendent, not perceived too much in anthropomorphic or human personal terms. He held a curious view of God as possessing personality 'clothed in laws' which he contrasted with the idea that God's personality was like human personality.[4] These laws in which the divine personality was 'clothed' were both moral laws and the 'scientific' laws which governed the universe, as may be seen from an argument about the existence of evil which Jowett constructed upon the foundation of this concept.[5]

This idea of the divine personality seems to owe something to both Hegel and Plato. One of the notes and jottings on theological subjects which survives among Jowett's papers speaks of 'God as goodness and wisdom, tending ever to realize itself in the world'. But he was always, as he had hinted in his revised essay on the

---

[3] *Sermons on Faith*, p. i.
[4] *Sermons on Faith*, p. 43.
[5] *Sermons on Faith*, pp. 43ff.

atonement, concerned to be practical where Hegel was metaphysical, to make things seem intimate rather than remote. And if, through Plato's influence, he thought of God as 'Law' or as 'Ultimate Truth', it was at this point that he was determined to reject abstractions and assert that the ultimate truth was embodied in the person of Christ.

This is the second and central point of his preaching. It saved his position from being simply barren and minimalist. He was entirely devoted to Christ both as the ideal and also as a present reality in everyday life. A kind of warmth infused everything he had to say about Christ, who 'went about doing good, not merely because he devoted himself to it as we might devote ourselves to some sort of philanthropy—but because he was what he was'.[6] He believed that the essence of religion was self-sacrifice and self-denial, the greatest moral power in the world. This power Christ embodied. Plans for writing a life of Christ figured again and again on Jowett's list of projects to be undertaken and *Imitatio Christi* was something that always fascinated him. The climax towards which his preaching moved was almost always the moral demand made by Christianity, to live the life of Christ.

The third point which recurs frequently in the sermons is the necessity to take account of established facts. He believed that it was impossible to defend or protect Christianity by being obscurantist or to try and overcome the truth by adopting an ever more rigid theological position. One has to meet the temptation to take refuge in dogma by having confidence in history.[7] And this, too, may be part of the continuing influence of Hegel.

What Jowett failed to see was that much of what he dismissed as mere dogma enshrined a vital part of the Christian tradition and that that tradition was based, in turn, upon the very experience in which he put so much trust. Prayer, sacraments, worship, and doctrine can all be ways of conveying a richness and depth of belief which are lost if religion is pared down too much by over-simplification. Jowett

---

[6] Balliol College: Jowett Papers: 'Notes for Sermons' in small red note book.

[7] Balliol College: Jowett Papers: 'Descriptions of the present state of theology'—notes written in a small note book marked 'F'; and cf. 'Criticism and Dogma' in Abbott and Campbell, ii, pp. 311ff.

A Liberal Gospel

always insisted that there must be a place for mystery, but the element of mystery itself was not very prominent in what he preached.

The theology which lay behind the sermons of the first ten or fifteen years of Jowett's mastership does not seem to have changed much from that expressed in the commentaries or in his contribution to *Essays and Reviews*. But if he continued to say much the same things, his dislike of systems was taking its revenge. There were considerable difficulties inherent in his approach, just because he insisted that logical coherence was unnecessary and that contradictions did not matter. As he continued to state his beliefs in his preaching the problems seem to become more intractable. Though he appears not to have recognised this openly, he put what he wanted to say in a form which pointed up the problem more and more sharply, so that the very way the matter was expressed seems to cry out for an answer which Jowett did not attempt to provide. His thought was not always serene; sometimes there was a deeply pessimistic, almost despairing tone to the notes he wrote, as though he had to struggle to maintain his faith.[8] And it may be that he was not as unaware of the difficulty as he seemed to be.

What was happening can be seen very clearly from an examination of two examples. The first is a pair of linked sermons from the middle of his first decade as master: the second comes from the end of that same decade. Both are crucial examples of his attempts to set out a clear approach to theology. They reveal the same difficulties and at the same time show how they became less easy to ignore.

The pair of sermons appear in the volume called *Sermons on Faith and Doctrine*. 'The Hebrew Conception of God' was preached in college chapel on 23 April and 'Christ's Revelation of God' on 21 May 1876. There was, apparently, a third sermon in the course. It was the first in the series, but it was not included in the book.

What is particularly interesting about these sermons is that they contain some rare information about Jowett's methodology. In the first of the two he described the considerations by which he would chiefly be guided. In understanding the biblical passages themselves

---

[8] See 'Changes in Religion', 'The New Christianity', and 'The Two Great Forms of Religion', in Abbott and Campbell, ii, pp. 311ff.

he would want to determine how they had come to take the form they did and what influences had shaped them. He would then want to ask whether the understanding of God contained in them needed to be modified by ideas received through classical philosophy. And finally he would also need to take account of those aspects of modern scientific thought which seemed to him to have a bearing on the point.[9] In other words, in trying to explain the *sense* in which he understood the New Testament assertions about the person and work of Christ, he would be continually asking himself how he could understand them in the light of what he had learnt from Greek metaphysics and modern physics.

This is not to say, of course, that Jowett had always got science, critical New Testament scholarship, or even Platonic metaphysics right. It is his own conception of what he was doing which is significant. He was prepared to give a weight to philosophy and science which most of his contemporaries would not have allowed to them. As Fremantle pointed out in his introduction, the question whether Jowett believed in Christ as saviour and as 'the expression of the divine nature in a human form',[10] is vital for determining whether his theology can be said to stand in the mainstream of Christian thought or not. But the question is complicated because in determining the truth of a theological proposition one has always to ask not only 'Is it true?' but also 'In what sense is it true?' Each of the assertions 'Christ is the son of God' or 'Christ is the saviour of the human race' can be made in a wide variety of different senses, some of which may accord with what has usually been intended by traditional orthodoxy and others of which may not. And anyone wishing to make a case for the orthodoxy of his own interpretation of those assertions would also need to show how he derived it from scripture.

It was Jowett's misfortune that the distinction between whether a belief is true and the sense in which it is true was not a distinction to which the nineteenth century was very sympathetic. As the attitude of bishops like Tait and Wilberforce shows, it was an era when the *sense* in which a truth was to be understood had become almost more

[9] *Sermons on Faith*, pp. 57, 61f., and 74ff.
[10] *Sermons on Faith*, p. v.

important than the truth itself. And for this the very atmosphere of the times was, no doubt, largely responsible. That the Bible is the word of God and what it says is true; that Christ is God incarnate in human form; that he redeems humanity from sin; all were regarded as crucial proclamations of divine truth without which the whole Christian faith would crumble. Any attempt to find a new way of stating these essential truths, if it appeared to throw the least doubt upon the traditionally sanctioned *sense* in which they had been asserted, was to seem to deny them altogether.

The first of Jowett's pair of sermons traced out, in brief, the way the Israelite concept of God had developed out of a primitive idea not much different from those of surrounding tribes. Without going into any technical detail, he confronted his audience with some of the questions raised by critical scholarship. 'Are the Books of Genesis or Exodus, or the oldest part of them, really of the same date with the Book of Deuteronomy, which has so much in common with the prophets?' And questions of this kind were raised, not gratuitously, but to throw light on the problem of the Old Testament's understanding of God. 'It is natural to ask how we can be sure to what period the Jewish conception of the divine nature can be really attributed, and how far they may have been affected by the ideas of foreign nations.' In attempting an answer, Jowett was concerned to show that the Old Testament does not have an idea of God wholly different from that of the New, pointing out that even the Old Testament speaks of God as father as well as king; as merciful as well as powerful; as the God of individuals as well as of nations.

Then he comes to what one feels is the heart of this particular sermon: what kind of God this is. Once again Jowett did not avoid the problems of transposing early Israelite ideas of God and nature into nineteenth-century terms, but nor did he go into any detail or burden his hearers with technicalities. The first thing about the Old Testament God is that he is the God of nature. 'The Israelites of course knew nothing of the fixed laws by which the world is governed; their heaven was above them, their place of the departed below; the earth was a large plain which divided them.' But the very things which make God the ruler of the physical world also make him the judge: 'this physical government of the world is also a moral government . . .' This was an important point for Jowett. He believed very firmly that there was an essential link between moral laws and the laws of nature. And that belief was a part of his conception of God's personality as 'clothed in laws'.

Then, after a brief look at other religions of the world in order to remind his hearers that God cares for everyone, the sermon ended with a very significant passage which contrasted Old Testament religion with Greek ideas and with modern Christian beliefs. The conception of God in the Old Testament, which 'attributes to Him the acts and feelings of a person', was contrasted with the fact that a Greek found it 'comparatively indifferent whether he speaks of God in the singular or in the plural, in the masculine or neuter'.

From this contrast Jowett drew a somewhat surprising conclusion. He did not, as his audience must have expected, insist that the Hebrew idea was right and the Greek one wrong. Instead he asserted:

The difference between the two modes of conception leads us to make the reflection that, while we know of no higher mode of representing the Divine Being to ourselves than under the forms of Unity and Personality, yet that Personality is not like a human personality, nor that Unity like the unity of the world. It seems as if we should not be so careful to *define* our terms as to *vary* them, lest we should become the slaves of words in matters which transcend words.

In other words he regarded each view as contributing something to a full and proper understanding of the nature of God. And when he came to relate Old Testament ideas to modern thought, his words must have been equally disturbing. He pointed out that, because the Israelite had no conception of the laws of nature, he simply 'thought of God as very near him—his Father, his King, the Inhabitant, when He was pleased to dwell there, of the land of Israel'.

But any notion of a Divine Being which did not embrace all knowledge and all power would be to us unreal. We cannot be satisfied with having one God in science and history, another in religion. And the reconcilement of these opposite aspects of the divine nature has hitherto been beyond our strength. Something we may have done for it, but not much. And while men are seeking after God, if haply they may find Him (though He be not far from any one of us), we cannot entirely cast out fear and doubt; we have sometimes to turn our eyes back again to earth and think of our duties there, which remain as ever plain and clear to us. . . .

In these days there are many things which we must criticize, although they are the foundation of our lives, for otherwise they would become mere words and have no meaning to us. We cannot expect that without any effort of thought we can understand the thoughts of 2,500 years ago. The realities which underlie our criticism, though manifested in different forms, remain the same; though the world grows old they change not; though at times obscured they are again revealed, deriving, as in the past so also in future ages, light and meaning from the history and experience of mankind.

His next sermon began by picking up a point from its predecessor, the close parallels between Old and New Testament; though Jowett was at pains to reject the practice of reading back into the Old Testament—by typology or the interpretation of prophecy—a meaning which it did not have but was really derived from Christian usage. The greatest difference between the two Testaments, he thought, was to be found in the 'inwardness' of the New Testament. Christ, as messiah, had times of suffering as well as glory;

A time when God seems to have forsaken him, and the meanness or the indifference or the wickedness of mankind are too much for him, and a time when the multitude cry 'Hosanna' before him, or he himself in his inmost soul has a more present vision of a kingdom 'not of this world'. This double thread runs alike through the prophets and the Gospels. Only what is more outward and visible in the Old Testament becomes more inward and spiritual in the New. . . . 'the kingdom of God is within you'. There, in the heart of man, its struggle is to be maintained, its victory won.

It was this emphatic individualism in Jowett's thought that had led him to omit the Church altogether from his theological purview, to adopt a subjective and exemplarist theory of the atonement and to place so much emphasis upon morality.

The next section of the sermon (relying heavily on Romans 7) was occupied with the spiritual struggle within a man and it ended with a kind of realised eschatology—the end of the struggle, 'the hope of good' as he called it, is not in some distant future but 'present and immediate; within the reach of everyone, if he will renounce himself and follow Christ'.

That brought Jowett to the crux of the issue. Christ, he pointed out, was a private, unknown, gentle, and innocent person.

He would have seemed like any other man, only calmer and deeper. He would not have made that great interval between Himself and other men which we sometimes attribute to Him; He would rather have sought to identify Himself with them.

And so he moved to the question 'What, then, do we mean, and what would He Himself have meant by declaring that He was 'the manifestation of God' or the 'Son of God'?'

He argued that God is beyond all knowledge and imagining and cannot be comprehended by the human mind. We may therefore be in danger of trying to imprison within human language what it is quite incapable of expressing. But all philosophy has tended to go on to say, nevertheless, that 'from this transcendentalism we must return to the earth, which is the habitation, not of our bodies only, but of our minds, and that through man we must ascend to God. . . . He is only known to us, so far as we can conceive him, under the form of perfect human nature. The highest we can imagine in man is not human but divine.' And then, as if to counteract immediately this rather dangerous claim, which seemed to suggest that God is only man writ large, he said, 'Perfect righteousness, perfect holiness, perfect truth, perfect love—these are the elements or attributes, not of a human, but of a divine being.'

Logically such claims made about Christ must raise the question of the evidence on which they are based, so Jowett then turned briefly to the question of the accuracy of the New Testament sources. The divine goodness is presented to us in a fragmentary way, in which 'we cannot altogether separate the thoughts of Christ Himself from the impressions which the disciples and evangelists formed of him.' Nevertheless, he maintained, it is possible still to form an idea of God even if we have to discard some things in the New Testament as being inconsistent either with itself or with what we know and its writers did not. 'Our duty as Christians is not to inquire whether this or that word of Christ has been preserved with superhuman accuracy, but to seek to form the highest idea of God which we can, and to implant it in our minds and in our lives.'

Having voiced that disconcerting thought, Jowett did not develop it. Instead, there followed a passage in which he seemed to be at his happiest and best, dealing with the characteristics of divine goodness as manifested in the kind of person Christ was—not concerned with power or intellect or happiness or success, but 'not of this world', wholly devoted to the service of the Father, converting law into spirit, finding within himself what he actually was, not needing to be taught the will of God.

While this sermon—and particularly the latter part of it—is, on the surface, clear and coherent and must have been extremely moving to hear, it does not reveal very precisely just what Jowett believed. He took account of critical study and admitted that it was impossible to get behind the New Testament to the actual words and thoughts of Christ himself. But he thought that what followed from that impossibility was that Christians ought to form the highest possible idea of God, implant it in their minds and lives, and model themselves upon Christ. Two enormous questions he simply did not face—how one was to model oneself upon someone about whom one's knowledge was so uncertain, and how that person was actually related to the God whom he is alleged to reveal.

On the second of these two questions what Jowett says is simply opaque. He was quite clear that Christ manifested the divine nature and spoke with divine authority but he used other phrases which it is difficult to reconcile with a belief that Christ actually *is* God. He slipped from an emphasis upon Christ as the divine manifestation to an emphasis upon the humanity which everyone shares with Christ, without making it at all clear how he thought these two aspects of Christ's person were related to each other. He was as difficult to pin down on this point as ever Schleiermacher was and the ambiguity was, no doubt, required by his belief that atonement and salvation consist in the individual's making Christ's life his own. He was forced to stress the common humanity and the reality of Christlikeness in everyone in such a way that it was difficult for him to say that Christ differed from other human beings at all. And that, in turn, made it impossible for him to say anything clear and precise about the presence of the divine in Christ.

One of the 'types' under which he asked his hearers to imagine the character of Christ was as follows:

'He lived in God'. He did not teach of Himself or act of Himself, but He was taught and inspired of God. His own soul was the mirror or reflection of the divine will. He looked inwards (not like the mystic seeking to be absorbed in some unreal enthusiasm); and finding within Himself love and right and truth without any alloy of earthly motive, felt instinctively that they were the word of God. 'This man had no letters,' said the Jews; but He saw farther and more truly than them all. 'Is not this the carpenter's Son?' Yet He spoke with a divine authority. For He spoke not of Himself but out of a Power which was independent of Himself, words which he knew to be the voice of God and the true law of the world. The truth never presented itself to Him as a matter of opinion or uncertainty or speculation; it was not a thing to be reasoned or argued about, but to be felt and known by all men. It meant not a system of doctrines such as the Christian community afterwards devised, but a spirit of life—the spirit of peace and love, the temper of mind which rests in God and is resigned to His will, which seeks also to fulfil His will actively in doing good to man.

To this simple life Christ invites us to return . . .

It is difficult to be certain what sort of Christology lay behind what Jowett was saying. Sometimes the sermons seem to assert that the divine authority belonged to Christ by nature, by virtue of who he was; sometimes that it came from outside himself. Jowett might have been expounding what Pusey would have called the simplistic Unitarianism of Joseph Priestley. Or he might have been attempting to convey to his undergraduates something of Schleiermacher's concept of the God-consciousness of Jesus, the sense of absolute dependence upon God. It might have been a deliberate attempt to return behind the 'system of doctrines' to the language of the Gospels. It might have been an essay in devising a Christology of inspiration in place of the traditional two-natures orthodoxy. Or it might simply have been the careless language of a preacher who was principally concerned to exhort to a vigorous morality. And it is almost impossible to tell which it is.

This particular sermon ended, much as the previous one had done, but with a rather firmer optimism. Jowett went back to the questions raised by critical scholarship, philosophy, and science and said

A Liberal Gospel

that whatever uncertainties there might be, 'there is no uncertainty about the Christian life'. But 'how the most fervent love of truth may be consistent with the deepest religious feeling; how the spirit of Christ may animate historical and scientific researches without being lost in them—this is a task which seems to be reserved for the coming generation to accomplish.'

The thought that, as a result of critical scholarship, the modern world was in a position to return behind the complexities of doctrinal systems to an original simplicity, was very like the kind of thing he had said in his contribution to *Essays and Reviews*. Indeed, the whole of this sermon is reminiscent of a good many passages in his earlier writings. In the second edition of his commentaries, in an essay on 'Paul and Philo',[11] he had argued for the necessity of learning from both Greek and Hebrew ideas. That work had also contained an essay on the 'Abstract Ideas of the New Testament',[12] which had devoted particuar attention to human ideas of the divine nature. And in the revised essay on the atonement,[13] he had concentrated especially on the indentification of the Christian with Christ. These two sermons of fifteen years later present an almost identical theology. Since the second edition of the commentaries, appearing as it did only a year before *Essay and Reviews*, was really a clarification rather than a modification of the first edition, it is possible, with some confidence, to assume that Jowett's theology had remained unchanged throughout twenty-five years. It may not have been crystal clear but it was essentially unaltered.

But there were two ways in which his liberal protestant concerns had taken a somewhat unusual form. First, he was asserting that one was perfectly entitled to develop whatever seemed to be the best and highest view of God—and associate it with Christ—regardless of whether it could be shown to be based on the Bible. This was, in fact, an essential part of his understanding of development or progress in religion. In other words, though he was plainly interested in the humanity of Jesus of Nazareth as it was described in the Gospels, he did not think that he—or anyone else—need be limited to what

---

[11] *Epistles*, 2nd ed., London 1859, i, pp. 448–514.
[12] Ibid., ii, pp. 96–109 and n.b. pp. 107ff.
[13] Ibid. pp. 547–96.

could be said on the basis of the Gospels alone. Concepts of goodness, truth, and perfection, wherever they might be drawn from, could properly be attributed to Jesus. Even less was he concerned about what could and what could not be justifiably said about Jesus on precisely established historical grounds. This fits entirely with his attitude to the use of history as a critical tool in interpreting the scriptures, as evinced in his contribution to *Essays and Reviews*. Once one had got back to what the authors of the New Testament had said, history's task was done. This attitude, of course, partly accounts for his tendency to read into rather than out of the text of the New Testament. It also accounts for the second main stress of his teaching, though it makes his blindness to the supreme problem he was raising even more inexplicable.

This second central theme was, of course, his belief in the continuing and permanent presence of Christ in everyday life. This presence he liked to work out in terms of 'friendship with Christ', so that—as in his understanding of how one would be guided by a divine faculty in one's reading of scriptures—he could sometimes sound like a veritable Evangelical. He would have been infuriated if this had been pointed out to him and equally furious if he had been told that his concept of a Christ-centred life was a sort of mysticism. Mysticism, for Jowett, belonged with all the activities he associated with priestcraft and mumbo jumbo, the things that were the opposite of English protestant common sense. His impatience with mysticism was, in fact, part and parcel of his apparent disregard of church and sacraments. Yet it was Jowett who insisted on celebrating the holy communion early each Sunday morning in the college chapel and there was an element of something which it is difficult not to call mysticism in the vividness with which he would talk about his sense of a close and continuing relationship with Christ.

In his commentaries he had developed the idea of 'putting on' Christ by analogy with the way in which late classical literature had talked of 'putting on' a friend,[14] and his attempt at developing an alternative to the penal substitutionary theology of the atonement had also used the concept of friendship with God through Christ.[15]

[14] Above p. 56.
[15] Above p. 65.

This is not surprising, for in purely human terms friendship mattered very greatly to Jowett, hence his frequent sense of having been betrayed by his friends. Only someone who thought of friendship as a relationship of total trust and reliability, could have reacted as he did.

He preached a sermon on friendship in 1873,[16] which opens with precisely that theme—'There are many things said about friendship in Scripture, and some touching examples of the fidelity of friends.' A post-Freudian world would find it difficult not to read into such a sermon all sorts of implications which were probably not there originally, but it is difficult to imagine anyone being able to preach it in a post-Freudian world, either.[17] At any rate Jowett looked at the friendships of Jonathan with David, Ruth with Naomi, Paul with Timothy, Christ with Mary, Martha, and Lazarus, and Christ with the beloved disciple. He also pointed out—significantly when one remembers his own relationship with his pupils—that Christ's name for his disciples as a whole was 'friends'. Then he turned to the world of classical antiquity and again mentioned specific examples of famous friendships, including Achilles and Patroclus, and asserted that 'the school of Socrates was quite as much a circle of friends as a band of disciples'.

This preliminary section of the sermon was intended to establish two things; the importance of faithful, intimate friendship in the development of one's intellect and character, and the fact that the best form of discipleship is friendship. Then came a very typical and lengthy piece of common-sense advice on forming good and desirable friendships, before he turned to his final section on Christian friendship 'which,' he said, 'in uniting us to a friend, at the same time unites us to Christ and God'.[18]

This final section on Christian friendship itself is almost disproportionately short, considering how packed it is with crucial material. Part of it is devoted to a favourite theme of Jowett's—the death of friends and the Christian hope in relation to them. But in

---

[16] Printed as an appendix to *Sermons on Faith*, pp. 337ff. For a possibly overly sympathetic treatment of Jowett's theology of friendship see Swanston, pp. 192ff.
[17] See Hinchliff in *Balliol Studies*, p. 156 n. 22.
[18] *Sermons on Faith*, p. 343.

this brief section he had some significant things to say. It is really about the inwardness of the Christian life. What makes a lfe a Christian life is its motivation and that cannot be defined in terms of the objective shape of what a man actually does. The same truth held, he argued, for Christian friendship, which he defined as serving God together in doing good to his creatures and as finding one's meeting point in Christ. Such a friendship ought to be based on religious motives and flow out of a religious principle but must not be 'lost in spiritual emotions or in unreal words'. 'Better that friendship should have no element of religion than that it should degenerate into cant and insincerity.'

Jowett then talked of the Christian's 'natural interest in the spiritual welfare of others . . . that they may become more such as God intended them to be in this world'. He pointed out very firmly that this Christian love is quite different from the 'ideal of the ancients' because it is, like God's love, 'the love of the weak and of those who can make no return'.[19] It is interesting to note that in making the distinction between Greek and Christian ideas of 'friendship' he argued firmly and clearly for the superiority of the Christian one. This, apparently, was not a point at which one had to broaden the biblical tradition with what was to be learnt from the classical. Though he said that this Christian friendship, because it was not for one or two but for many, was 'less personal and individual, and more diffused towards all men', the example he gave to illustrate it was a far from impersonal one—a man nursed back to health from mental illness by a friend.

Friendship, therefore, was the category under which Jowett was most easily able to consider Christian life and its motivation. The atonement is the great declaration of God's friendship towards humanity. It was, as he had pointed out in his essay in the commentaries, as real as the love of a human friend but greater, more powerful, unshakable and ever-present. This divine friendship for human beings, Jowett believed, was declared vividly in the life and death of Christ and embodied in his relationship with his disciples who were also his friends. The Christian shares in that friendship. And the friendships of Christians, if motivated by love of God, will

[19] *Sermons on Faith*, pp. 351f.

be an attempt to serve God together in serving his creatures. Thus Christians live out in their own lives that friendship of God towards man from which the whole Christian gospel springs.

One gets the impression that Jowett was somewhat uneasy with the word 'love'—or, at any rate, that he was happier to use the language of friendship. Perhaps, since he was usually talking to audiences of late adolescents, he thought it less misleading. But it was not intended to be a weak or cool word: friendship was one of the most powerful of all emotional concepts for Jowett. He avoided 'charity', on the whole, for that very reason: it was too chilly a word for what he wanted to convey. And it was this theology of the divine friendship which gave Jowett's personal religion its real warmth and vitality. He was not just a liberal protestant moralist with an interest in the historical Jesus. The love—the 'friendship'—of God revealed in Christ was of immense importance to him; and his human friendships—which were just as important—were a vehicle for returning that love.

These two aspects of his Christology—his warm consciousness of an everyday friendship with Christ and his strange belief that one was free to find in Christ all that one thought of as best and highest regardless of its derivation—seem to have been partly responsible for the lack of movement in his thought after 1870. Problems connected with the historicity of the Gospels were becoming more and more pressing in the period between the publication of Seeley's *Ecce Homo* in 1865 and the year of Jowett's death. That year, 1893, has been identified as the very point at which 'the majority of scholars and a fair proportion of educated laity in each of the British churches came round to a critical view of the scriptures, at least in principle.'[20] Such a critical view was inextricably linked with an interest in what actually could be said about Jesus as an historical person. Moreover, the last years of Jowett's life were also the period in which the 'scientific revolution' in the writing of history was taking place, in the sense that historians were asking philosophical questions about how far it was necessary to apply the assumptions of

---

[20] D. L. Pals, *The Victorian 'Lives' of Jesus*, San Antonio 1982, p. 152.

a scientific world-view to documents which antedated the development of that understanding of reality.[21]

In one sense it is surprising that Jowett failed to get to grips with these issues systematically. He was, after all, the author of a notorious contribution to *Essays and Reviews* which had made much reference to the significance of history. He frequently talked about the importance of living with history,[22] about relying on history, and taking the facts of history seriously. He even continued to include writing a life of Christ as among the things he planned to do.[23] But there is another sense in which his failure to get to grips with the problem of historicity is not surprising. The life of Christ which he would have liked to have written would have been not at all like other lives of Christ of the period. For he thought it ought to be idealised and he cited, as his authority for this unhistorical approach, St Paul himself. 'Did not Paul idealize Christ?', he asked. He thought, in fact, that it was a very good thing that the life of Christ was only partially known. 'We have enough to assist us and not enough to constrain us.'

> Instead of receiving Christianity as once given, all mankind from the first should have been endeavouring to improve it, to adapt it to the wants of other ages, to get rid of its eccentricities and peculiarities. We fancy that it came in perfection from Christ and therefore are afraid to touch it. But even if we knew exactly what came from Christ, it is in perpetual process of depravation and needs to be restored; it is in process of being narrowed and needs to be enlarged, or rather in any case needs to be enlarged, if it is to comprehend the world. There is a fallen Christianity, if there is a fallen man, and man is always falling.[24]

A man who held such views was not, in spite of everything he said about history, likely to concern himself with an attempt to establish the historicity of the Gospel narratives in detail. The life of Christ he might have written would be presented, he said, not 'as a history of wonders but as a history of truths'. The 'truths' that he was concerned with, however, were eternal rather than historical, for he

[21] V. A. Harvey, *The Historian and the Believer*, London 1967, pp. 68ff.

[22] For a discussion of what Jowett meant by living with history see Swanston, pp. 151ff.

[23] Abbott and Campbell, ii, pp. 84ff.

[24] Ibid.

believed that such a work ought not to be critical, any more than it ought to be sentimental or picturesque. It should 'seek to bring the mind and thoughts of Christ a little nearer to the human heart' but 'in the spirit not in the letter'.[25] Such a 'life' is, of course, almost impossible to imagine but what Jowett was doing was only a more honest and self-conscious version of what many others have done. It must always be a temptation for a devout believer to take the Gospel narrative as it stands and to flesh it out by reading into it his own ideas. Jowett was turning that temptation into a virtue. But the fact that he was aware of what he was doing made it almost impossible for him to face up to the problems of historicity. He was freeing Christianity from its historical roots while claiming that he believed the facts of history to be of crucial importance. He was also insisting that one should model oneself on Christ at the same time as he was asserting that one could never actually know what Christ was like. It is not difficult to see why he never quite felt able to face up to the central issue.

There was yet another implicit contradiction in what he was doing in these sermons. He appears to have been trying, as he had done in the commentaries, to give an account of crucial Christian doctrines (like the atonement) while breaking free from the particular forms which those doctrines had traditionally taken. But, as we have seen, his statements on the central question of Christ's person and nature tend to be vague and muffled. He wished to be able to claim that Christ embodied the divine friendship towards mankind, manifested the divine nature and possessed the divine authority. Therefore it was necessary for him to assert the divine in Christ. Yet he could not explain what he meant by this claim because he felt compelled to insist that the God-related humanity possessed by Christ was possible for all human beings. No doubt his refusal to make room in his theology for the sacramental and the mystical was partly responsible for this ambiguity for it left him with no easy or obvious way of describing the manner of the believer's union with Christ. He believed that much of the dogma of traditional Christianity was an unnecessary elaboration upon the original simplicity of the Gospel. He wanted to be able to say that simplification itself

[25] Abbott and Campbell, ii, pp. 84ff.

was all that was needed for human beings to discover their identity with Christ and their full and perfect relationship with God. He would do nothing that might appear to make the Church—as a theological concept—an essential part of man's path to God.

As the decade wore on he came to state the paradoxes of his theology more and more sharply. It was as though he was determined to force them upon his hearers' attention while at the same time refusing to give the least help in resolving the problems. The sermon, for instance, in which he made his most determined stand against dogmatic elaboration was also the sermon in which he committed himself most clearly to a belief in the divinity of Christ. This was the sermon entitled 'The Permanent Elements of Religion' and preached in 1879.[26] The particular form of words he chose for his affirmation was peculiar, not to say eccentric, in the sense that one cannot imagine anyone else dealing with the matter in quite that way. Jowett might have argued—with some justice—that he was clearly affirming both the divinity and the humanity of Christ, yet he entirely evaded the question of how Christ could be God and man.

His affirmation appeared in a context which was as vigorous a rejection of deism as anything he had said in the 1840s. And then, having quoted a string of sayings, mostly his favourite verses from the Gospels, Jowett went on, 'This is the religion of Christ; not the religion consistently taught by any section of the Christian Church, nor practised by any considerable number of Christians. But it is the religion in which Christ lived and died—the religion of a person whom we believe to be Divine.' What it could mean for a 'divine person' to 'have a religion', he did not explain at all.

Part of what was exercising Jowett's mind in this sermon was a problem that has a very modern ring to it.[27] But it was also a problem with which the nineteenth century wrestled and Newman's *Essay on the Development of Christian Doctrine*, published shortly after his conversion in 1845, was one attempt to deal with it. The Christian religion—Jowett pointed out—has not been static and unchanging

[26] A copy is bound up with the copy of *Sermons on Faith and Doctrine* in Balliol College library, though it was not actually part of the volume.
[27] See e.g. M. F. Wiles, *Faith and the Mystery of God*, London 1982, pp. 5ff.

through the centuries, so that 'if we could imagine a single individual living from the Christian era until now, he would have been, not of one religion but of several, and several times over would have anathematised and excommunicated himself.' If that is the case, what constitutes the essential or continuing Christianity? Anyone familiar with Jowett's sermons could, almost without hesitation, provide not only his answer but the actual phrases in which he was going to clothe it. The essential Christianity lay in the simplicity of Christ himself who 'went about doing good'.

But Jowett was aware that it would be somewhat naive to leave it at that, so he examined some other possible hypothetical answers that he believed to be false. He made no direct reference to Newman, in spite of the fact that the revised edition of the *Essay on Development*—so extensively revised as to be virtually a new work, and one which made considerable use of an analogy with biological evolution—had appeared in the previous year. Nor did he directly confront any of the classic attempts to define an 'essence' of Christianity.[28] But he showed some degree of sophistication, nonetheless, arguing that true Christianity could not be found in institutional forms, for these are 'relative to the age and state of society which gives birth to them'. Nor can it be found in the 'internal certainty which good men have of the truth which has been vouchsafed to them' because people with a wide variety of different beliefs have all had an equally intense conviction that their beliefs are true. Nor can it 'be supposed to consist in historical facts' because these—like any historical facts—are subject to historical enquiry and must be judged by the rules of historical evidence. And if this is true of the ordinary facts narrated by the Old and New Testaments, it must be just as true of the extraordinary.

We cannot say, with some writers, that they are more probable than other facts; or, with Butler, that all facts are antecedently so improbable that the difference between the improbability of the ordinary and the extraordinary 'cannot be estimated, and is as nothing.' Nor can we require the evidence for them to be supplemented by belief in them; for this would destroy the very nature of evidence. The certain knowledge that in the universe is a fixed

[28] For a discussion of these see S. Sykes, *The Identity of Christianity*, London 1984, n.b. pp. 81ff., 102ff., and 211ff.

order makes a great difference in our manner of regarding them. If we saw them with our own eyes and in the full light of day, we should have a difficulty in verifying them or appreciating their import; how can we see them more clearly when they are far away in the distance?

Instead he asserted that the true, essential Christian religion had three characteristics. The first of these was what he called 'the perfection of the Divine nature'. Since everyone agrees about what is holiness, right, love, and truth, and since everyone also agrees that one 'cannot have too much' of these, Jowett thought we could all agree about what God is like and need not be be too concerned about metaphysical questions about the origin of evil or the being of God.

Secondly, among the fixed points of religion is the life of Christ Himself, in whose person the Divine justice, and wisdom, and love are embodied to us. It may be true that the record contained in the Gospels is fragmentary; and that the life of Christ itself far surpassed the memorials of it which remain to us. But there is enough in the words which have come down to us to be the rule of our lives; and they would not be the less true if we knew not whence they came, or who was the author of them.

Jowett's third fixed point in the essence of Christianity ought to have forced his hearers and himself to face the crucial question which he had been refusing to tackle for so long. For his third point is 'that we must admit all well-ascertained facts of history, or science. For these, too, are the revelation of God to us, and they seem to be gaining and accumulating every day.'[29] Coming immediately after his assertion that the first two essential points of Christianity are the perfect nature of God and the embodiment of that divine perfection in Christ, it ought to have forced him to attempt a reconciliation between the categorical nature of those assertions and the problematic character of the New Testament evidence.

In one sense, of course, he was simply reiterating in a sharper and clearer way a point he had been concerned to make over and over again for almost forty years. That the facts of science, if true, must not be denied, he had been asserting since the 1840s. In the commentaries he had insisted that there cannot be two kinds of truth, one for religion and another for the real world. And, along with that refrain, he had also been saying that true faith cannot be assailed by other

---

[29] See Swanston, pp. 151ff.

aspects of truth. Previously, when the 'well-ascertained' facts of science or history had actually seemed to assail the truth of faith, he had always taken refuge in an appeal to morality—how one actually lived the Christian life was what mattered, not the intellectual problems. Every time he had felt obliged, in his early days as master, to remind the undergraduates that the Gospel evidence was fragmentary or uncertain, he had gone on to say that that was really unimportant because there was no uncertainty about how Christians ought to live. Moreover, he was also accustomed to insist that it did not matter if the Bible seemed sometimes to convey a picture of God which conflicted with our own ideas of what was best and highest. We were entitled to maintain the highest possible concept of God and to believe that it was *this* God which had been revealed in Christ. And that was precisely what he did again in 1879, in spite of having stated the problem in what appears at first sight to be an inescapable form. This is the force of his insistence that 'there is enough in the words that have come down to us to be the rule of our lives; and they would not be the less true if we knew not whence they came, or who was the author of them.'

Jowett summarised the whole argument of the sermon in one telling sentence. 'This, then, is what we believe to be the sum of religion: To be like God—to be like Christ—to live in every true idea and fact.' In essence this was what he had been trying to say all along but had never enunciated quite so clearly, comprehensively, and without obfuscation. But the very fact that he thought he could put the whole thing in this one sentence suggests that he was not aware of the problem he was creating—or, perhaps, he did not think it was a problem. He hated and feared systems, as we have seen. He did not believe that logic could overrule common sense. And he did not believe that paradox in the metaphysical realm was undesirable. But did he really think that one could, as it were, invent one's own idea of Christ, read it back into the gospels, and still claim to be living 'in every true idea and fact'?

In the sermon on 'The Permanent Elements of Religion' Jowett was restating all his favourite themes, asserting them more precisely and clearly than usual, and putting them bluntly side by side even when they appeared to contradict one another. Not only did he make a much clearer statement of his belief in the divinity of Christ, he firmly rejected as never before all reliance upon authority whether of Bible, Church, tradition, or orthodox doctrinal formulations. The whole edifice of faith has become the achievement of the individual. One wants to ask, therefore, how it is that Jowett *knows* that Christ is God. Moreover, the truths of science and history he had now almost declared to be *de fide*. They had become the third essential element in religion because it was in them that one had to live. But he seemed to display a much more sceptical attitude than he had shown before towards the narrative material of the Gospels. He was no longer simply saying that the record was uncertain: he was asserting that a great deal of it cannot be true. Yet this did not alter his appeal to Christ. 'And if anybody asks,' he said, 'Where, after all these assaults of criticism and science, and the concessions made to them, is our religion to be found now? We answer, Where it always was—in the imitation of Christ.' He gave no hint of being aware that it might be difficult to imitate a Christ about whom one could learn little: or, worse still, that it might be far too easy to imitate a Christ whom one had virtually invented for oneself.

Jowett probably failed to see the problem because it was possible for himself, having started with a traditional and unquestioning attitude towards Christianity, to reinterpret his faith in terms of the new facts of science and history which he encountered and still be able to cling to his previous understanding of the God revealed in Christ. It is not so clear that he was able to expound it to a new generation, which did not share those assumptions, to whom he was not prepared to teach the old certainties, and to whom he was yet looking to solve the problems.

Amid all the changes to which, during centuries to come, the Christian faith may be exposed, either from the influence of opinion or from political causes, the image of Christ going about doing good, of Christ suffering for man, of Christ praying for His enemies—this, and this alone, will never pass away.

Obviously he believed that, in spite of any detailed criticism which the Gospel narratives might suffer, there would survive an unassailable sense of a *person* which could be conveyed to future generations.

A Liberal Gospel

He might not be able to expound precisely by what means that was to be done nor to justify his methodology. Nor would he even have wanted to systematise it. To him it was just a matter of common sense that it was so.

Perhaps, then, it was not surprising that the sermon ended with what sounds almost like a return to the position he had advanced to Benjamin Brodie nearly forty years earlier:[30]

> To have a firm conviction of a few things is better than to have a feeble faith in many, and to live in a belief is the strongest witness of its truth. For he is not a Christian who is one outwardly; neither is that Christianity which is in the letter only. But he is a Christian who is one inwardly, and walks, as far as human error and infirmity will allow, in the footsteps of Christ.

Faced with an insoluble problem, Jowett seems to be saying that one would just have to give up believing a few more things while continuing to live as though one were certain of everything.

That this was not really a tenable position was obvious to some at the time. Leslie Stephen did not understand what Jowett was trying to do, but his sketch for a life of the master of Balliol reveals very clearly why so many members of a younger generation found his approach impossible to accept. Jowett's admirers were compelled to take his thought much further and to devise a philosophical underpinning for it. Those, like Stephen, who found Jowett's position totally unconvincing, moved on towards agnosticism.[31]

It is simply not possible to estimate how much Jowett's theological opinions, expressed in his regular sermons, may have influenced prospective clergymen educated at Balliol. His reiterated opinion that it was better for such men not to engage in theology presumably meant that he had no conscious desire to disturb their orthodoxy. The fact that he did not wish to be the leader of a party, his Broad Church individualism, and his very firm belief that educators ought not to make disciples among their pupils, would all have tended against his imposing his beliefs on others. This, no doubt, partly explains why he had so few obvious clerical heirs. But there is

---

[30] Above pp. 22f.

[31] L. Stephen, 'Jowett's Life', *Studies of a Biographer*, 2nd edn., 2 vols., London 1910, ii, pp. 123ff., and n.b. 131ff.

another possible fact to be borne in mind as well. What had happened to Tait and Temple would have inclined Jowett against grooming bright and critical undergraduates for bishoprics: they, too, might betray the truth by submitting to the constraints of the received creed. But he did not hide his hatred of obscurantism and his ideas were bound to leave some mark upon the minds of his regular undergraduate audience.

W. H. Fremantle himself, the editor of Jowett's posthumously published sermons, was probably the nearest thing there ever was to a Jowett protégé in high ecclesiastical office. He was an undergraduate at Balliol in the early 1850s and was therefore about ten years younger than Jowett, who was his tutor. From Balliol Fremantle went to be a fellow of All Souls, where (with two other Balliol men) he conducted a vigorous campaign to force his new college to accept Jowett's ideal of open competition for fellowships. They were even prepared to go to litigation in order to do so. Fremantle went on to be Tait's chaplain in London in the 1860s and then became incumbent of St Mary's, Bryanston Square—where Jowett once preached for him and caused a great furore by 'sneering at Elisha's miracles'.[32] He was to go back to Balliol as fellow and chaplain from 1882 to 1894 and afterwards became dean of Ripon.

He was a somewhat humourless man and not always very acute in his judgements but he had obviously conceived a great admiration for Jowett during his time as an undergraduate. The master himself plainly thought Fremantle worthy but a bit tiresome. And Fremantle for his part sometimes found the master very difficult to deal with. As a young man he had been anxious to rush heroically to Jowett's defence during the controversy that followed the publication of the first edition of the commentaries. Amongst the minor campaigns against Jowett in the university was the provision of a prize for the best essay to be written on the atonement, the obvious intention being to encourage the entrants to write against Jowett. Fremantle wrote an essay *in support* of Jowett's view and was only prevented from submitting it because his uncle, whose curate he then was, virtually forbade him to do so.[33] He was convinced both of

[32] Tait Papers: Personal Letters, vol. 90, fo. 199.
[33] *Recollections* [*of Dean Fremantle, chiefly by himself*, edited by the Master of the

A Liberal Gospel

Jowett's intellectual stature and the depth and genuineness of his religion behind what he regarded as a reticent facade.[34] Yet, when Fremantle returned to Balliol twenty-five years later as chaplain and tutor in theology, Jowett seems to have been the chief obstacle he encountered. This was the more surprising because Jowett had chosen Fremantle for the job, secured his election, and put such enormous pressure on him to accept that he felt obliged to abandon offers of preferment in order to do so.

Fremantle went to Balliol as chaplain with two chief goals in mind. First, he wanted to correct the impression current in the university that Balliol had become almost entirely secular through Jowett's influence. And secondly he wanted to build up the theology school in the college and demonstrate that it was a good place for the training of clergymen. Both these things he obviously intended, in a somewhat clumsy fashion, by way of protecting Jowett from himself. Jowett consistently seemed to frustrate all his efforts. Whenever Fremantle hoped that the master would show some public interest in chapel-going or theological teaching in the college, Jowett snubbed him.

Fremantle appears to have only partly perceived what was happening. His account of the matter is as follows:

> when the setting up of the school of theology as one of the subjects of examination for degrees was under discussion it was opposed by Jowett. His position and influence were peculiar. During the time in which he was the subject of ill treatment he seemed to take no interest in the religious part of college life. It would seem that he was so much afraid of the ecclesiasticism which seemed to beset it that he thought that no good was to be expected except from the fortuitous good influences of a University life. When he became master in 1870 a sudden change took place; he took up the habit of attending the chapel morning and evening with great regularity and administering the communion every Sunday. But this could not obliterate the past; it could not but appear as a mere appanage of his official position. The respect for his great qualities remained; many of his sermons told, though somewhat indirectly, upon the conscience of young men; but the college was looked upon in the public estimation as completely secularized.[35]

Temple, London 1921,] pp. 51ff.
[34] *Recollections*, pp. 37f.
[35] *Recollections*, p. 103.

It is possible to detect behind this account two things at work. As regards the theology school, Jowett was plainly doing one of his sulks. He had, after all, been outwitted by Pusey in this matter. He had appointed Fremantle because he knew that that would ensure that Balliol men were taught liberal instead of Tractarian theology; but he was not going to be seen to give the slightest acknowledgement in public of the existence of the school.

On the matter of chapel services, Jowett's reaction was probably more complex. It is quite clear that the new master was in no sense a secular person nor would he have wanted Balliol to be a wholly secular place. What Fremantle says about his reticence is borne out in other sources: Jowett did not like to talk about religion but this was at least partly because he thought it too important to be a proper topic for conversation. He also, for whatever reason, stayed determinedly clear of public theological debate and—because he was a controversial figure so far as theology was concerned—it would be difficult for him to discuss religion without becoming involved in argument. He was, moreover, quite frank about the reasons why he now liked to go to chapel whereas earlier he had not. Once he had become the master he was in a position to ensure that the services were as he liked them to be.[36] And one of the things he liked was that some, at least, of the services and particularly the communion services were voluntary.

Jowett was far happier to see thirty volunteers early on a Sunday morning than a more or less compulsorily full chapel later in the day. But Fremantle, as part of his campaign to demonstrate that Balliol had not become secular, would have preferred the latter.[37] Jowett's horror of 'eccleciasticism' probably went deeper than Fremantle perceived and included even Fremantle's own Broad Church ecclesiasticism. The last thing the master would have wanted was for the college to acquire the only kind of reputation for piety which would have stilled outside criticism. He knew very well that, if he allowed Balliol to conform once more to the accepted pattern of behaviour for a 'religious' college, he would have lost his opportunity to create

[36] Abbott and Campbell, ii, p. 31.
[37] *Recollections*, pp. 107f.

the kind of liberal Christian institution which had been his goal for so long.

What the new master was doing through the sermons and services in the college chapel probably had more influence on future laymen than future clergyman. Some, like T. H. Green, Edward Caird, and Lewis Campbell (an exact contemporary of Fremantle's and, in effect, Jowett's literary executor as well as his biographer) had been deeply influenced by him even before he became master. They acquired an expertise in theology which was critical, open-minded, and constructive—if not always very orthodox. They did not feel that it was necessary to be ordained in order to have something to say and to do in the field of religion. After Jowett's election, his sermons and the kind of services he devised became an instrument in spreading his ideas far more widely than ever before. Whole generations of Balliol undergraduates would grow up with a sense that religion was something one should take seriously as a matter of significance for everyday life, think about independently and critically for oneself, and even be prepared to pronounce on in public. Lay sermons and lay theology became a Balliol tradition. The college was very much what Jowett had wanted it to be.

Colleges, moreover, possessed a considerable degree of autonomy and were now in a position to reform themselves, so it may even be that Jowett believed that university reform had gone far enough. The essential things had been done. Just as he had never thought that the university was as important as the college so he had never thought professorships as important as tutorships, even though he was a professor himself. But he came to believe that new chairs ought not to be endowed unless it could be guaranteed that the professor would have a class to lecture to. And he was no more inclined to support research or private scholarship than he had ever been. Though he had begun to think that it would be a good thing for there to be readerships in the university, it was so that there should be some means of rewarding the faithful college tutor.[38] But he was convinced that there were so few people capable of pure research that it was not worth endowing it.[39]

[38] Engel, p. 180f.
[39] Engel, p. 191.

Living in lodgings had been permitted since 1867 and Balliol, with Jowett already in a position to force Scott's hand, had then gone ahead and built and furnished lodgings which could be let cheaply to poorer students who would receive free tuition and even small bursaries from the college. That scheme had to be shelved because it aroused opposition from other colleges who feared that Balliol might come to absorb the whole university. Jowett, had then backed a proposal to open a Balliol hall, with T. H. Green, his chief lieutenant, in charge. As master he still pursued this policy but, again baulked by the opposition within the university, turned his attention to a scheme for the extension of universities in the English provinces as well.

In 1874 he produced yet another memorandum on education and reform.[40] Now that he was firmly in control of Balliol, he began to give consideration to the place of universities in English society as a whole. He urged that new colleges should be planted in the great centres of population, the new industrial cities. Doing this would provide a proper means of continuing education beyond school level and 'would afford to the more active minded of the working classes the opportunity of self-culture'. He also apparently thought that such colleges would solve the problem of higher education for women, 'about which so many difficulties are felt at the present time. (For there could surely be no impropriety in young persons of both sexes living at home with their parents meeting together in lecture rooms or at an examination.)'

The memorandum, in fact, reveals that many of the quirks and prejudices of Jowett's social attitudes survived. The right to confer degrees in arts, he thought, should be restricted to the old universities, though certain concessions might be made to those who had attended the new urban colleges in terms of the length of time they would have to be in residence in order to qualify for an Oxford or Cambridge degree. But, in general, his proposals were very practical. He had a genuine interest in the extension of opportunities for higher education and a grasp of the realities of English industrial

---

[40] Campbell, pp. 183–208, 'Suggestions for University Reform: Memorandum by Professor Jowett'.

society. He may not have been desperately anxious to have working-class students or scientists in large numbers—or women at all—at Oxford, but he was prepared to use the academic prestige and expertise of Oxford and Balliol to create institutions where they were most needed. There is no means of telling whether he secretly perceived that this was precisely the best way of keeping undesirables elsewhere and that affiliating the new colleges to the older institutions was a recipe for preventing them from competing for the better student. At all events, as master of Balliol, he put a great deal of effort into helping to found new universities.

So far as Oxford itself was concerned, further reform was still in the air. Gladstone had appointed a commission to examine university and college finance in 1871, though actual reforming legislation was not to be enacted for a further decade. But Jowett was no longer (if, indeed he had ever been) a militantly radical reformer: perhaps he was never really radical in any sphere. By the 1870s, with fellowships open to competititon, the improvement of college teaching, the abolition of religious tests and most other restrictions, and with greater opportunities for poorer students to come to Oxford, he had really got everything he had wanted in 1854. From that point he became far more conservative about the university.[41]

[41] Ward, pp. 271 and 298f.

7

Disciples

Jowett's relationship with Fremantle is significant because it reveals something about the master's personality. He always said that he did not approve of teachers who 'made disciples'. Yet it was implicit in his whole strategy as a tutor and as master that he should exercise a compelling influence on the young men whom he taught. It was probably also the case that he found it personally very satisfying to be the object of a certain amount of hero-worship. The very fact that he had expected, in 1854, that his own former pupils would automatically vote for him and not for Scott suggests that he regarded personal loyalty as his due. At the same time, his impatience with poor Fremantle indicates that sheer, blind hero-worship was not enough. He expected his admirers not simply to agree with him, certainly not to try and save him from himself, nor even to need to be told what they ought to do to win his approval. They were expected to be perceptive enough to see what he was aiming at without being told. It was almost as if they had to think for themselves, yet never arrive at independent conclusions.

Fremantle was by no means the conventional clergyman of his generation. In spite of the fact that he could never quite satisfy Jowett, he was something of a radical. Coming from an Evangelical and Tory family, he became—largely through Jowett's influence—liberal in both theology and politics. He interested himself in ecclesiastical reform and, maintaining that the Church must involve itself in social and political matters, put into practice the ideas he advocated.[1] As chaplain of Balliol Fremantle was best known in wider Church circles for his championing of the view that there could be

---

[1] L. E. Nettleship, ['William Fremantle, Samuel Barnett and the Broad Church Origin of Toynbee Hall', *Journal of Ecclesiastical History*, 33 (1982),] pp. 564ff.

no genuinely Christian distinction between the sacred and the secular: all existence was the sphere of the divine operation. The very titles of his two books, *The Gospel of the Secular Life* and *The World as the Subject of Redemption*, hint at this belief.

The second of these works was his Bampton lectures and Jowett was enthusiastic in his praise of them, at least if Fremantle himself is to be believed.[2] But he also perceived that the master's expressed enthusiasm did not carry over into any sustained interest. Fremantle thought that this was because Jowett really was not at all interested in missions—nor even in Fremantle's rather liberal approach to other religions, which got him into trouble with Evangelicals.

In fact, by the time he became master, Jowett had for nearly twenty years been interested in other religions in the broadest sense. Hamish Swanston has assembled the evidence for dating that interest to the period between the first and second editions of the commentaries.[3] Jowett had two brothers in the Indian army and had perceived that the Indian mutiny had implications for missions. He had been consulted about the reform of the Indian Civil Service. Inevitably he took some interest in the religions of India. He was to think in terms of an essay on the history of religion for the planned second volume of *Essays and Reviews*.[4] He was involved in the creation of the Indian institute in the university and the setting up of the chair of Sanskrit. But his interest was rather vague and unspecific and the planned essay came to nothing. Jowett remained interested in religions in general, in Buddhism as well as in theistic religions. As he grew older he used to talk more and more about the importance of what he called the 'science' of religions. But he never acquired any very precise, systematic, or thorough knowledge, whether practical or academic, of other religions.

Yet it was clearly important to Fremantle that Jowett should approve of his Bampton lectures. Again and again he was hurt by the master's lack of interest in things which he, Fremantle, was doing. When he was engaged in a translation of Jerome, Jowett once asked

---

[2] *Recollections*, p. 102.
[3] Swanston, pp. 144ff.
[4] Abbott and Campbell, i, p. 405.

him, 'How do you get on with the works of St Chrysostom?'[5] Fremantle thought that Jowett was clumsily trying to be gracious while not really finding the chaplain's work worth bothering about. Jowett may even have derived some slightly malicious pleasure from a disingenuous enquiry of that kind. His behaviour, at all events, was gratuitously wounding; and yet, surprisingly, he was able to retain Fremantle's admiration. Nor did Fremantle ever abandon the belief that Jowett was 'a truly Christian man'.[6]

In spite of the master's demanding and difficult attitude to his disciples, it emerges very clearly from Fremantle's account of his undergraduate days that Jowett did not use the opportunities provided by his role as tutor to force his ideas upon the young. Fremantle says that the devotional addresses given by Jowett to his pupils consisted of simple teaching on prayer and Bible reading. His more formal academic lectures were rather over their heads.[7] Jowett does not seem to have put any pressure on them to accept his theology. Fremantle himself took up liberal theological ideas after he had ceased to be an undergraduate. No doubt his obvious hero-worship of Jowett played some part in this, but that does not seem to have been Jowett's fault. It was personal loyalty from his pupils which Jowett desired—and largely got: their opinions were less important.

Jowett's ideals as a teacher were very high indeed. In a sermon preached in college chapel almost ten years after he became master, he said:

Some persons may never have understood that teaching has anything to do with sympathy. The gifts which they look for in the teacher, are knowledge of the subject, clearness in the arrangement of materials, power of illustration, accuracy, diligence, nor can anyone be a good teacher in whom these qualities are wanting. And yet much more than this is required. For the young have to be educated through the heart as well as the head; the subtle influence of the teacher's character, his love of truth, his disinterestedness, his zeal for knowledge, should imperceptibly act upon them. Dry light, without any tincture of the affections, may truly under a figure describe science. Of teaching it would be truer to say that it must be clothed in the

[5] *Recollections*, p. 107.
[6] *Recollections*, p. 36.
[7] *Recollections*, pp. 32f.

language of affection and enthusiasm, that it must be warm as well as light. Further the relation of the teacher is a personal one, and human beings are much more easily led by feeling than by reason. He who is capable of taking an interest in each of his pupils individually, who by a sympathetic power can reach what is working in their hearts or perplexing their understanding; who has such a feeling for them that he has acquired the right to say *anything* to them, has in him the elements of a great teacher. He will be sanguine about them too, because he feels confident in what he and they by a perfect understanding of one another can jointly accomplish. And in general to think better of mankind than they always deserve is a safe as well as a generous rule in the conduct of life; most men have some virtues which are not recognised at first sight, and a degree of intelligence which requires to be drawn out. And generous feeling in an elder is sure to be met by generous response in a younger person.[8]

No one, of course, manages always to live up to his own ideals. Jowett certainly did not. He was not renowned for his accuracy or his clarity and the barbed wit in which he indulged is not evidence of a constant generosity. But, at least, he knew what he ought to be doing and it is probably fair to assume that he tried. His very considerable reputation as master and the real affection which so many undergraduates felt for him were the measure of his success. He clearly aimed to create such an affection. He was angry if he failed to get it. He was less scrupulous in giving loyalty himself. But his expressed intention was not to impose particular beliefs on his pupils and if, in spite of himself, he 'made disciples' this was probably because he quite simply underestimated the effect of his own powerful personality upon the young.

Obviously Jowett could not have appealed in the same degree to all the undergraduates nor they to him. A few seem to have disliked him very much indeed. They were chiefly those who—like Mallock—were intellectually undistinguished, zealously 'orthodox' in religion, and either rigidly *laissez-faire* or high Tory in politics. He would naturally tend to become more friendly with those who shared his interests and attitudes. His obvious liking for aristocrats, preferably Whig aristocrats, did not prevent his being sharp with precociously self-important young men even when they belonged to

---

[8] *College Sermons*, pp. 157f.—the italics are mine.

the leading Whig families. Henry Scott Holland's description of Jowett's first sermon suggests that it was possible for undergraduates who disliked his approach to religion nevertheless to find him personally attractive. There is, indeed, some evidence that even those who, at first sight, seem least likely to be in sympathetic accord with Jowett got on quite well with him. Gerard Manley Hopkins, for instance, who was an exact contemporary of Scott Holland's in the years just before Jowett became master, must have been the kind of introspective young man, intensely agonised and mystical about religion, with whom Jowett might be expected to be impatient. But, in fact, Jowett seems to have approved of him, at least as a scholar. Years afterwards he wrote warmly in favour of Hopkins's candidature for the Greek professorship at Dublin.[9]

Undoubtedly Jowett's greatest failing in dealing with younger people was that he was inclined to take their devotion for granted and exploit it, while being impatient and somewhat disloyal in his dealings with them. The way he treated Fremantle was not an isolated case. It was, in fact, almost the normal pattern for his dealings with his disicples. The pattern recurs, for instance, in his relationship with R. L. Nettleship. Like Fremantle, Nettleship was generally regarded as one of Jowett's men. He was a layman and a tutor. He was undogmatic and something of a free-thinker in religion, while exercising a strongly pastoral role among undergraduates. He was also deeply admired by them as a man who lived, in practice, a genuinely Christian life. Jowett seems to have taken him for granted in precisely the same way as he took his other disciples for granted. In Nettleship's case, his extreme diffidence and the fact that his memoir of Green was almost the only work he ever brought himself to publish seems to have caused Jowett to underestimate his ability. And Jowett admitted this, in a sermon preached after Nettleship's death, with the kind of frankness that makes it possible to understand why his ill-treated admirers so often remained faithful to the master.

I am afraid that I did not always do him justice, because I did not altogether understand him. For he was of such a temper, and sometimes tended, as I

[9] C. Schmidt, 'Classical Studies at Balliol in the 1860's: The undergraduate essays of Gerard Manley Hopkins', in *Balliol Studies*, pp. 162 and 169f.

thought, too much to depreciate himself and the usefulness of his own work.[10]

Nettleship was to be the memoirist and literary executor of T. H. Green, perhaps the most important of Jowett's disciples. Green's importance is that he became the acknowledged leader of the Idealist school,[11] which dominated British philosophy in the last quarter of the nineteenth and until well into the present century. Moreover the beginnings of the welfare state can credibly be traced to its influence.[12] Since Jowett was responsible for setting Green upon the line of thought from which the religious, philosophical, and political ideas associated with British Idealism all developed, Green was instrumental in propagating much that Jowett stood for. Indeed the biographers of Edward Caird—somewhat implausibly—describe Jowett as the John Henry Newman of the Idealist movement: the man who initiated it, became critical of it, yet always defended it against its enemies.[13] But Newman moved away from most of his followers because *his* ideas developed beyond the original position of the Tracts: Jowett parted company with the Idealists because *their* thinking developed away from *his* position. And, probably for that reason, the familiar pattern reappears in Jowett's relations with Green.

Green went from Rugby to Balliol in 1855, the year after Scott became master, and Jowett was his tutor. These were, at least in Jowett's own estimation, his years in the wilderness when he cut himself off from his fellows in hall, senior common room, and

---

[10] *College Sermons*, p. 268 and cf. article on Nettleship in *Dictionary of National Biography*.

[11] A recent article by H. D. Lewis, 'The British Idealists', in N. Smart, J. Clayton, P. Sherry and S. T. Katz (eds.), *Nineteenth Century Religious Thought in the West*, Cambridge 1985, ii, p. 275, contains a curious error, asserting that Green was a fellow of Balliol during the mastership of the other eminent Idealist Edward Caird. Caird was, in fact, Green's pupil and did not become master of Balliol till a decade after Green's death.

[12] [A. M.] Quinton, ['Absolute Idealism', *Proceedings of the British Academy*, 57, London 1971,] pp. 303f. and [A.] Vincent and [R.] Plant, [*Philosophy, Politics and Citizenship: The Life and Thought of the British Idealists*, Oxford 1984,] pp. 4f.

[13] [H.] Jones and [J. H.] Muirhead, [*The Life and Philosophy of Edward Caird*, Glasgow 1921], p. 126.

chapel. He does not, however, seem to have neglected the cultivation of his pupils—rather the reverse in fact. They were his real friends and associates. It is quite clear from Green's own account that tutor and pupil stood in something other than the older, very formal relationship. To Jowett he owed, as he said, 'the greatest and most lasting debt'.[14] That debt was personal as well as academic.

Green's friends often compared him with Arthur Hugh Clough, the poet. Jowett, himself, did so in a sermon he was to preach after Green's death.[15] The point of the comparison is obvious. Clough, too, had been a product of Rugby and Balliol, where he had moved in the same circles as Jowett and Stanley in the late 1830s. Having become a fellow of Oriel in 1841, he resigned seven years later because he could not conscientiously reconcile his religious doubts with his tenure of that office. Those doubts were not caused primarily by intellectual difficulties nor because he found Christianity morally repugnant.[16] He found, rather, that he had no fervour for religion as conventionally understood. He was also disenchanted with English politics and came to regard the whole established order of society as in need of drastic reform. He needed a quite other understanding of the world to evoke commitment.

The frequent comparison of Green with Clough was, in part, straightforward. Green was, as Clough had been twenty years earlier, precociously mature, highly intelligent, seriously engaged in theological questionings even before he took his degree, something of a radical in both religion and politics, a highly moral and sensitive man, and a lay tutor while still very young. But behind all these obvious parallels, lay an even more significant point. Clough's resignation had shocked all his friends not simply because doubts were shocking in themselves. What upset the liberals was that Clough had seemed so obviously to be a naturally religious person,

---

[14] 'Memoir' in R. L. Nettleship (ed.), *Works of Thomas Hill Green*, 3 vols., London 1886–90, iii, p. xvii. When the reference is, as here, to the 'Memoir' it will be cited below as 'Nettleship' with the page number in Roman numerals: when it is to Green's own writings it will be cited as *Works* with volume and page number.

[15] Published in *Sermons: Biographical*, pp. 210ff.

[16] P. G. Scott, 'A. H. Clough: A Case Study in Victorian Doubt', in D. Baker (ed.), *Studies in Church History*, ix, p. 387.

unworldly and high minded. That he should be lost to theology and to the university because he could not accept the whole system of traditional orthodoxy seemed an appalling waste. There is a note of pride in Jowett's mention of the comparison. Green did not have to resign his tutorship. He became a highly professional, if lay, theologian and his influence for good among the undergraduates was incontestable. What Jowett tried to do for Green as his tutor had been worth doing. Green's life had been a kind of vindication of Jowett's determination to make Balliol a centre of liberal religion.

Green's time as an undergraduate was also the years between the first and second editions of the Pauline commentaries. Jowett had not yet written the revised essay on the atonement in which he began to distance himself from German metaphysics. He was still in the phase of his thought in which he had begun to temper Kant with Hegel. And it was Jowett, in his lectures, who had introduced Green to Hegelian ideas. There really was no other source, at that time, from which an English undergraduate could learn about Hegel.

Green clearly took up and developed these ideas very quickly. As early as 1862 he was asserting them, in a prize essay on novels which gave him an opportunity to discourse on the two senses in which a world may be said to be the creation of the mind—Kant's and the novelist's.[17] The essay contains many words and phrases which sound as if they are echoes of Jowett but it also foreshadows Green's whole technique of using Kant's thought as his starting-point and then developing 'Hegelian' ideas from it. In fact, Kant was to figure far more prominently than Hegel in Green's writings and almost all his contemporaries were aware that his method was to proceed from Kant along lines parallel and similar to, but not identical with Hegel.[18] It is possible that this technique owes its beginnings to the particular point Jowett had reached when Green was his pupil, the transition from an enthusiasm for Kant to an equally temporary enthusiasm for Hegel. Green certainly first encountered the ideas of

---

[17] *Works*, iii, p. 22.
[18] See e.g. E. Caird in A. Seth and R. B. Haldane (eds.), *Essays in Philosophical Criticism*, London 1883, p. 5 and Nettleship, pp. lxxxvf.

F. C. Baur—of whom he said that he was 'nearly the most instructive writer I ever met with'[19]—through reading Jowett's commentaries. And this, too, was of considerable significance for the later development of Green's idealism for it seems to have been from Baur that he took the idea that God's self-realisation in history is never complete.

But, if it was Jowett who first introduced Green to German Idealism, Green seems fairly soon to have begun to develop and sytematise the ideas he learnt from his tutor. The eclecticism and the inconsistencies of Jowett's approach were simply inadequate for someone of Green's intellectual capacity. It was important for him that all thought should be worked into a single coherent system. 'He was not', as one of his colleagues said, 'a mere discoverer of sporadic good ideas; his tendency was to form his conclusions into a whole, in which nothing was isolated or out of relation to the rest.'[20]

Nor did Jowett's reliance upon common sense seem a satisfactory defence of the Christian position which was under attack from critical historical enquiry and from the discoveries of the scientists. Green was certainly very acutely aware of the problems raised—which Jowett so consistently evaded—by critical doubts about the historicity of Jesus. What he did was to take the very sources from which Jowett had developed his own critical approach (such as Hegel and Baur) and make them the basis of a new presentation of the Christian faith in a form which was not vulnerable to a critical attack upon its basic documents. The Gospel, in Green's view, was an account of metaphysical rather than historical truths. In a reversal of Jowett's position, he seemed to be saying that the untruth of certain supposed historical facts did not prove the untruth of the idea.

Nevertheless Green by no means departed wholly from what Jowett had taught him. It was always his ambition to state the Idealist vision in a less esoteric way than Hegel had done, so as to make it acceptable to serious and scientific men.[21] There was in him, as in Jowett, an 'English' impatience with the remoteness and

---

[19] Nettleship, p. xxxvii.
[20] Quoted in Nettleship, p. lxiii.
[21] Vincent and Plant, p. 12.

abstraction of German metaphysics. Indeed, much of Green's work can be seen as an attempt to provide a solid systematic framework in support of positions which Jowett, more intuitively, had adopted. Green, for instance, provided a clear argument against any naturalistic theory of morals and insisted that a sense of moral obligation implies, ultimately, a belief in the operation of an eternal intelligence.[22] The practicalities of the moral life, he also insisted, are the real test of religion. Both these ideas are to be found in Jowett, but without the supporting system of thought, nor as a rationally defensible Christian system that could be passed on as a positive and communicable whole.

In the 1850s the college was still struggling to provide itself with fellows who were academically respectable and with tutors who could actually teach. Fairly soon after he graduated Green was appointed to lecture in the college and two years later he was elected a fellow. In 1866 he was appointed to tutorial office, which in those days still meant delivering lectures to smallish groups of undergraduates, marking their exercises, and being generally responsible for their welfare. Green, who was never ordained and was the first layman to be a tutor in the college, nevertheless functioned as spiritual adviser to his pupils and delivered devotional addresses to them, as other tutors did.[23]

As a tutor in Balliol he lectured regularly on the New Testament. He followed Baur in believing that Paul provided a path to a conception of Christian faith which would not be vulnerable to historical criticism: Paul, after all, had not known the historical Jesus.[24] He worked out a concept of God as the 'ideal self', using Pauline language about the witness of God, and arguing—much as Jowett had done—that it was necessary 'to reproduce with as much exactness as modern phraseology admits of, and without any conventional use of theological language, the essence of St. Paul's belief in Christ'.[25] And one is bound to admit that Green's account of Pauline thought seems to bear as little resemblance to the original as

---

[22] Vincent and Plant, p. 19.
[23] Nettleship, p. xcii.
[24] Vincent and Plant, p. 13.
[25] *Works*, iii, p. 235.

Jowett's had done. Each man, he believed, has to re-enact in himself the eternal act of God—a death to life and a life out of death—in order to be conformed to the being of God to whom he is at every point related.

He was as uneasy about miracles as Jowett was. Founding religion upon supposedly supernatural events seemed to imply a belief that the energy which creates the order of nature 'reveals itself by annulling the order in which it is implied and apart from which it has no reality'.[26] Unlike Jowett, however, he disliked attempts to reconstruct the character of Jesus from 'uncertain documents', preferring to base what he said on a reinterpretation of Pauline or Johannine theology. He was happier—to use modern jargon—with the Christ of the earliest Christian kerygma than with the historical Jesus. But in one respect, at least, he always remained very obviously Jowett's pupil. His favourite religious theme was:

> if there can be an essence within the essence of christianity, it is the thought embodied in the text, 'The word is nigh thee;' the thought of God not as 'far off' but 'nigh', not as a master but as a father, not as a terrible outward power, forcing us we know not whither, but as one of whom we may say that we are reason of his reason and spirit of his spirit; who lives in our moral life, and in whom we live in living for the brethren [27]

In Green's political thought there was the same mixture of ideas that were like Jowett's and those which were quite unlike. This is true even in his attitudes to the political figures of the time. Like Jowett he was an admirer of Mazzini but, unlike Jowett, he thought Louis Napoleon a 'successful brigand'.[28] His serious political passions were concerned with what was happening in British and even local society. As D. M. Mackinnon has pointed out, Green was a pioneer among Oxford dons in accepting responsibility for the conditions of the city.[29] He became a member of the city council as if the drab details of local government, too, were an expression of the universal mind.

[26] *Works*, iii, p. 128.
[27] *Works*, iii, p. 221.
[28] Nettleship, p. xxiii.
[29] [D. M.] Mackinnon, ['Some Aspects of the Treatment of Christianity by the British Idealists', *Journal of Religious Studies*, 20 (1983),] pp. 134f.

But, of course, Green also enjoyed teasing out the broad moral principles governing political action. He was never content, as Jowett often was, to understand political morality primarily as a matter of having the right men in the right jobs. It is true that he regarded Greats as a means of inculcating in undergraduates a sense of the importance of service to society rather than as a training ground for scholars or professional philosophers. But he was really attempting to devise a political philosophy which would have something more to offer than the *laissez-faire* liberalism derived from Mill, and ultimately from Locke, which was the dominant school of thought at the time.[30] And his object was to advance a new vision of liberalism and a more positive and attractive concept of society. Utilitarians desired a society in which the individual would be able to serve himself and, by his efforts to do so, contribute to the whole. This gospel of individualism was reinforced, after Darwin, by the teaching of those who thought that the evolutionary hypothesis could be applied to the social and political sphere. Chief among these, perhaps, was Herbert Spencer who opposed state provision of social welfare or education on the ground that it would interfere with the natural elimination of weak and uncompetitive individuals. It would, he thought, fill the world with fools.[31]

Green urged his pupils to 'close up Mill and Spencer and turn to Kant and Hegel'.[32] Real freedom, he maintained, lay not in the absence of restriction or in limiting the sphere of the state's activity, but in maximising the power of all members of society to make the best of themselves. He believed passionately in the appropriateness of state intervention to secure that freedom from want without which the moral life could not be lived.[33] Real liberalism, in other words, was to be understood as 'the removal of all obstructions

---

[30] The first hundred pages of his 'Introductions to Hume's Treatise of Human Nature' is a critique of Locke's philosophy (*Works*, i, pp. 5–130). Green also dealt with Locke in 'The Principles of Political Obligation' (*Works*, ii, pp. 274–385). There is a critique of Mill and a disquisition on freedom in 'Lectures on the Philosophy of Kant' (*Works*, ii, pp. 195–334).

[31] Green's chief critique of Spencer is 'Mr Herbert Spencer and Mr G. H. Lewes: their application of the doctrine of evolution to thought', *Works*, i, pp. 373ff.

[32] Quinton, p. 311.

[33] Vincent and Plant, p. 28.

which the law can remove to the free development of English citizens'.[34]

Thinking of this kind marked a considerable advance on the ideas held by Jowett. Jowett's was a kind of Platonic, elitist liberalism. He was not, as we have seen, a radical in any sphere and, in politics in particular, his sense of justice seems to have stopped in practice at the frontiers of the middle classes. He recognised that the structure of society played a very important part in the development of man's moral nature. His own job, however, was to enable clever but not very wealthy boys from middle-class homes to receive a university education, move up the social ladder, and achieve positions of importance and influence where their moral character might have some effect upon the nature of society as a whole. Green moved well beyond such an approach. No doubt, the middle classes rather than the working classes engaged his chief sympathy. His main concern, in matters of education, was to provide adequate grammar schools for middle-class children. But the vigour of his social ideals and the systematic way in which he worked them out, provided a vision of a kind of society which was concerned to develop *all* its members.

Green's friends and pupils set up settlements in the slums of the east end of London in the hope of providing education and opportunities for very un-middle-class people. And the fact that Green insisted that religion was the middle term between political philosophy and social action meant that it was possible for a new generation of Christians, some of whom had very different doctrinal beliefs from his, to be inspired by his thought. No doubt, both he and they were often patronising in the way they expressed themselves. One gets the impression that they were most at ease when they had managed to instil middle-class values in the minds of working-class boys. But they had perceived the fact that social morality meant changing society, giving it new structures, using it for the benefit of all its members.

The year after Jowett gained the mastership, Green was married and soon afterwards was re-elected to his fellowship, another indication of the way in which the college was to develop under the new regime. In the last years of Scott's mastership he had been Jowett's

[34] Nettleship, p. cxx.

Disciples

closest ally and supporter in the college so that when Jowett became master in 1870 Green was thought of as his right hand man. In that very year Jowett was writing to Tait complaining still of the inadequacy of most of the ordained fellows who were not up to the standard required for tutoring. But Green, he said, was excellent.[35]

Fairly soon, however, relations were less easy and it is plain that the cause of the trouble lay in Green's idealism. Jowett, who had been responsible for introducing Green to Kant and Hegel, was alarmed by the systematic way in which he had devloped his ideas. He also suspected that Green was forcing that system upon his defenceless pupils. In Jowett's letters to Florence Nightingale in 1872 and 1873 there is a note of sarcastic complaining about Green. 'I am in better heart about the college,' he told Miss Nightingale, 'than I was when I last saw you. I am thinking about new buildings and have persuaded the Revd Hegel Green [Jowett loved having nicknames for people] to give up lecturing for a year and take to writing—whereby the minds of our undergraduates will be greatly clarified.'[36] Six months later he was still complaining. In a letter which asserted that there was 'an opportunity in Moral Philosophy and Theology such as there has never been before', he went on to say, 'The wordy platitudes of Mr H. Spencer do not fill up the void. And I sometimes fear that our Hegelian friends Professor Caird and Green are resting on some metaphysical subtleties and not on common sense or experience. Our undergraduates are constantly bringing in Kant in their essays which they derive from their aforesaid teachers.'[37]

Five years later Green was made Whyte's Professor of Moral Philosophy. His health began to deteriorate almost immediately but this illness did not soften the master's complaints. In 1880 Jowett wrote to a mutual friend:

> We have been anxious about Green: though he seems better at present. I wish that he would take a different line in his philosophical teaching: He intoxicates himself and others with Kant and does not see that these dead

---

[35] Lambeth Palace Library: Tait Papers Personal Letters: vol. 88, fo. 165.
[36] Balliol College: Jowett to Florence Nightingale, 15 Dec. 1872.
[37] Balliol College: Jowett to Florence Nightingale, 25 June 1873. His comments on Kantian metaphysics, already quoted in an earlier chapter, followed at this point.

German philosophers cannot be revived and end—in nothing; but this is between ourselves. His character does great good here; his teaching almost harm. His pupils get confused, retain no interest in other kinds of knowledge and after a few years find that they have lost much and that there is no compensating gain. . . . I am afraid that Green can never make a great and solid reputation unless he alters his method and thinks more for himself; and also until he recognises the greatness of men like Locke and other masters of philosophy.[38]

Green died, after contracting septicaemia, in 1882. He was only forty-six. But Jowett continued to criticise him, even in the sermon he preached to mark his death. It was an extraordinary piece of work. It began with some general remarks about the death of friends, which applied with particular aptness to Jowett's own relationship with Green. Jowett said:

The bitterness of party spirit is hushed over the grave. We can hardly imagine how we ever came to entertain a feeling of jealousy or dislike towards one who is gone. We may regret that we did not understand or appreciate him better; or that through some fancy or pride we did not do more for him or see more of him . . . There may be some forgiveness, too, which we should have wished to ask.[39]

Later in the sermon he was surprisingly frank and direct about the disagreements which had arisen between them:

He may be gently censured for not having treated with proper reverence the great Englishman, John Locke—like himself, a lover of liberty and toleration. (I am sure he would have forgiven me for saying this.) It is very difficult for anyone who has a very strong conviction, whether in speculation or in life, to see its relation to other truths in right proportion . . . What his pupils and friends saw in him may have been partly a philosophical system, but it may much more truly be described as a Christian and a philosopher. . . . of great capacity and uncommon intensity of mind . . . who seemed to respond to their own higher and better aspirations. . . . And whether or not they take as great an interest hereafter in the subtleties of philosophy as in the days of youth (for such impressions are apt to fade away with advancing years) I venture to think that this general impression will remain . . .[40]

[38] Balliol College: Jowett Papers: Box F, Jowett to J. A. Symonds, 28 Dec. 1880.
[39] *Sermons: Biographical*, pp. 210f.
[40] *Sermons: Biographical*, pp. 216f.

It is possible that Jowett had been—as the sermon seems to admit—subject to simple jealousy. Through all the years in which he had been the leader of the opposition in Balliol, Jowett had had very close relations with his own pupils and had been the person whom the young men had wanted to follow. Now, as master, though he continued to take a close interest in the undergraduates, it was not possible for him to have that sort of role. Green, in some sense, had taken his place.[41] But there was probably also a genuine fear that Green was not teaching his pupils so much as force-feeding them with his ideas. Jowett may also have resented the fact that the Balliol which he had tried so hard to establish as a centre for free but religious thought, had become a vehicle for disseminating a new and triumphant *system*.

Green had certainly made many disciples, whether he intended to or not. It is generally agreed that he was the pivotal figure in the Idealist school. Almost every significant member of the group, whether of Green's own generation or of the next, was at least partly educated at Balliol while he was a don there. Scottish as well as English chairs of philosophy came to be occupied by his former pupils. But he also influenced leading politicians and others who were to be prominent in public affairs. And, as has often been pointed out, his ideas were of considerable importance for the group of mostly young theologians who contributed to the collection of essays published under the title *Lux Mundi*. Two of the contributors, Charles Gore—who edited the volume—and Henry Scott Holland had been Green's pupils.

Charles Gore arrived at Balliol as an undergraduate in 1871, a year after Jowett became master. Not a great deal is known about his academic development at the college nor about his relations with the master.[42] But he was Jowett's pupil and his essay in *Lux Mundi* was on the same subject as Jowett's contribution to *Essays and Reviews*— the authority of scripture. It is curious, therefore, that the link

---

[41] The letters to Scott Holland, quoted in Paget, pp. 29ff. are evidence of the close relationship that Green had with at least some of his pupils.

[42] For such evidence as there is see [P.] Hinchliff, 'Jowett and Gore[: Two Balliol Essayists', *Theology*, 87(1894,] pp. 251ff.

between them is so seldom mentioned while Green's influence on *Lux Mundi* is regularly noticed.[43]

Lux Mundi, which appeared in 1889, was a series of studies by a group of young Oxford Anglo-Catholics who were attempting to relate traditional 'catholic' orthodoxy to contemporary critical and scientific thinking. They conceived of the doctrine of the incarnation as the key concept which, because it was the classic Christian statement of the relationship of the human to the divine, would enable them to bring together the two—usually opposed—approaches to theological study. Tractarians had held to one of these approaches, that truth was given in revelation which possessed a divine authority: liberals had held that religious truth, like all other kinds of truth, was a proper subject for human enquiry and must be subjected to the tests of human reason. The contributors to *Lux Mundi* aimed to find and to justify a position from which they could both recognise the validity of secular scholarship and maintain the truth of the cardinal beliefs of classical Christianity. The volume was, as *Essays and Reviews* had not been, a genuine attempt to present a common understanding and also to cover all the main issues. It was Gore, however, as the editor of the book and the author of the essay 'The Holy Spirit and Inspiration' who attracted most attention and most hostility.

The actual argument of Gore's essay started from a discussion of the doctrine of the Holy Spirit. Perhaps this was an attempt to soften the blow of his critical approach to scripture but it also enabled him to talk about Christian experience as a present reality and thus to claim that the faith was not just about something that lay in the past. This became important when he came, well into the essay, to deal with the question of the scriptures themselves. He argued that much of revelation took place in the history of the people of Israel but its meaning is largely to be found, not in the facts themselves, but in the way in which the writers interpreted them as the hand of God in

---

[43] [J.] Carpenter, [*Gore: A Study in Liberal Catholic Thought*, London 1960,] pp. 28f. and 71f.; and [G. L.] Prestige, [*Life of Charles Gore* London 1935], p. 15; even standard reference works tend to mention this fact, e.g. the article on Green in *The Oxford Dictionary of the Christian Church*, 2nd edn. 1974.

history. The records may contain factual errors because the inspiration of the writers did not consist in a miraculous communication to them of the facts as they originally happened. Nevertheless, he insisted, the account of events from the time of Abraham onwards is, in a general way, 'really historical'. Holding such views, he could accept the work done by the moderate critics on much of the Old Testament because he believed that one should read scripture 'in the same spirit in which it was written'. That sounds very like Jowett; but the point Gore was making was that it was the spiritual truth contained in the Old Testament, and not necessarily the supposedly factual detail of the narrative, which was authoritative.

About the New Testament he was much less radical. He believed that the Church was entitled to insist on the historical character of the Gospels and that the miraculous element could not be lightly dismissed. This difference of attitude towards the historical and factual aspect of the two Testaments created a logical problem since, on a surface reading at least, Christ appears to accept the Old Testament as literally true. Gore's kenotic answer was to assert that Christ's teaching did not go beyond knowledge natural to his time and place in history except in revealing the spiritual truths about God and his relationship to creation and to man. He could claim, in other words, that he was consistently maintaining the distinction between fact and spiritual truth.

Lux Mundi was regarded by the older generation of Tractarians as a kind of treason because it admitted the validity of the liberals' critical understanding of the biblical writings. Gore bore the brunt of the attack. H. P. Liddon, who was thought of as the spiritual heir and successor of Pusey, wrote to *The Spectator* on 5 April 1890 seizing upon the very point of the relationship between the Old and New Testaments. He alleged that those who accepted, with Gore, the findings of biblical criticism were, in effect, implying either that Christ was fallible and fallacious or that the Gospels were an inspired forgery. It was Liddon's favourite argument and he had employed it against Colenso in his Bampton lectures as long before as 1867. If Christ quoted or referred to the books of the Old Testament as if Moses had really written the Pentateuch or David the Psalms, when they had not, then Christ could not be God incarnate: God could be neither ignorant nor deceived.[44]

Gore's reply to Liddon, in the same paper, was courteous and gentle but yielded no ground at all, insisting that there was 'a very large opportunity of escape between the two horns of the dilemma' as Liddon had framed it. He was prepared to make certain '*corrigenda*' in his essay in order to remove misconceptions but he was not prepared to move from the position he had taken up.[45] He was quite clear, at least as regards the Old Testament, that there was nothing blasphemous or heretical in accepting the findings of critical scholarship.

Gore was deeply hurt by the attacks of the old guard,[46] and at one time felt obliged to tender his resignation as principal of the house built in Oxford as a memorial to Dr Pusey. What is equally significant is that this pressure from the guardians of the Tractarian tradition did not apparently make him doubt the validity of a proper critical scholarship. Two questions, therefore, arise. Why did he come to accept the importance of such scholarship? What part did Jowett's Balliol play in the formation of these convictions?

Gore had already become an Anglo-Catholic by conviction before he even went up to Balliol. Father Stanton at St Alban's, Holborn, one of the most 'advanced' of London churches, had taught him to make his confession and he delighted in full catholic ceremonial. At Oxford he worshipped regularly both in the Cowley fathers' chapel and at St Barnabas.[47] But Anglo-Catholicism was not the only thing he brought with him to Balliol. David Newsome has suggested that the teaching and example of Brooke Foss Westcott may well have been the chief formative influence in his early years.[48] And Prestige asserts that while still a boy at Harrow, Gore had learned from the

---

[44] H. P. Liddon, *The Divinity of Our Lord*, 8th edn., London 1878, pp. 454ff. and 469ff.

[45] The *corrigenda* were reported in a variety of newspapers, e.g. *The Ecclesiastical Chronicle* of 23 Apr. 1890.

[46] Prestige, pp. 102ff. and 112ff.

[47] Prestige, p. 15.

[48] D. Newsome, 'The Assault on Mammon: Charles Gore and John Neville Figgis', *Journal of Ecclesiastical History*, 17(1966), pp. 238ff. and the same author's *Two Classes of Men*, pp. 120ff.

future bishop, then an assistant master at the school, 'the moral value of exact scholarship; the insight to be gained from a religious study of history; the spiritual glories of simple living; and a love of the poor'.[49] It is possible that Westcott's influence was also the source of his determination to adopt a critical approach to the scriptures but it is equally possible that the passionate insistence on the 'true facts of science and history' which was such a feature of Balliol teaching had much to do with it, too.

Gore would have found Jowett's liberal protestant approach defective. The master's determination not to answer the crucial problem of how one could love God in Christ when one could not be sure just who the historical Jesus Christ actually was, would have filled Gore with impatience. But he would not have been entirely unsympathetic to the master's emphasis upon the value of history to theology nor to his concern for the underprivileged (limited and patronising though, no doubt, it was). As late as 1927, Gore was quoting with approval Jowett's habit of denouncing those who thought that 'the fabric of our laws, the machinery of our government and the methods of our industry' had no bearing upon the moral development of men and women.[50]

We happen to know that Gore was always present when the master preached in Balliol chapel.[51] We also know that during Gore's undergraduate years he would have heard Jowett preach about evolution and the problems raised by this and other scientific advances; about the truth and authority of the Bible and how it ought to be understood and interpreted; about the duties of a scholar and a clergyman. There is no direct evidence as to his reaction to any of Jowett's sermons. He would not have liked everything that he heard but he would, nevertheless, have found much of it stimulating. A great deal of it, too, would have been consonant with what he had already learnt from Westcott.

Certainly there was nothing about Jowett's theology which would make it less acceptable to a young Anglo-Catholic than that of T. H. Green, whose influence on Gore and Scott Holland is so

[49] Prestige, p. 9 and cf. Carpenter, pp. 25f.
[50] C. Gore, *Christ and Society*, London 1928, p. 154.
[51] Prestige, p. 16.

widely acknowledged. There is no reason to doubt that influence, of course, and it extended beyond the purely theological to their political thought also.[52] What is more questionable is the suggestion that Green was a source of much inspiration to the authors of *Lux Mundi* but that they derived nothing from Jowett, whom they found faithless and arid. Michael Ramsey's well-known account of Anglican theology from the publication of *Lux Mundi* onward, describes Jowett as 'devoted to philosophic speculation, utterly detached from interest in doctrines and religious institutions, and, when asked what would be his attitude to subscription, saying only, "Give me a pen" '.[53] In fact, Ramsey's description would really fit Green better than Jowett. Jowett was far from being a devotee of philosophic speculation: that was precisely what upset him about Green. Admittedly neither man had much time for ecclesiastical institutions but much of the metaphysical underpinning of *Lux Mundi* is actually closer to Jowett's Platonism rather than to Green's 'Hegelianism'.[54]

In the religious sphere, Green's influence seems to have affected two rather different circles. On the one hand, there were those who continued directly in his own line of thinking, handling traditional Christianity rather freely within the context of an idealist metaphysics. On the other, there were the members of the *Lux Mundi* group, who took much from Green but were orthodox Anglo-Catholics so far as doctrine was concerned, and found Green's treatment of the historical basis of Christianity somewhat cavalier. R. L. Nettleship, editor of Green's published works, seems to have come somewhere between the two groups. He was, like Green himself, one of those tutors of Balliol who were laymen but exercised a religious and pastoral influence over their pupils. But he was also a friend of Scott Holland and, like the *Lux Mundi* men, sometimes impatient with Jowett's reductionist tendencies.

It is clear, of course, that Gore and his friends warmed chiefly to

[52] Vincent and Plant, pp. 52 and 85f.

[53] A. M. Ramsey, *From Gore to Temple*, London 1960, p. 60. Quite apart from the quite unfounded implication that Jowett was totally unscrupulous about subscription, neither Gore—nor for that matter Ramsey himself—would have been able to subscribe in the 'plain and literal sense' demanded from Jowett.

[54] Newsome, p. 84.

the general tendency of Green's metaphysics—which Jowett did not share—rather than to the specifics of his theology. It has been said of *Lux Mundi* that 'Darwin and Hegel, who have in common an emphasis on development, if nothing else, are always on the authors' minds.'[55] But Green's metaphysics led him to such an immanentist understanding of God's relationship with the universe that he found it difficult to distinguish between the divine presence in all human beings and that same presence in Christ. Green's thought, therefore, is not an obvious source for the incarnational approach of Gore and his friends. Indeed, Jowett's view of development—a continuum with its peak in the life of Christ to which subsequent Christian thinking ought to look back—was much closer to the thinking of the *Lux Mundi* essayists than Green's adaptation of Hegelianism in which the self-realisation of the divine was never to be finalised in history at all. And an interest, albeit an uneducated interest, in Darwin is much more characteristic of Jowett's theology than Green's.

It is, in any case, very doubtful whether undergraduates in the early 1870s would have been aware of the disagreements between Green and Jowett about 'Hegelianism', which at that stage were only just beginning to develop. When Jowett became master, the year before Gore came up to the college, Green was still regarded as his chief supporter. The letters to Florence Nightingale, which first hint at Jowett's unease, are dated in Gore's penultimate year as an undergraduate. It would be some time before the divergence of opinion became sufficiently marked for it to be noted publicly. And if Jowett came, in the end, to be known to disapprove of too much Hegel, he continued to use him in thinking and writing about Plato. Presumably, therefore, he did not eliminate every reference to Hegel from his teaching. Those members of the *Lux Mundi* group who were undergraduates at Balliol are unlikely to have made any very sharp distinction between what they were taught by Green and by Jowett.

As it happens, some of the actual lectures delivered by Green in the

---

[55] S. H. Major, 'Lux Mundi: A Reassessment', *The Church Quarterly Review*, 166 (1965), p. 76.

years in which Gore was an undergraduate at Balliol are preserved in Nettleship's edition of Green's collected works.[56] His theology can therefore be compared very easily with what Jowett was preaching at the same period in his college sermons. Though there are points of difference, it would be extremely difficult to argue that Jowett was propagating a dead and faithless religion while Green, though doubtless somewhat unorthodox, was proclaiming a Gospel which was full of encouragement and inspiration for the young. Apart from anything else, undergraduate comment on Green's teaching was as varied as it was on Jowett's. The young Gerard Manley Hopkins, for instance, in his High Anglican days, described Green as possessing an 'offensive style of infidelity'.[57]

Of the three courses of lectures, of which fragments were preserved by Nettleship, the one on Romans is that which Gore is most likely to have heard in the form actually recorded in print. Green's remarks were evidently arranged, like the traditional catechetical lectures, as a series of comments, verse by verse, on the text to be studied. Commenting on Romans 8: 1–11, he expounded a theology of the atonement,[58] which was very like Jowett's, though perhaps more clearly and directly expressed. It is just as honest about doubts and difficulties and at least as 'agnostic' as anything Jowett said. It is just as clearly a denial of the theology of substitution and satisfaction as that for which Jowett had been attacked, not only by the Evangelicals but by Pusey also.

Quite apart from the question of whether Green's theology was intrinsically more likely to commend itself to an undergraduate who stood in the Tractarian tradition than Jowett's, there is also the apparent difference in their approach and teaching methods. Gore was quite intelligent enough to perceive that Jowett's eclecticism—his mind of his own—had its value. We are told that, when Gore had

[56] Nettleship wrote in his preface, 'The lectures on the New Testament were delivered several times while [Green] was a tutor at Balliol; the extracts printed are taken from his notes supplemented by those [i.e. taken by undergraduates during the actual lectures] of A. C. Bradley in the Galatians, R. W. Macan in the Romans, and C. E. Vaughan in the Fourth Gospel; these gentlemen completed their academical courses severally in 1873, 1871, and 1877.' (*Works*, iii, p. vi).
[57] Schmidt in *Balliol Studies*, p. 171.
[58] *Works*, iii, p. 194.

become principal of Pusey House in 1884, he kept a picture of Jowett hanging on the wall of his study there.[59] 'When I feel I am stressing an argument too far,' he said. 'I look at Jowett and he pulls me up.' It may be worth looking a little more thoroughly into this matter because of Jowett's belief that undergraduates should be taught to think for themselves and his complaint that Green 'made disciples' of them instead.

In all Gore's writing the passage in which Green's influence is most obvious comes, not in the *Lux Mundi* essay, but in *The Body of Christ* of 1901. At any rate it is a passage in which Green's epistemology and the characteristic features of Green's technique—of picking up points from Kant and then working them out in quasi-Hegelian terms—seem very clearly to be echoed. 'God', Gore wrote, 'creates things in nature, and he creates mind. But in fact the two creations are inseparable. The things have no existence apart from the minds which know them, for it is only as held together by the mind that all sensations are held together in relation to the whole orderly world.' From this he concluded that the reality of our ordered world requires a universal mind which holds it together. But, though this may be an example of Green's influence, for Gore—as for Jowett—the universal mind was no remote Absolute but the truth revealed in the personal and accessible Jesus of Nazareth of the Gospel narratives. And in so far as Gore's kenotic Christology was concerned to recover a deeper and more genuine understanding of the real human character of Christ, it owed much, as John Macquarrie has pointed out, to 'what may be called the humanistic bent of theology since Schleiermacher'.[60] That 'humanistic bent' was very characteristic of Jowett.

Indeed, so far as Gore was concerned, the master need not have worried lest Green turn him into one of his disciples. Gore obviously learnt a great deal from Green, and later acknowledged his debt openly,[61] but there is no real sense in which he could seriously be described as an Hegelian. Like many other leading Christian thinkers of his generation, he was deeply impressed by Green's

[59] Prestige, pp. 75f.
[60] J. Macquarrie, 'Kenoticism Reconsidered', *Theology*, 77 (1974), p. 117.
[61] Carpenter, p. 73.

defence of theism. But, if Jowett's version of Christianity failed to appeal to the new generation of Anglo-Catholics because it was too little concerned with the splendour and the agony of faith, Green's system *taken as a whole* held few attractions just because it attempted to protect Christianity from attack by cutting it free from its historical roots. And Green presented his system precisely as something to be taken as a whole, whereas Jowett hated systems. He left his pupils free to pick and choose. Gore would not have wished to accept all the opinions of either man: he had another criterion by which to judge the truth—the catholic faith.

In spite of the fact, therefore, that Gore's thought was not a free-ranging eclecticism like Jowett's, there were many ways in which his cast of mind was much more like the master's than like Green's. The appeal to broad reasonableness, based on common sense and experience—so typical of Jowett—was equally characteristic of Gore throughout his life. It is to be found in the *Reconstruction of Belief* trilogy as much as in the essay in *Lux Mundi*. Such and such is true, Gore tended to assert, and it is reasonable to believe it, because the fathers said similar things in the fourth century, the findings of modern science look as though they will confirm it and it is *what we all know anyway*.

If such an appeal to general common sense and what we all know from experience is very typical of Jowett, the priority given to the fathers is not. But then Gore was simply not *anyone's* disciple. One can find points at which his debt to Green's idealism is very marked and other points where he seems to have affinities with Jowett. But there are, equally, many points where he is far apart from either of them. What is interesting is that he is sometimes all three within a very short space.[62]

Precisely how much Jowett's Balliol contributed to Charles Gore's thought and the liberal catholicism of *Lux Mundi* it simply is not possible to determine. W. R. Ward, who does not disguise his antipathy to both Tractarianism and to Oxford liberalism of Jowett's type, has argued that the *Lux Mundi* liberals were really a product of the complex relationship between Gladstone and the

---

[62] For an example of this see Hinchliff, 'Jowett and Gore', p. 256.

Anglo-Catholics between 1847 and 1869.[63] During that time, he maintains, the Tractarians had been split into two wings, in one of which an innate conservatism triumphed, while the other remained faithful in its attachment to Gladstone and the liberal politics to which the party had been driven by one crisis after another in the course of twenty years.

This theory might account for the radical politics of the contributors to *Lux Mundi*. It does not explain why they should also have been willing to embrace with some enthusiasm both critical biblical scholarship and the findings of the natural sciences: Gladstone was no advocate of those aspects of liberal theology. It also involves Ward in treating 'Balliol Hegelianism' as a problem which Gore and Scott Holland were compelled to encounter and overcome, in the same way that the philosophy of John Stuart Mill was a problem for E. S. Talbot, the oldest of the *Lux Mundi* group.[64] And that hardly seems to do justice to their attitude to Green. It seems at least as likely that Jowett's Balliol was a setting in which young men were encouraged to think about their faith over against the advances of the sciences, biblical scholarship, and liberal politics. Gore, at least, seems to have found this an encouragement rather than a problem. Just because he was being told to think for himself he put together an amalgam which was different from (and, he would have said, much richer than) both Jowett's and Green's and yet owed something to them both.

The chief difference between Gore and Jowett is revealed in a passage towards the end of the *Lux Mundi* essay in which Gore seems to be echoing a favourite sentiment of the master's. Jowett used frequently to say in his sermons that it was impossible to defend Christian truth by taking refuge in dogma.[65] In his essay Gore wrote, 'If the Christian Church has been enabled to defeat the critical attack

[63] W. R. Ward, 'Oxford and the Origins of Liberal Catholicism in the Church of England', in C. W. Dugmore and C. Duggan (eds.), *Studies in Church History*, i, London 1964, pp. 233–52.

[64] Ibid. p. 249 and cf. D. Cupitt, 'Darwinism and English Religious Thought', *Theology*, 78 (1975), p. 128, who argues that liberal catholicism was really a putting together of bits of T. H. Green, Darwin, and patristic theology.

[65] Balliol College: Jowett Papers: note book F, 'Description of the present state of theology' and cf. Abbott and Campbell, ii, p. 310.

... it has not been by foreclosing the question with an appeal to dogma, but by facing in fair and frank discussion, the problems raised.'[66] But there was a sense in which, tacitly, the whole of Gore's essay *was* an appeal to dogma. The creeds, which in his later writings were to be overtly treated as the final arbiter of truth, were already in the essay being given something of that role. For the whole of Gore's argument proceeds from an exposition of the credal statement, 'I believe in the Holy Ghost . . . the giver of life', which serves as a kind of text for everything that follows.

It is worth noting, though, that even in this matter of the creeds Jowett and Gore were not wholly opposed to one another. The creeds were the one part of the tradition to which Jowett was prepared to give a special place. Nothing, he thought, was to be gained from contrasting them with or opposing them to scripture itself, 'in which the germs of the expressions used by them are sufficiently apparent'.[67] But this willingness to treat the creeds as an extension of scripture was not the same thing as Gore's belief that they had a kind of sacrosanctity as enshrining the early Church's understanding of what scripture *meant*. On such a view they were, indeed, vital to a true interpretation of it.

There is a well-known passage from Gore which sounds almost like a riposte to part of the argument advanced by Jowett in *Essays and Reviews*. Gore once said, when Jowett had been dead for over thirty years, that to treat the Bible *like any other book* is to behave as if it had just been 'dug out of the Syrian sand'.[68] And what Gore meant, of course, was that to do that would be to fail to perceive that Christian tradition was essential to a proper understanding of the Bible's meaning.

Jowett seems to have understood very well where the arguments of *Lux Mundi* were tending. In his oft-quoted judgement on the book, he said:

The point on which the High Church party tend to give way is the Scripture and especially the Old Testament. They feel that as the Bible is seen more

[66] *Lux Mundi*, London 1889, p. 361.
[67] *Essays and Reviews*, p. 353.
[68] Carpenter, p. 274, quoting from Gore's *Can We Then Believe?*, London 1926. The italics are mine.

and more to be *like any other book*, the greater the need for the Church, an aspect of the question which is not wholly displeasing to them.[69]

This comment, which Ieuan Ellis regards as the most interesting judgement passed on *Lux Mundi*,[70] was followed by Jowett's well-known remark about the volume being 'the same old haze and maze' to which High Church theology, as he thought, was always prone.

It is perfectly clear, then, that, whatever affinities there may have been between Jowett and Gore, there was also this very wide difference between them about the value to be placed upon the Church's traditional orthodoxy. But one should not assume that Jowett's view of *Lux Mundi* was as entirely negative as the 'haze and maze' remark suggests, for he was able to give Tennyson an informed and sympathetic account of the arguments contained in the volume,[71] and he also, after all, added a qualifying clause to 'haze and maze', saying that the High Church theologians were now more friendly than formerly to the liberal point of view.[72] And while everyone remembers the unkind remark, Prestige's story about Jowett's last letter to Charles Gore is largely forgotten. In 1893, the year in which the master died, Gore resigned as principal of Pusey House. Jowett wrote to say how sorry he was to hear that Gore was leaving and invited him to dinner. There would be just the two of them together. The letter is signed, 'Yours truly and affectionately'.[73]

If it is true that Gore and Jowett were less at loggerheads than has usually been supposed, what is one to make of a story of Fremantle's that, when he was the chaplain in Jowett's Balliol, 'opposite to the side of Balliol in St Giles's the Pusey House had been erected for the object of perpetuating the influence of Dr Pusey; and as Balliol was not esteemed an adequate place for young men who looked forward to ordination, I found there was a constant influence which drew them away from us.'[74] Gore was then the principal at Pusey House and it was he who was drawing away young men from Balliol.

[69] Abbott and Campbell, ii, pp. 377f. The italics are mine.
[70] Ellis, p. 263.
[71] Prestige, p. 122.
[72] Abbott and Campbell, ii, p. 377.
[73] Prestige, p. 147.
[74] *Recollections*, p. 110.

Fremantle plainly felt that there was an implicit condemnation both of himself and of Jowett in what was happening. Gore would certainly have believed that he could give the young men from his own old college a fuller and richer theology and faith than either Jowett or Fremantle could. (The specific case cited by Fremantle is of an undergraduate who went off to Pusey House because Fremantle wanted him to study the Reformation and he 'had set his mind upon the old liturgies'.) But this is not at all the same thing as seeing Balliol and Pusey House, Jowett and Gore, falsehood and truth, facing each other across St Giles's in a spirit of bitter enmity.

There is one other tiny scrap of evidence which may conceivably throw a little light on the relationship between Jowett and Gore. Among the relatively few surviving Gore papers at Mirfield is a note from Jowett saying, 'Mr Poole Hughes has my permission to become a Candidate for the Junior Mathematical Scholarship.'[75] It is dated 13 March 1886, which is when Gore was principal of Pusey House and six years before Jowett died. W. W. Poole-Hughes, a young Welshman, did indeed win a mathematics scholarship to the college for 1886, took a degree in mathematics and became a schoolmaster in 1889. He was ordained in 1890 and died in 1923 as headmaster of Llandovery College and a canon of St David's. It seems possible that this young man was known to Gore,[76] who put him in touch with Jowett in the hope that he, too, would end up at Balliol. It is hard to imagine any other explanation for the survival of such a letter from Jowett among Gore's papers. And if that *is* the explanation it does not suggest that Gore regarded Jowett's Balliol (from which, by this time, death had removed T. H. Green) as a disastrous place for a young man to be. And if he had so regarded it, it is difficult to understand why on at least one occasion he declined to encourage someone who might have brought a more 'catholic' influence into the college.[77]

Part of the difficulty, if one is attempting to trace a theological influence across two generations, is that one cannot compare two

---

[75] I am greatly indebted to Canon Norman Blamires, CR for finding this for me.
[76] However the Right Revd John Poole-Hughes, formerly Bishop of Llandaff, knows of no connection between Gore and his father.
[77] Below p. 207.

minds at the same stage in development. Charles Gore was exposed to Green and Jowett when he was very young and they were mature (in Jowett's case middle-aged) men. One cannot, therefore, simply set out their thought side by side and see where it agrees and where it differs. One has rather to try and recapture the context which Green and Jowett provided for Charles Gore and within which he did some of his early thinking.

There would be no point in arguing—for the evidence is clearly against it—that there was some direct connection of developing thought between *Essays and Reviews* and *Lux Mundi*. But the evidence does support the belief that—for all his failings—Jowett won the affection of even those undergraduates who might seem, *prima facie*, most likely to resist him and had considerable influence upon them just because he encouraged them to think for themselves. It is at least possible that Gore learnt from Jowett not, admittedly, specific theological ideas, still less a system of thought, but an attitude of mind which he retained for the rest of his life.

Gore was to become, of course, an eminent churchman. It is often pointed out that he became rather more conservative in his later years, when he was Bishop of Birmingham from 1905 to 1911 and then Bishop of Oxford till 1919. He would have argued that, as a bishop, he had the responsibility of guarding the faith: Jowett might have said that he was simply behaving as all liberals did when elevated to the episcopate. What Jowett would have thought of his founding of a monastic community within the Church of England, can only be guessed at. But there is a sense in which Gore, whose theology was widely read until at least the middle of the present century, helped to make it possible for the Church to accept and even enjoy much of what Jowett had advocated.

8

Darwinism and Faith

Ever since before the publication of *Essays and Reviews* Jowett had been saying that the true or well-ascertained facts of history and science must be positively taken into account by theologians. On the other hand, he had never shown much disposition actually to acquaint himself with those facts. His sermons had frequently stated the problems raised by making the historical Jesus the focal point of one's religion, without attempting any resolution of them. In a similar way he had never faced the problems inherent in relating scientific knowledge to religious belief. Neal Gillespie has pointed out the short-sightedness of those theologians 'who thought successful accommodation of a divinely revealed religion to the new science was a simple matter of shedding a few antiquated superstitions'.[1] The crucial thing, Gillespie argues, was to recognise that the natural sciences could only be done at all by assuming two things. The first is that the natural world is a regular, predictable, and constant system in which exceptions simply do not occur. The second is that everything must be explicable simply in terms of natural causes. These assumptions not only exclude the possibility of miracles, since such events must be treated either as impossible or as 'natural': they also remove God from the way people think because he is no longer required for the purposes of explanation. Though one may continue to believe that he exists and though science in no way precludes his existence, the positivist assumptions, Gillespie asserts, 'took God out of nature (if not out of reality) as effectively as atheism'.[2]

If this is true, Jowett must certainly be counted as being—for most

---

[1] [N. C.] Gillespie, [*Charles Darwin and the Problem of Creation*, Chicago 1979,] p. 153.

[2] Ibid. and cf. Jowett's letter to Brodie, above p. 22.

of his life—among the theologians who assumed that all one need do was to shed a few superstitions. At the time when he was writing the commentaries he does not seem to have excluded the *possibility* of miracles. He simply took the line that they did not prove anything and needed to be treated with caution. His determination to counter deistic tendencies made him extremely reluctant to remove God from everyday reality. But he showed remarkably little interest in the sciences as such and throughout his life he retained his old rather snobbish attitude towards them.

Benjamin Brodie was the scientist whom Jowett knew best but only one of his letters to Brodie is about scientific matters and it is an attempt to elucidate his friend's attitude to Faraday's 'doctrine of forces' rather than any expression of his own opinions.[3] He seems to have lost touch with Brodie after about 1850, perhaps because he did not think him serious enough—too 'artistic'—on the subject of religion.[4] Through *Essays and Reviews* he must have had some contact with Baden Powell, the most eminent and the most thoroughly 'scientific' scientist within Oxford's theological world. Baden Powell, who had treated Chambers's *Vestiges* seriously and had warmly welcomed Darwin's *Origin of Species* in his contribution to *Essays and Reviews*,[5] was to insist upon the important fact that what makes a miracle a miracle is not the event itself but the alleged (though scientifically unidentifiable) cause of the event.[6] But Jowett does not ever seem to have been very close to Baden Powell and it was not really until the later 1870s that he was prepared to state clearly that he regarded miracles as 'the most improbable of all things', irreconcilable with science and, by implication, one of 'many other superstitions'.[7]

In 1871, soon after becoming master, Jowett had preached a long sermon on 'Darwinism and Faith in God' in which both his anxiety

---

[3] Abbott and Campbell, i, p. 117.

[4] Ibid. p. 161.

[5] B. Powell, 'On the Study of the Evidences of Christianity', *Essays and Reviews*, London 1860, p. 139.

[6] Gillespie, p. 150.

[7] Abbott and Campbell, ii, p. 87, the document is not dated but Abbott and Campbell assert that it was written some 30 years after Jowett's association with Stanley in the preparation of the commentaries.

about and his basic ignorance of the scientific hypothesis are very apparent.[8] We are told in books, which are in everyone's hands—he said—that man is descended from the lower animals. The danger is that man, if he is told that he is only an animal, may resolve to live like an animal. In a passage with a delightfully characteristic overtone of snobbery, Jowett likened humanity reading Darwin to 'some scion of a noble house who is suddenly informed that all his life long he has been mistaken and that he was really of ignoble birth'. Equally characteristically he refused to join the obscurantists. Harking back to Samuel Wilberforce's debate with Huxley of ten years earlier, he said that there was no harm in opposing Darwin with jokes about having 'for your ancestor, a monkey or an angel . . .' provided they were not too often repeated. But 'no one does more harm to religion or tends more to undermine the Christian faith than he who appeals eloquently to our religious feelings on behalf of scientific untruth, or a conclusion not warranted by fact.' The new scientific theory must be accepted for what it was—but not for more than what it was. It could not be regarded as proved nor could it explain the whole origin of man. There were about man certain things that the theory could not explain, his intellect and his moral sense, even some of his physical characteristics.

One of the things that worried Jowett was the catch-phrase 'survival of the "strongest" '—and he actually used 'strongest' rather than 'fittest'. It is easy to see why it upset him. As one who accepted the Darwinian hypothesis and continued to be a theist, he felt himself being forced into the belief that God had made a world in which the fundamental creative principle was a fiercely competitive, wasteful, and destructive one. Whatever Darwin's own attitude to religion may have been, it is apparent that there was a strong inheritance from the tradition of natural theology in his *Origins*,[9] and he himself perceived quite clearly the moral implications of his hypothesis.[10] Nature red in tooth and claw is not a morally attractive concept, yet it looked as if God had chosen this essentially immoral mechanism as the foundation upon which the whole world had been

[8] *Sermons on Faith*, pp. 1ff.
[9] [J.] Durant, [*Darwinism and Divinity*, Oxford 1985,] pp. 16f.
[10] Gillespie, p. 126.

erected. If, moreover, one wrongly assumed that Darwin had demonstrated that it was always the *strongest* who survived, it must have seemed that anything which contributed to the victory of the stronger over the weaker could conceivably be justified as congruent with God's plan. It might seem, in other words, that the universe manifested a divine nature which caused might rather than right to triumph. For someone like Jowett, who regarded morality as the chief ground for belief, this would threaten the heart of Christianity. So he looked for loopholes. 'And may not the instincts of animals, like the reason of man, have had the effect sometimes of preserving the weakest as well as the strongest?'

He also began to revise his thoughts about the laws of nature. In his commentary on Romans he had argued that the concept of a world governed by laws was a comforting one and that it ought to deliver believers from fear of the arbitrary and unpredictable. Many of his contemporaries attempted to reconcile religion with the new science by accepting the idea that God had impressed laws upon his initial creation which ensured that it evolved and developed, through secondary mechanisms, to the goal which he had purposed for it.[11] What Jowett had to say about laws in nature is not incompatible with such a view, though it does not necessarily imply it. Indeed, it might have seemed to him too deistical and his concept of the divine personality clothed in laws may have been an attempt to devise a version of this approach which escaped that difficulty. Personality clothed in laws seems to be a concept of God, directly expressing himself through both the moral laws which command humanity and the mechanical laws which control the universe, as a human personality would be expressed through mind and body. This suggests an attempt to assert that God is always personally and immediately present in the life of his creation in a way which is neither the originating but otherwise absent being of deism nor the continually but extraordinarily intervening God of contemporary orthodoxy.

Jowett also seems to have been anxious to exclude Spencerian ideas which were widely held at the time. Herbert Spencer, whom

---

[11] Gillespie, p. 130 and Durant, p. 15.

James Moore has called 'the Eeyore of Victorian science',[12] was attempting a grand 'synthetic philosophy' as an alternative to the traditional theological understanding of life. Spencer's was a system 'in which ethics was grounded in sociology, sociology in psychology, psychology in biology, and biology in metaphysical first principles that were overtly religious. Spencer believed that the whole of evolution was the progressive manifestation of an Unknowable Power that makes for righteousness.'[13] In practice he was a vigorous champion of individualism and *laissez-faire*, asserting that wealth was a symptom of individual worth.

Many Christian theologians who sought to come to terms with evolution found the superficial attractions of Spencer's holistic and 'religious' approach a temptation they were unable to resist. Even Frederick Temple, Jowett's former friend and ally, was to become more a Spencerian than a Darwinian.[14] But Jowett seems, in his sermon on Darwinism and faith, to have been anxious to combat any such architectonic since it ignored real differences in the way concepts were used in different branches of knowledge:

the terms which are used in these speculations are to a great extent ambiguous. When we speak of 'evolution', or 'development', or even of more familiar terms, force, cause, law, we are insensibly generalizing in a single word processes which may be infinitely various and belong to different spheres of knowledge. The laws of mind are not the same as the laws of external nature. The evolution of thought is altogether different from the evolution of the animal creation. Are we not transferring the language of physics to metaphysics? Nor is the expression 'survival of the fittest' free from ambiguity. For who are the animals fittest to survive? Not necessarily those who are most in harmony with their circumstances or framed on the most symmetrical model. In animals, as in men, there may have been some hidden force which would more than compensate for adverse external conditions, like that hidden force in human constitutions which gives longevity, and is partly the same with health and strength, partly different from them.[15]

[12] [J.] Moore, ['Herbert Spencer's Henchmen: The Evolution of Protestant Liberals in Late Nineteenth Century America',] in Durant, p. 79.
[13] Moore in Durant, p. 80.
[14] Durant, p. 22.
[15] *Sermons on Faith*, p. 13.

It is worth noting that at this point Jowett reverted to 'fittest' from 'strongest' but it is still not clear what he was trying to say in this connection. He asked, clearly expecting a negative answer, whether the animals fittest to survive are those most in harmony with their circumstances. But had he understood that this was precisely how 'fittest' was defined in Darwin's theory? If he had, why did he allow himself to become confused in the earlier passage and assume that evolution was about the triumph of the 'strongest'? If he had not misunderstood, then his argument must be one which is directed *against* Darwin and was intended to be an alternative view. But in that case what would his own definition of 'fittest' have been? He must have had some theory of 'hidden forces' which preserved some species. It is all very confused and confusing.

Jowett was, perhaps, not entirely to be blamed for his misunderstanding of the evolutionary hypothesis. The phrase 'survival of the fittest' seems to have been Herbert Spencer's summary of what the hypothesis meant. And Spencer had applied evolutionary theories to the social and political area in a way which did seem to imply that it was the strongest who were entitled to survive. Moreover, it was Spencer rather than Darwin who claimed that evolutionary biology had direct implications for one's understanding of ethics. Jowett would have hated a view of society which gave the strongest the moral right to trample on everyone else and he would have thought Spencer's view of biological ethics even more threatening than the moral implications of Darwin's theory.

In fact, and this was probably in his own mind neither an evasion nor an accident, his sermon turned back to one of his favourite themes—morality and religion. He will recognise no true opposition between science and religion, only 'false oppositions as there are false reconciliations . . .' But too much concentration upon the natural sciences may have a 'materializing' effect and there are higher goods than the material ones. 'There is a voice within us which is always repeating, in fainter or louder accents, that we must avoid the evil and choose the good; that we were placed here not to do our own will, but to follow Christ; that we are not to pass our lives in indolence, but to be up and doing in the service of God . . .' And he ends on the same note as that employed in his sermon on belief and unbelief of twenty years earlier. We ought not to be 'too much the servants of the hour, falling under the dominion of this or that theory which happens to be in the air . . .' Those for whom all truth is a revelation of God 'in the hour of death, when their eyes close upon external nature, . . . know that He is mindful of them, and that to Him they will return'.

That this reversion to the demands of morality, death, and eternity is not simply an attempt to evade the problem is suggested by the context in which he developed his concept of the divine personality clothed in laws. He was there dealing with the problem of evil within a world created by God. He made no attempt, as others might have done, to argue that the imperfections of creation were to be seen as the products of a necessary process towards the perfect goal designed by God from the beginning. Instead he maintained that it was in another world and another life that God's justice would be revealed. Nor was this, for Jowett, a sort of placebo for he maintained that, meanwhile, it was in the hands of human beings to ensure that there was more good, less evil in the world.[16]

Jowett may even have been fortunate in his unclarity of Darwin. One of the consequences of his eclecticism, combined with his tendency to go his own way regardless of criticism or counter-argument, was a tendency to seize on ideas and then to reiterate them obstinately and without alteration. But whatever it was that he thought were the moral implications of evolution, he plainly found them deeply distasteful. There could be no question of his being tempted, as so many were tempted in the 1860s, to indulge in wild attempts to apply evolutionary theories to ethnology and anthropology. A plethora of 'scientific' societies came into being and spent their time listening to papers on such subjects as, for instance, the relevance of the Darwinian hypothesis to language; or whether negroid people could be a species separate from Europeans because half-castes were not infertile.[17] Jowett possessed neither the inclina-

---

[16] *Sermons on Faith*, pp. 40ff.

[17] See e.g. J. Crawfurd, 'On Language as a Test of the Races of Man', *Transactions of the Ethnological Society*, New Series, 3 (1865), pp. 1ff; F. W. Farrar (Dean Farrar), 'Language and Ethnology', ibid., 4 (1866), pp. 196ff.; J. Crawfurd, 'On the Supposed Infecundity of Human Hybrids or Crosses', ibid., 3 (1865), pp. 357ff.

tion nor, probably, even the half-knowledge to indulge in theories of this kind.

Bishop Colenso, on the other hand,[18] had felt himself obliged to reply to some supposedly Darwinian ideas being aired on the subject of Africans' capacity to accept Christianity or Western civilisation. It was even held by some that the presence of a 'superior' race, representing a higher religion and civilisation, would cause an inferior to disappear by 'natural selection'. The bishop had been in England between 1862 and 1865 taking legal action against the attempt at excommunicating him. He was present when a paper was read at a meeting of one of the societies and, before his return to Natal, made it his business to reply. The contrast between his approach and Jowett's is significant.

The bishop seems to have familiarised himself with Darwin's work and to have mastered the details of the surrounding controversy with considerable speed. On 23 May 1865 he delivered a lecture to the Marylebone Literary Institute which was a reply to the argument that Darwinism proved that the inhabitants of Africa were not only incapable of understanding Christianity but might actually be destroyed by it.[19]

In this lecture Colenso demonstrated that he was at ease with the evolutionary debate, understood the hypothesis, and perceived its limitations in a way that Jowett was still unable to emulate six years later when he preached his sermon. Colenso seized on the fact that the very belief that man had *evolved* implied that Western Europeans were once primitive, too: the primitive character of a people cannot be used as evidence for a racial incapacity to develop. He also argued, with considerable force, against the assumption that the evolutionary hypothesis implied that contact between races must involve the destruction of the 'inferior' by the 'superior'. The contact, he

---

[18] The substance of the remainder of this chapter is based on 'Ethics, Evolution and Biblical Criticism in the Thought of Benjamin Jowett and John William Colenso', in *Journal of Ecclesiastical History*, 37 (1986), pp. 91ff.

[19] University of the Witwatersrand: Archives of the Church of the Province of South Africa: AB 223, MS lecture (it is actually catalogued as a 'sermon') on missions to the Zulus.

thought, could not be avoided. Primitive people were going to encounter more 'civilised' men and would inevitably pick up their vices and diseases. But, he said, even if it were true that they were 'bound to pass away by the inexorable law of natural selection' it would still be better that 'while they yet lived' they should receive the benefits of civilisation as well as its horrors.

It was a clever reply to a particular version of social Darwinism and it showed a bishop and theologian unruffled by the heat or the technicalities of the debate. Like Jowett, Colenso insisted that Darwin's hypothesis was only a hypothesis. But, just because he perceived that fact so clearly, he was not to be rushed into making up his mind about scientific matters nor would he pretend to a knowledge and expertise which he did not have. With a sideways glance at Disraeli's variant on Wilberforce's joke, Colenso said, 'Though I am not with Mr D'Israeli on the side of the angels, yet I confess, I am not on the side of the apes—or rather I should say, I do not feel competent to pronounce any decisive judgement on the question. But I do not feel at all distressed or shocked about it.'

There is a relaxed sure-footedness about Colenso's performance that contrasts sharply with the mistaken assertiveness of Jowett's sermon. For all that Jowett was, so to speak, on the same side as Colenso, he displayed much more of the rather tense, opinionated attitude of Wilberforce whom he so much despised. Nor would Jowett have been capable of the imaginative conclusion to Colenso's lecture. For the bishop ended by asserting that Africa might have as much to contribute to Christianity as Christianity to Africa.

James Moore has argued that the orthodox, and particularly orthodox Calvinists, were far better able to come to terms with Darwin than the liberals.[20] More recently he has asserted that 'Fundamentalists, ecologists, feminists, Marxists . . . will continue to seek a basis for human values transcending the present realities that society experiences as "natural". True religion for them consists in being neither the junior partners of evolutionists nor their henchmen.'[21] The force of this somewhat surprising list of bedfellows

[20] [J. R.] Moore, [*The Post-Darwinian Controversies*, Cambridge 1979,] e.g. pp. 340ff.
[21] Moore in Durant, p. 97.

seems to be that it is only the non-evolutionists who are able to escape the limitations of assuming that the future is already contained in the present. Neither Colenso nor Jowett quite fits this paradigm. Colenso was no Darwinian in social or political terms because he was able to imagine a situation in which the 'environment' would contribute something positive to the development of ideas which was not already contained within them. Jowett failed to cope with Darwinism, not because he was a liberal but because he failed to understand what it was saying and did not like what he *thought* it was saying.

It is clear, however, that in the last decade of his life Jowett began to take a much more serious interest in the natural sciences than he had ever done before. It was as though, at last, he had begun to feel an obligation to take his own insistence on the importance of true facts seriously. And it is possible that this new determination may have created problems for his religion.

In part, his new interest in science may have had something to do with his time as vice-chancellor, since it seems to be agreed that one of the things he achieved was the advancement of science in the university.[22] And in the list of things to be done, which he drew up for himself during the long vacation before he took office, were the establishment of a physiological laboratory and a medical school.[23] It must not, however, be thought that Jowett had changed his opinion of science in any radical way. Two years after taking office as vice-chancellor he wrote to Lewis Campbell, 'It seems to me that all those who, like ourselves, are entrusted with the care of ancient studies, have a hard battle to fight against the physical sciences which are everywhere encroaching, and will certainly lower the character of knowledge if they are not counteracted.'[24] In the same year, Frederick Temple—then Bishop of Exeter—delivered his very significant Bampton lectures on the relations between science and religion. Jowett presumably presided as vice-chancellor at some, at least, of the lectures but his biographers do not record that he thought them worthy of any comment or reaction.

[22] Engel, p. 221.
[23] Abbott and Campbell, ii, p. 214.
[24] Abbott and Campbell, ii, p. 268.

In the curious way in which each phase of Jowett's life seems to coincide with a further stage in the reconstruction of the university, his four years as vice-chancellor came just after the completion of the final reforms of the nineteenth century. The Gladstone administration had appointed a further commission in 1871, under the chairmanship of the Duke of Cleveland, to enquire into the revenues of both universities and colleges at Oxford and Cambridge. Jowett's biographers, possibly reflecting Jowett's own opinions, report that 'many felt that a great danger had been averted when the Gladstonian Government fell from office before the Report of the Commission was published.'[25] Jowett was on the whole satisfied with what had already been achieved by way of reform and was certainly opposed to any radical interference with the way in which colleges ruled themselves.

Cleveland's commission of enquiry had been intended by the Liberals to be the preliminary to a further reform of the universities. The change of government, though the Tories had also declared themselves sympathetic to reform, led to further delays and it was not until 1877 that a commission was appointed to reallocate college income and provide each college with a new set of statutes, which on this occasion the commissioners had the power to compel the colleges to accept.[26] A restriction on the number of prize fellowships, permission for fellows to marry (which in Balliol was applied very generously),[27] a reduction in the number of fellows required to be in orders, the use of fellowship endowments for professorships, the creation of faculty boards to control university lecturing (as opposed to college teaching), and a general reduction of the influence of the clergy in the university and its government, were the main features of the reform.

The reforms were not put into effect until 1881 and 1882 and Jowett became vice-chancellor in the autumn of 1882. He was therefore responsible for seeing that the new aspects of university government were made to work smoothly and he was, at least, sufficiently committed to the latest reforms to be anxious that they

[25] Abbott and Campbell, ii, p. 121.
[26] Engel, p. 157.
[27] Ibid. p. 160.

should do so. He seems to have enjoyed being vice-chancellor and behaved in the university in the same autocratic and decisive manner that he was accustomed to use as master in his own college. If he thought something should be done, he would insist on immediate action and find the necessary authorisation from relevant committees afterwards. If he thought that something should *not* be done, he simply ignored its appearance as an item on agenda papers.

He had always been interested in even fairly small-scale and local political affairs,[28] though, in comparison with Green's, his interest tended to be in the theory rather than the practicalities. As vice-chancellor he had to tackle several such issues at a practical level (the flooding of the river; the creation of a pensions scheme for employees of the university press), besides the more academic questions of university development in which he was interested (the setting up of the Indian Institute in connection with the training of candidates for the Indian Civil Service; the organisation of non-collegiate students).

It is difficult to make any proper assessment of Jowett's vice-chancellorship. Abbott and Campbell claim that he was effective, full of ideas and energy, and achieved a great deal.[29] Faber represents this period of his life as a melancholy one of fading powers and growing doubts and anxieties.[30] Yet each biography contains sufficient evidence to suggest that the overall picture it gives is not quite accurate. Each time Abbott and Campbell record any specific activity undertaken by Jowett as vice-chancellor, one actually gets the impression that he devised a programme far more elaborate than was really needed, tried to force it through autocratically, found that he could not manage the project effectively, and was compelled to abandon it without achieving the goal he had set himself. Faber maintains that 'the effort of filling the office broke and helped to kill him.'[31] Yet the impression actually conveyed by his accounts is of a Jowett who, though wearied by the pressures of work, age, and ill-health, was chiefly notable for a serenity that seems to have come

[28] Above p. 103.
[29] Abbott and Campbell, ii, pp. 212–35.
[30] Faber, pp. 406ff.
[31] Faber, p. 406.

from a consciousness that he was doing what he ought to be doing.

One thing is very clear. By the mid-1880s Jowett was an important, influential, and very respectable person. Even in matters of religion and theology he was no longer quite the suspect figure he had once been. This was partly, no doubt, a result of the change in public attitudes toward a critical approach to understanding the Bible which has already been noted. Dean Farrar, whose *Life of Christ* of 1874 had been an even greater publishing success than the famous *Eric; or Little by Little* which had appeared in the year before Darwin's *Origins*, dedicated his Bampton lectures to Jowett in 1885.[32] Farrar was a liberal Evangelical and, therefore, in some ways held views which were not totally unlike Jowett's own.[33] Though he had been under attack for some of his beliefs, his *Life of Christ* was obviously pious and devout in intention and had been extremely popular with respectable middle-class readers. Whether Farrar was aware that Jowett would have written a very different *Life* from his own does not appear. But he dedicated the lectures to Jowett 'with sincere respect for the services which he has rendered to the cause of education, theology and literature'. That Jowett should be publicly thanked for his contribution to *theology* indicates, as nothing else could, the remarkable change that had taken place since the 1860s.

It is not easy to determine precisely how Jowett's own religious thought was moving in that last decade of his life. He seems to have continued to hold the clear, if problematical, position which he took up in his sermon on 'The Permanent Elements of Religion' of 1879. Yet one cannot escape the feeling that the sharp way in which Jowett had come to state the problem, made it difficult for him to continue to evade a resolution of it. He also seems—and the two things may be connected—to have found it difficult to maintain his earlier sense of a warm and vivid relationship with the Christ of the Gospels. There seems to be something of a change in the content of his sermons in these final years. Many of them were 'biographical', not just eulogies on friends and colleagues who had died, but talks about such a bewildering range of people as Wycliffe, Loyola, Bunyan and

---

[32] F. W. Farrar, *History of Interpretation*, London 1886.

[33] I. Ellis, 'Dean Farrar and the Quest for the Historical Jesus', *Theology*, 89 (1986), pp. 108ff and n.b. pp. 110 and 113.

Spinoza (in the same sermon), Richard Baxter, Pascal, John Wesley, Leon Gambetta and Archbishop Tait (also in a single sermon). Others were much more concerned with common sense than religion, what Nettleship would have called good advice to raise the quality of the commonplace, money-making lives of the ordinary men in the street.[34] They were about courage and sympathy, life in the college, the joys and aspirations of youth, study, and the right use of money.

The point is very neatly illustrated by a reminiscence of Jowett in the life of Cosmo Gordon Lang, who was an undergraduate at Balliol from 1881 to 1885 so that part of his time coincided with Jowett's vice-chancellorship. The future archbishop was not the kind of young man likely to find Jowett entirely sympathetic. He had been brought up in a Scottish manse, was seriously religious, and became a High Church Anglican. He found the master formidable and a little frightening though he also knew that he could be kind and generous and was an outstanding teacher. Lang thought that in matters of religion Jowett was something of a spent force.

> Once he had been a very real influence in the religious life of his time, but in my day that had largely passed. At least such influence never reached me. His sermons in Chapel excited my curiosity rather than impressed either my mind or my spirit. Two sermons I remember. One began with the text: 'Man shall not live by bread alone but by every word that proceedeth out of the mouth . . .' Then he stopped, and quietly resumed: 'I propose to-day to omit the familiar and profound concluding words of this text and to address to you some remarks on Conversation.' And very good and shrewd remarks they were.[35]

Though Lang was relatively complimentary about it, the sermon[36] was a rather strange piece. Not only was it a travesty of the text (Luke 4: 4) which it claimed to expound, it was also one of the sermons which had little to do with Christian life and faith. It was about good behaviour and was very much the sort of lecture an old-fashioned headmaster might give, in a purely secular way, about what a gentleman does and does not do. It was, no doubt, very good

[34] Above p. 116.
[35] [J. G.] Lockhart, [*Cosmo Gordon Lang*, London 1949,] pp. 27f.
[36] *College Sermons*, pp. 202ff.

of its kind but is nothing like the sermons which Jowett had preached in earlier years. And it may be precisely this difference which made Lang say that Jowett was no longer a powerful influence on Oxford religion and that his sermons made no very spiritual impression on him.

This is not proof, of course, that the old warm, vivid, almost mystical, personal devotion to Christ had come to occupy a less prominent place in Jowett's religion. There were still some sermons, even in that last decade, which dealt with the life of Christ or with his authority or his unity with the Father, which pick up all the old themes from the master's early sermons and seem to be part of the same theology that he had been proclaiming since the days when he had been writing the commentaries. And he wrote to Lady Tavistock in December 1884 that the basis of religion was the life and death of Christ:

that means the life and death of Christ in the soul, the imitation of Christ—the inspiration of Christ—the sacrifice of self—the being in the world but not of it, the union with God and the will of God such as Christ had. And this is all to be worked out without mysticism in society and in the daily routine of life.[37]

Yet it is certainly the case that, among Jowett's *published* sermons of the decade between 1882 and 1892, there is a preponderance of pieces which consist chiefly of common sense and good advice. Whether this is sheer chance or whether it reflected a genuine change in the content of his preaching it is not now possible to determine. But it does suggest that something of the vividness of his personal religion had faded.

But this is not to say that he had become a sceptic or an unbeliever. Here, too, Faber creates an unnecessarily confused and depressing picture. He quotes Jowett as saying, at about the time he became vice-chancellor, (and treats it as part of the evidence that 'his confidence is still at the lowest point of the ebbing tide') 'Morning and evening prayers are almost impossible to me. Church is difficult. But I desire more and more never to let a day pass without some idea or aspiration arising in my mind. And this appears to be retained. I

---

[37] Abbott and Campbell, ii, p. 273.

am always thinking of death and of God and of the improvement of human nature, though sometimes interrupted by false and petty conceits of self.'[38]

It is just possible to interpret this, as Faber does, as the thinking of a man whose faith is wavering. But later jottings, which Faber also quotes, suggest that what Jowett said about the difficulties he had with prayer were the self-criticisms of a penitent rather than the desperations of a doubter. 'Nothing makes me more conscious of poverty and shallowness than the difficulty in praying or attending to prayer. . . . If I had any real love of God, would not my mind dwell upon Him, like the believer in Wesley's Hymns?'[39] And again, 'I must try to revive religion if possible in Oxford, and to concentrate my thoughts.' And 'I have no idea except that of fulfilling my duty to the University and of devoting the remaining years to the service of God.'

Faber also makes much of a story, originally told in the Abbott and Campbell biography, of Jowett's words to Edward Seymour in the last years of his life when he was already far from well.[40] Faber says that Jowett told Seymour, who was wondering whether to resign his orders because of religious doubts, 'Holiness has its sources elsewhere than in history. The true use of authority is this; it is due to one wiser than oneself and to an expert. All else is a mere matter of conduct.' Faber then adds:

The report is exasperatingly imperfect. Jowett must have said, or have meant to say, more than this. For what did he mean by 'holiness'? The whole of religious argument turns upon this single mysterious word. It may be a word of supreme value or a word of hocus-pocus. Just at the moment when Jowett seemed to be on the point of telling Seymour what he thought 'holiness' to be, either he failed to complete his sentence or Seymour failed to understand what was being said.

In fact, if the report is exasperatingly imperfect, it is because Faber has made it so. As originally told by Seymour himself, what Jowett actually said was:

Religion is not dependent upon historical events, the report of which we

[38] Faber, p. 405.
[39] Faber, p. 407.
[40] Abbott and Campbell, ii, p. 307 cf. Faber, pp. 410ff.

cannot altogether trust. Holiness has its sources elsewhere than in history. The true use of authority is this: it is due to one wiser than oneself and to an expert. All else is a mere matter of conduct. Faith in the perfect will of God rests upon a basis which can never be shaken. If you sever yourself from the Church you are isolated and useless. . . . Your position is a difficult one; it requires a [strong?] man to fill it. Your ideal is higher: you need loftier motives than those who lean upon the supports which conventional religion supplies.[41]

The meaning of the passage is actually quite clear, in this form. Jowett was talking, in much the same terms as he used in his sermon on the permanent elements of religion of 1879, about the authority upon which religious faith ought to be based. And in the same sermon he had said that holiness was something we all know the meaning of and cannot have too much of. Indeed, in all his sermons he uses 'holiness' to mean moral behaviour and nothing at all of the 'mysterious' kind that Faber imagines. But faith and morality, he was telling Seymour, do not depend upon a belief that the Gospel narratives are historically accurate in detail. And one ought not to ascribe to those narratives, or to anything else, an authority they are not entitled to. One can only properly appeal to authority—to make good an uncertainty—if one is appealing on the ground that it possesses an expertise or wisdom that one lacks oneself. (The sort of appeal that Jowett is thinking of—this or that must have happened because the New Testament says it did—is not an appeal to either expertise or wisdom.) But faith in God does not rest on that sort of appeal to authority, in any case. Difficult though it is to be motivated by nothing other than one's own self-substantiating faith, that is a higher ideal than a conventional religion based upon an appeal to the authority of Church or Bible.

Though he had come to see that reference to the human Jesus of history was a much more elusive thing than it had once seemed, Jowett had not deviated from his insistence that man's moral dimension—holiness—required belief in God. His passion for morality had, indeed, been the reason for his concern with the 'undoubted facts of history and science'; his motive for developing a new understanding of the interpretation of scripture; his purpose in defending

[41] Abbott and Campbell, ii, p. 306. The lacuna is in the original.

theism against the criticisms of agnostics; one of the principal themes in his preaching; and the cause of his very real and patent devotion to the Christ of the Gospels. But it is also possible that the diminution in the vividness of his faith and the apparent uncertainties of his last years are connected with his having to rethink the relationship between morality and religion. And that, in turn, was connected with his coming to grips with some aspects of the natural sciences as he had never done before.

Ironically Jowett's new interest in science seems to have arisen out of one last friendship which was almost of the same kind as the theological friendships he had had in the 1840s and 1850s with people like Temple and Stanley. This friendship was with T. H. Huxley, professional scientist and biologist in his own right, champion and exponent of Darwin's theories, a vigorous critic of Christianity and notorious for his debate with Wilberforce, and an expert on the philosophy of Hume. It was an unusual friendship for Jowett, though they had some things in common. Huxley disliked Comte as much as Jowett did and he had been a friend of Baden Powell.[42] But Huxley represented so many things of which Jowett normally disapproved. He was not a product of the older English universities and he represented the new kind of scientist for whom a rigorous technical competence replaced a rather amateurish interest in the natural world. He was also the embodiment of the determination of these new scientists to gain control of the establishment.[43]

The two men also had completely opposed views on education. Jowett had never regarded science as having any very great educational value and he had always maintained that it was no substitute for a proper training in classical scholarship. Huxley, on the contrary, insisted that a training in the arts contributed nothing to an understanding of science, while scientific education held the key to all human need. The philosophy of Hume, whose expositor Huxley made himself, was poles apart from the kind of philosophy Jowett normally interested himself in. Above all, Huxley was entirely unsympathetic to theism—as Darwin had not been. It is extremely

---

[42] [T.] Cosslett [(ed.), *Science and Religion in the Nineteenth Century*, Cambridge 1984], p. 16.
[43] Cosslett, p. 10.

difficult to imagine what drew the two together, particularly as this was an unusual friendship for Jowett in that it was with someone who was not a Balliol man.

Nevertheless the two apparently became quite close friends and when Jowett heard in 1893 that Huxley, who was to give the second Romanes lecture, had chosen as his topic 'Ethics and Evolution', he wrote him a letter which said:

No one has yet represented adequately the antithesis of the moral and the physical. Is not the word 'evolution' rather unfortunate? There are so many kinds of progress in the world and in human nature and it does not distinguish them. I do not think we can give up the great traditions respecting truth and right and respecting divine and human perfection. When simplified and purified all religions agree on them; and all good men and the better part of all philosophies. We cannot do without that necessary basis of morality, nor can we imagine how natural science (though it transforms the destinies of man in various ways, and may do so yet more in the future) can possibly supply it.[44]

The Romanes lectures had been founded by G. J. Romanes in 1891 and were to be given annually by a man 'of eminence' on a scientific or literary topic. Gladstone gave the first lecture in 1892 and the choice of Huxley, who was universally regarded as the expert on Darwinism, was presumably a sign that it had become respectable. But there was also considerable interest in the fact that Huxley proposed to talk on the relationship between evolution and morality. The immediate enthusiasm for trying to apply the principle of natural selection in all sorts of inappropriate areas had begun to die down but Spencer was still insisting that Darwin's scientific discoveries and the hypothesis derived from them could be erected into a system in which all knowledge—including ethics—could be comprehended.

It is difficult to determine how far Huxley's lecture may have been influenced by an interchange of ideas with Jowett. It has been argued that the lecture was largely motivated by Huxley's political concerns, and that he had been working on it for at least a year before it

[44] [Imperial College London:] Huxley Papers: Scientific and General Correspondence: vii, fo. 91. There is a copy of the letter in Balliol College: Typescript copies of Jowett Letters [3].

was delivered.[45] But although Jowett's letter just quoted is dated only a month before the lecture was delivered, he had been in touch with Huxley on the subject for some time.

Huxley had engaged in a number of theological controversies since his clash with Wilberforce thirty years earlier and, inventing the term 'agnostic', maintained that it was quite impossible even to know with any certainty what Christ himself had believed and taught. Even Mr Gladstone had been rather badly mauled by him. By the time of the Romanes lecture he was insisting that he was giving up controversy and was anxious to make a more positive contribution to the debate. In fact, Jowett and Huxley had each been interesting himself in what was really the other's speciality. Jowett had disapproved of Huxley's involvement in theology and biblical criticism. But when Jowett had begun—about his seventieth year and just at the time when Huxley was taking up theology—to interest himself in biology there was no suggestion that Huxley disapproved of that.

Not long before Huxley began to work on the Romanes lecture Jowett had been to stay with him. In February 1892 he wrote to Mrs Huxley saying that he doubted whether her husband would find biblical criticism a permanently satisfying subject for study. How much more useful it would be 'to elevate somewhat (not by preaching) the moral standard of mankind . . .'[46] To Huxley himself he wrote in the same month, not specifically referring to the Romanes lecture but saying that he had enjoyed Huxley's 'three lectures on evolution'—presumably 'On the Natural Inequality of Men', 'Natural Rights and Political Rights', and 'Government: Anarchy or Regimentation', all delivered in 1890.[47]

Jowett went on to say:

you should try to find a new basis for morals now when it seems likely to be buried under physics . . . All men are asking on what principles they must live; and they want an answer independent of the traditional theology. Will

---

[45] [M. S.] Helfand, ['T. H. Huxley's "Ethics and Evolution": The Politics of Evolution and the Evolution of Politics', *Victorian Studies*, 20 (1977)], pp.159ff.
[46] Huxley Papers: Scientific and General Correspondence: vii, fos. 81–2.
[47] T. H. Huxley, *Method and Results*, London 1893, pp. 240ff.

you give them a helping hand? The good in all religions and in all things; the example of the lives of the best men; the necessity of admitting all the facts and problems of history and natural science; the duty of resignation to all true facts withersoever they lead; the impossibility of basing religion on the uncertainly [sic] record of past facts; the value of ideals; are some of the principal topics which would have to be considered.[48]

In July of that year he wrote again to Huxley saying, 'I hope that you have not forgotten and will be able to fulfill your intention of writing on the constructive side of religion and morality now that you have renounced theological controversy.'[49]

It has been argued by Michael Helfand that Huxley's thesis, in effect, represented an abandonment of his earlier Spencerian ethical relativism and that its:

> main purpose was to deny the authority of evolutionary science to both the individualist ethic of Spencer and the land socialist cause . . . while using that authority to bolster the specific causes he supported. . . . Far from limiting and depoliticising the authority of evolutionary science, Huxley used it to justify the modified laissez-faire social policy which later Victorian Liberals proposed to solve the problem of the 'Great Depression' and the Irish nationalist movement.'[50]

Jowett was no admirer of Spencer—the 'wordy platitudes of Mr H. Spencer' are dismissed in one of his letters to Florence Nightingale as of no use in filling up the void left in contemporary theology and moral philosophy.[51] And Green had devoted considerable attention to a thorough critique of the ideas of Spencer and G. H. Lewes (George Eliot's partner) in the *Contemporary Review* between December 1877 and January 1881.[52] One cannot therefore suppose that Jowett would regret Huxley's rejection of Spencer.

Whether Jowett was still, at that date, in any sense a political Liberal is somewhat doubtful. He seems to have doubted it himself, telling Lady Abercrombie in 1882 that he was 'in danger of becom-

---

[48] Huxley Papers: Scientific and General Correspondence: vii, fos. 83f.
[49] Huxley Papers: Scientific and General Correspondence: vii, fos. 88f.
[50] Helfand, p. 177.
[51] Balliol College: Jowett to Florence Nightingale, 25 June 1873.
[52] 'Mr Herbert Spencer and Mr G. H. Lewes: Their Application of the Doctrine of Evolution to Thought', *Works*, i, pp. 373–520 n.d. cf. p. vi.

ing a Tory (though I struggle against this as much as I can)'.[53] And it seems to have been Gladstone's policy on Ireland that was chiefly responsible for his doubts. He had always held strong views on Ireland but they seem to have changed somewhat as he grew older. In 1868 he had told Florence Nightingale, 'Irish grievances are 1 loss of nationality; 2 tenure of land; 3 Irish Church. That is the Irish order, but the Englishman takes them in the reverse order. Irishman wants really 1, 2: Englishman says you shall only have 3.'[54] That sounds as though he believed that Irishmen should be given their own nationality, land, and religion. If that is what he meant, he soon changed his mind on the first point though not on the other two. At the famous meeting at Camperdown, which preceded Gladstone's removal of Scott to Rochester, Jowett had thought the politician 'so unsound' on Ireland. And after Gladstone had committed himself to introducing a Home Rule Bill, Jowett seems to have taken to voting against the Liberals.

Edward Seymour's recollections of Jowett in 1888, from which the remark about holiness not having its source in history comes, also contained this comment:

Jowett was alone, with the exception of Lord Camperdown, who had come to speak at a Unionist meeting. Very interesting conversation the whole time; politics predominating.[55]

This may indicate that Jowett had openly become a supporter of the Unionist cause. If so he was not alone: disenchantment with the Liberals over Home Rule was widespread not least in Oxford. Many even of their most solid nonconformist supporters deserted on the same issue because they feared that Roman Catholicism would weaken the sense of British national identity.[56] Little though Jowett would have wished to be associated with nonconformist tradesmen in their opposition to home rule, he is only too likely to have shared such a sentiment. He thought the 'peasant priests' the real source of Irish hatred of England, though he also regarded the disestablish-

---

[53] Abbott and Campbell, ii, p. 210.
[54] Balliol College: Jowett to Florence Nightingale, 24 May 1868.
[55] Abbott and Campbell, ii, p. 306.
[56] D. W. Bebbington, 'Nonconformity and Electoral Sociology, 1867–1918', *The Historical Journal*, 27 (1984), pp. 640ff. and 648f.

ment of the Church of Ireland as a blessing.[57] But his most considered analysis of the Irish question suggests that he thought it an intractable problem to which there was no solution compatible with both justice and safety.

But it is improbable that he was really very much concerned with the political implications of Huxley's lecture. The moral and theological issues were at the forefront of his mind. And, in view of his continuing contact with Huxley on these themes during the preceding months, it is difficult to escape altogether from the idea that he may have had some influence on what Huxley said. Part of the Romanes lecture seems almost to be developed as if in answer to Jowett's doubts and fears. The distinction between 'fittest' in the biological and moral senses was clearly drawn. Though Helfand's analysis is in many ways an attractive one, then, it is possible to take the view that, whatever political motivations Huxley may have had, he had also been listening to Jowett. His vigorous defence of a morality wholly independent of religion, whether deliberately so designed or not, reads as though it was an answer to Jowett.

In the lecture Huxley was to argue that so far from there being a natural morality to be derived from the evolutionary principle which would sanctify the depredations of the strong against the weak, there was a paradox about ethical development. Every advance in civilisation and morality was made by deliberately going counter to the principles apparently to be detected in the evolutionary process. The evolutionary theory cannot do more than show how the good and evil tendencies in man have come about. It cannot show us why we should prefer one course of action to another.

But Huxley did not draw from this the conclusion that no moral standards are desirable. He proceeded to make the point that Jowett himself was so anxious to stress. 'Fittest' in the sense in which it is used in the theory of evolution, was not necessarily the same as 'strongest' and had nothing to do with 'best' in any moral sense. 'Fittest' meant those best adapted to survive in given conditions—'if our hemisphere were to cool again, the survival of the fittest might bring about, in the vegetable kingdom, a population of more and

---

[57] Abbott and Campbell, ii, p. 210.

more stunted and humbler and humbler organisms until the "fittest" that survived might be nothing but lichens, diatoms, and such microscopic organisms as those which give red snow its colour.'[58] The evolution of morality and of civilisation follows a very different course and there is nothing to justify the 'fanatical individualism' in which 'the duties of the individual to the state are forgotten, and his tendencies to self-assertion are dignified by the name of rights.'

This, as Helfand has pointed out, is a development of a position he had taken as early as 1888 in 'The Struggle for Existence in Human Society'.[59] There Huxley had begun to oppose to each other the selfishness of a non-moral nature and the moral objectives of corporate society. The same kind of approach is also present in a paper called 'Natural and Political Rights', delivered by Huxley in 1890. There, after pointing out that laws of nature were in no sense commands 'to do or to refrain from doing anything', and that 'The proper object and effect of moral and civil laws are to benefit all those who are subjected to them by bringing about a state of peace and mutual confidence', he had gone on to say that 'consistent and thoroughgoing action based upon the law of nature and the natural rights which flow from it, tends to benefit the individual at the expense of all other individuals whose needs and desires are of the same kind . . .'[60]

What was new in the Romanes lecture, however, was Huxley's deliberate development of the dialectical approach already described. 'Let us understand, once and for all, that the ethical progress of society depends, not on imitating the cosmic process, still less in running away from it, but in combating it.'[61] So by 1893 he had come to advance the quite overt view that every growth in civilisation had to be won by a deliberate countering of the competitive and destructive tendencies of biological evolution.

If it is difficult to avoid the impression that Jowett had some influence upon Huxley's approach to his subject, it is equally difficult to avoid the impression that Huxley's arguments had some—

[58] [T. H. Huxley,] *Evolution and Ethics* [*and Other Essays*, London 1894,] pp. 80f.
[59] Helfand, p. 168.
[60] T. H. Huxley, *Method and Results*, London 1893, p. 349ff.
[61] *Evolution and Ethics*, p. 83.

possibly much more significant—effect on Jowett's actual beliefs. The two had obviously been talking together about religious belief, morality, biblical criticism, and biology. Huxley's opinions were vigorous and well known and had been expressed in public controversy. He rejected theism and, as a disciple and interpreter of Hume, maintained the impossibility of metaphysics. He had also argued, in relation to the critical study of the New Testament, that it was not possible to determine with any certainty what Jesus had actually said or taught.

These are precisely the areas in which Jowett would be most vulnerable to attack. His letters to Huxley revert to the ideas he had expressed in his sermon on 'The Permanent Elements of Religion' and in his remarks to Seymour, that one must live in the true facts of science and history. His dislike of Huxley's venture into biblical criticism and his increasingly enthusiastic pressure upon Huxley to formulate a new approach to religion and morality, make one wonder whether Jowett did not—in his last months—find it impossible to maintain his earlier conviction that morality and religion were inextricably bound together. It may be that, as his sermons after 1880 suggest, he had begun to lose some of the vividness of his personal devotion to Christ precisely because he had come to insist too firmly that faith could exist quite independently of any historical rooting in the Gospel narratives.

Huxley had found—or thought he had found—a way of defending morality without religion. He was also driving a wedge between the two halves of Jowett's concept of the divine personality clothed in laws, separating the laws of nature from the laws of morality. And, ever since his first reaction to the philosophy of Kant fifty years earlier when he had insisted that man's knowledge of himself as a moral being and his perception of the external world were inseparable, this belief had been the foundation of Jowett's faith. He must have felt that his last defences were being threatened. He was too ill and died too soon afterwards for us to know what he thought about Huxley's lecture. Even if he had had no answer to the arguments contained in it, he might not have been able to accept that his perennial defence of a liberal Christianity had failed. But his correspondence with Huxley must inevitably raise some doubts about precisely what he did believe at the very end of his life. It was, after all, a risk implicit in Jowett's whole approach that it might lead to doubt rather than conviction. He had always insisted that religious enquiry, like all academic enquiry, must be free from dogmatic preconditions. If Gore's determined adherence to patristic orthodoxy created inconsistencies within his theology, Jowett's liberalism insisted that all questions must remain open. It is true that he had been convinced that belief would emerge unshaken from the quest but, in terms of his own premiss, he could have no guarantee that that would happen.

Whatever Jowett's beliefs may have been at the very end of his life, it does seem that he had begun to realise that his liberal but rather negative approach had serious limitations. Lang's biography contains another anecdote about Jowett which reveals this very clearly. In 1893, the last year of the master's life, when Lang was a fellow of All Souls, Jowett asked him to come to Balliol as Fremantle's successor.

> I felt greatly honoured. I have often remembered and quoted some words he said in describing what my duties would be. The last sentence is an epitome of wisdom for pastoral work, and indeed for life: 'You will try to make young men as good as young men can be made. *Don't expect too much and don't attempt too little.* . . . I frankly told the Master what I felt—that my theological position was rather different from his, and that I had such respect for him that I could not bear to take any line against his views in his own College. He surprised me by saying: I know this. It is just why I am asking you to come. My friends and I had our work to do in Oxford. I think it was worth doing. But it is largely done; and there are some things we don't seem able to do, and which I want done. We don't seem able now to inspire the young men. *We may have truth*—I think we have—*but we have no fire.* It was said very simply, quietly, rather pathetically . . . I was greatly touched . . .[62]

After consulting Gore and others, who thought he was right about the theological incompatibility between himself and Jowett, Lang turned the offer down. He told his mother that he regarded it as 'most significant of the change of tone in modern Oxford that Jowett, the old chief of the extreme Broad Church Liberals, should even think of a man of my views to take on the religious supervision

[62] Lockhart, p. 101.

of Balliol College'.⁶³ And he might have added that it was just as surprising that the High Church party did not leap at the opportunity to carry the battle into the enemy's stronghold if, indeed, they still regarded Jowett as an enemy. Lang, of course, may have been correct in judging Jowett to have become something of a spent force. If he was, that may, in itself, have been responsible for a softening of former enmities. No doubt, also, the fact that the university had been opened to people of a wide variety of religious opinions had something to do with it. In a society where those who openly declared that they would have nothing to do with religion of any kind were growing in numbers, even a liberal like Jowett might have seemed preferable to the unbelievers. Or, it may be, twenty years of being master had made him respectable. At any rate, when Jowett died only a few months later—on 1 October 1893—Frederick Temple, Archbishop of Canterbury, officiated at the funeral with Fremantle's assistance. It was another sign that old controversies were losing some of their virulence.

There is a mildly ironic postscript to Huxley's lecture on ethics and evolution. Romanes, himself a well-known biologist, had been persuaded after correspondence with Darwin that religious beliefs were untenable. This view, expressed in his *Candid Examination of Theism* of 1878, he seems to have begun to modify towards the end of his life. He died in 1894, the year after Huxley's lecture and Jowett's own death. Notes he had written, apparently accepting the view that it was reasonable to be a Christian believer, were handed to Charles Gore who edited them for publication. Mrs Romanes, a strong-minded lady of High Church persuasion who was much involved in the movement to provide university education for women, seems to have been instrumental in this. But in a concluding note Gore felt able to assert that Romanes had 'returned before his death to that full, deliberate communion with the Church of Jesus Christ which he had for so many years been conscientiously compelled to forego'.⁶⁴

---

⁶³ Ibid p. 102.
⁶⁴ G. J. Romanes, *Thoughts on Religion*, ed. C. Gore, London 1896

9

After Jowett

Jowett was succeeded as master of Balliol by Edward Caird, Professor of Moral Philosophy at Glasgow and a leading figure in the British Idealist school. Those who thought of themselves as striving to preserve the Jowett style of mastership would have preferred another candidate.[1] In spite of the fact that one of the college's lecturers assured Caird that he had been 'among those from the outside whom [Jowett had] named as possible successors',[2] Caird would probably not have been Jowett's own choice. Only three letters addressed to Caird and dating from the period after Jowett became master are included in the Abbott and Campbell biography. There may, of course, have been others which have not survived but the first letter, written in 1887, contains an admission that the two men were not in touch with each other very often. It also contains a remark which was an implied criticism of Caird's Idealist philosophy.[3] A year later Jowett wrote to tell Caird that he had just been reading Nettleship's memoir of T. H. Green. In spite of the fact that Caird and Green had been particularly close friends, Jowett repeated the criticisms he had included in his memorial sermon on Green.[4]

On the other hand, the third letter was written to thank Caird for the dedication of his Gifford Lectures 'by an old pupil who owes much to his teaching and friendship'.[5] Since this letter belongs to the very last year of Jowett's life, it is clear that some degree of friendship and sympathy between the two had survived to the end but the

---

[1] A fascinating collection of letters relating to the election has been assembled by John Jones, 'A Contested Mastership: the Election of Jowett's Successor', *Balliol College Annual Record*, 1977, pp. 49ff.
[2] Ibid. p. 52.
[3] Abbott and Campbell, ii, p. 325.
[4] Ibid. p. 340.
[5] [E. Caird, The] *Evolution of Religion*, [Glasgow 1893].

overall impression one receives is that Jowett's relationship with Caird had followed the usual pattern—admiration on one side and a tendency to be hypercritical on the other. Jowett's praise of Caird's book was noticeably muted. He might well have preferred the mastership to pass to someone less likely to use Balliol to propagate a system. He had, moreover, always insisted that the college existed for the benefit of undergraduates and not of those who were primarily concerned with scholarship for its own sake. And Caird was primarily a scholar.[6]

In fact, Caird seems to have perceived, and to have been sympathetic to, Jowett's plan for creating a free but distinctly religious institution. He acknowledged that his predecessor's great reputation was founded not upon 'the worldly success of a select few of his pupils, but in the spirit of consecration to truth and to the higher forms of social service which [he] had cherished in himself and his colleagues, and had made a tradition of the College'.[7]

Caird was a Balliol man, but not at all a typical one. He had been born in 1835 and his father had died when he was very young. His education had been interrupted by general ill-health and it was not until 1860 that he went to Balliol on a Snell exhibition. He was, therefore, much older even than most of the Scots who came to the college and, since postgraduate students in the modern sense did not exist, he read Greats, completing the school in 1863. Scott was the master and Jowett was still in the wilderness though about to gain control of the governing body. He taught Caird Latin and Greek composition—'the very best in the University', Caird told his mother,[8] a strangely complimentary remark since Jowett was not noted for his accuracy in the classical languages.

Caird also first encountered Hegel through Jowett's lectures,[9] but it was Green who was the pre-eminent influence in his undergraduate life. They were much of an age in spite of the fact that Green was

[6] Besides the Gifford Lectures, Caird had written a book on Hegel (1883), and *A Critical Account of the Philosophy of Kant* (1877), revised and extended as the two-volume *Critical Philosophy of Immanuel Kant* (1889). Both were recognised as substantial contributions to philosophical scholarship.

[7] Jones and Muirhead, p. 184.

[8] Jones and Muirhead, p. 27.

[9] Quinton, pp. 321ff.

already a fellow and, indeed, Caird's tutor. They thought alike: the Idealism which Green expounded seemed to his new pupil to be what he had already half perceived as the proper way to understand existence. For Caird had already fallen under the spell of Carlyle;[10] not the later advocate of autocracy and oligarchy but the early Carlyle, the moralist who opposed poverty and oppression, the hater of dogmas who yet proclaimed that 'the Religious Principle' was to be found within all good men. Caird was later to say that Carlyle, like the great German thinkers, broke open all constraints upon ideas and gave Europe a sense of vision because he expressed 'disgust at the mean achievements of what we call civilization, . . . generous wrath at the arbitrary limitations of its advantages, [and] deep craving for a better order of social life . . .'[11] Through Carlyle's influence and the example of his own elder brother John who 'liberalized and humanized Scottish theology and secured faith against scepticism by revealing its intrinsic reasonableness',[12] Caird was already predisposed to sympathise with Green's approach.

Jowett had some hand in Caird's appointment to the Glasgow chair in 1866 though he seems not to have been the candidate of his first choice.[13] It was an appropriate appointment for Caird was always pre-eminently a *moral* philosopher. Like Green, he took Kant as the starting-point for all his philosophy,[14] but he did so because he believed that Kant proclaimed the essential truth, that life is moral. He also believed that Kant's ideas were insufficiently related to the real and corporate life of human beings: they needed to be 'materialised and socialised'. And it was precisely this that he thought Hegel had achieved by securing the moral and religious basis of human existence.[15] Caird's moral theory was, therefore, essentially a religious one. At its heart was the belief that human life

---

[10] Jones and Muirhead, pp. 23ff.
[11] E. Caird, 'The Genius of Carlyle', *Essays on Literature and Philosophy*, Glasgow 1892, pp. 230ff.
[12] Jones and Muirhead, p. 20.
[13] Abbott and Campbell, i, p. 399; Jones and Muirhead, p. 48.
[14] Quinton, p. 322.
[15] Jones and Muirhead, pp. 61ff.; Quinton, p. 309.

was truly 'idealised', not by the ethereally spiritual, but by realising the infinite in commonplace, everyday relationships.[16]

Caird's only directly theological work was his Gifford Lectures, an attempt at a 'science' of religion. He set out his motive in the preface.

> I have specially had in view that large and increasing class who have become alienated from the ordinary dogmatic system of belief, but who, at the same time, are conscious that they have owed a great part of their spiritual life to the teachings of the Bible and the Christian Church. To separate what is permanent from what is transitory in the traditions of the past is a difficult task which every generation has to encounter for itself. In the present day there are many . . . who are divided between two feelings, perplexed on the one hand by a suspicion that in clinging to the orthodox forms of the creed of Christendom, they may be untrue to themselves, and may even seem to assent to doctrines which they have ceased to believe; and checked on the other side by a fear that in discarding those forms they may be casting aside ideas which are essential to their moral and spiritual life.[17]

This might almost be Jowett talking about religious doubters of the generation of Arthur Hugh Clough but Jowett could not have added Caird's next sentence. 'What they want, above all, is some principle or criterion, which will make it possible for them to distinguish what is tenable from what is untenable in the opposite claims which are made upon their belief.' Jowett had never thought that the answer lay in some universal system. He told Caird that he expected the book to be widely read and to create a great deal of interest,[18] but he was careful not to say that he thought that Caird had actually laid down the right principles or that he, himself, agreed with what the book contained. Instead he said that, when he had finished it, he might venture to send Caird 'a few remarks'. In retrospect his rather moderate enthusiasm for Caird's work was probably justified.

Caird's lectures were concerned with the possibility of constructing a science of religion on the basis of what he called 'the idea of development'. The very first sentence of the book defined what he

---

[16] [E. Caird,] *Lay Sermons [and Addresses delivered in the Hall of Balliol College, Oxford,* Glasgow 1907,] pp. 70f.

[17] *Evolution of Religion,* i, p. viii.

[18] Abbott and Campbell, ii, p. 446.

meant by science—the discovery of 'law, order, and reason in what seems at first accidental, capricious and meaningless'. But orderliness, rational explanation in terms of causality, and the consistency of things in terms of 'law', though they existed throughout the universe, were not always on the same level: moral science or a science of religion would be different from the physical sciences. This is not unlike the warnings Jowett had been in the habit of attaching to his comments on evolution. But Caird went on to argue that what had made it possible to treat religion scientifically, were two concepts which had only recently been generally accepted, the *unity* of man and human *development*.

It appears that Caird intended the word 'evolution' in the title of his lectures seriously. Though he did not precisely analyse and apply the concept of evolution—in its biological sense—to the study of religion, he often employed its language.[19] And, in spite of the fact that it proved to be impossible to show that religion had evolved in a form precisely analogous to biological evolution, he held that all religion could be regarded as part of a 'development', even when there was no historical connection between its different manifestations. What mattered, indeed, was not the tracing out of the historical development of religions but an examination of the developing way in which the human mind *conceived* of religion. He believed that it was possible to demonstrate that there was a common course followed by such development and that each phase evolved out of what went before it.

Essentially what enabled him to treat religion thus 'scientifically' was his belief that the spiritual manifested itself with a consistency analogous to the consistency which is assumed as the basis for all scientific enquiry. Spirit manifests itself through everything that exists, consistently and not erratically. It does so, supremely, through the human mind. Because religion is an aspect of the human mind and because the rational is the spiritual, religion will also manifest a consistency and a unity which makes it possible to treat it scientifically, as a developing, living organism. Surveying religion in this way; tracing its development and understanding why it has taken the forms it has; perceiving which are the 'higher' and which

[19] E.g. *Evolution of Religion*, i, p. 40.

the 'lower' forms of religion; will enable one to distinguish what are the permanent features of genuine religion and exclude those aspects of it which are merely conditioned by the needs and the limitations of earlier times.

The two volumes of the book surveyed in some detail what Caird obviously believed to be the most important stages in the development of religion. Much of what he wrote was hardly scientific, in the sense of being objective and demonstrable. A great deal of it was simply an expression of his own view of the nature of the religions he was considering. For instance, he attributed to Paul and to the author of the fourth Gospel the 'separation of Christ from humanity and a kind of identification of him with God, which is practically a return to the Jewish opposition of God and man'.[20] Caird himself believed that one of the essential aspects of the Gospel of Jesus was the unity of the human and the divine, not in the classical sense of the two natures in one person, but because man cannot be true to himself unless he is able to see himself in God. He was not, of course, alone in holding such views. But they are hardly self-evident; nor did he attempt an objective consideration of the evidence for them. Moreover, though he made much of the concept of evolution as the basis for his scientific approach to religion, he found it difficult to use in practice. He was forced to admit that it was impossible to define religion in terms of either the most highly developed or the most primitive of its forms.[21] In the end he had to argue that the only kind of biological development analogous to the development of religion was the growth of an individual member of a species. So he was able to argue that it was neither in its most primitive origins, nor in its most highly developed form, but in its developing continuum that the essence of a religion was to be found.

A good deal of orthodox doctrine he rejected and more he transmuted into a mythological representation of eternal truths. He was willing to be visitor of Manchester College, the Unitarian training institution, an indication that he sat somewhat lightly to the doctrine of the Trinity. But his moderate temperament disguised the radical character of some of his beliefs. After he became master he read a

[20] *Evolution of Religion*, ii, p. 214.
[21] *Evolution of Religion*, i, p. 42.

paper on Christianity and the historical Jesus to the Oxford Society of Historical Theology,[22] in which he tried to apply the methodology developed in his Gifford lectures to the problem so persistently evaded by Jowett. He believed that it was possible to define an essence of Christianity in spite of uncertainties concerning the historical Jesus. But, in fact, he used the concept of 'development' as a justification for choosing what was attractive to himself in the orthodox tradition and abandoning the rest. It may be worth remembering, too, that the body to whom he was delivering this presidential address chose to call itself the Society of *Historical Theology* precisely in order to indicate that it assumed no *dogmatic* presuppositions.

There is a problem in determining how far Caird set himself to propagate his system among his students: even his biography contains contradictory statements about this. Though Caird in Glasgow is described as being like 'a master with disciples', it is also said that he was scrupulous in not exerting undue influence upon his students.[23] And, indeed, he seems to have been like Jowett in not *wishing* to impose ideas on others. Yet, perhaps,—again like Jowett—he underestimated the force of his own personality and the attraction exercised by the clear, coherent, and optimistic system he expounded. At Balliol he seems to have been awkward and shy with undergraduates. His biographers point out that Jowett had no easy small talk either, but they admit that at least he made an effort while Caird appeared to make none.[24] So, in spite of their shared dislike of 'making disciples', the effect of the two men may, in fact, have been totally different. Jowett really did make every effort, even in his later years, to get to know the undergraduates individually. It was their personal loyalty he wanted, rather than that they should agree with his ideas. But Caird seems to have impressed them with his ideas rather than his personal interest and, therefore, it would be the thought rather than the man which they came so much to admire.

Caird, moreover, had become during his years at Glasgow a

---

[22] Jones and Muirhead, p. 148. The lecture is printed in *Proceedings of the Oxford Society of Historical Theology*, 22 Oct. 1896, pp. 5ff.

[23] Jones and Muirhead, pp. 77 and 128.

[24] Jones and Muirhead, p. 144.

lecturer rather than a tutor. In Oxford he made real efforts to be a 'good college man', devoting himself to Balliol to an extent which made some of his admirers feel that he was not playing as large a part in the university as he might have done. But he was always at his best when addressing a larger audience on a set theme rather than with individual undergraduates. Undramatic though his style undoubtedly was, it seems that it was through his public speaking that he most impressed others.

It is not surprising then that his connection with Balliol is most often remembered through his *Lay Sermons*, delivered in the hall which he may have thought a more appropriate setting for the preaching activities of the first layman to be head of the college. They became a regular annual event, on the first Sunday of each academic year. What he had to say could have left no one in any doubt as to his attitude to Christianity. Though he was no controversialist, he made little attempt to modify or soften his divergence from traditional orthodoxy. He expounded in simple terms the comprehensive system of thought which he had developed. His concern for morality was as obvious as Jowett's and so was his anxiety to take science seriously. Like Jowett, too, he used the results of biblical criticism in making his points. And his tendency to assume the steady progress of humanity is even more marked.

Caird's mastership lasted for fourteen years (he died in 1908, a year after retiring from office). He had developed the college which he had inherited from Jowett along lines of which Jowett would, on the whole, have approved. Though his religious beliefs were actually much less orthodox than Jowett's, this fact was obscured by their systematic character. He seemed to be revitalising religion, liberating it, and making it more coherent and intelligible. Many of those who were at the college during his time remembered it as just the kind of institution Jowett had set out to create, one in which a positively religious environment was deliberately combined with an open, enquiring, and liberal approach to theology.

It is possible to see how his vision of a religious but real world could be captivating and exciting to his students, particularly since he related it to practical things and to politics, in particular. Like

Green, he took local politics seriously and saw it as one of the ways of uniting the finite with the infinite. He was interested in the reform of the national educational system, and particularly in education for women. He became an open opponent of free market economics in his outspoken attacks upon the working conditions of women and children. He had also been involved in the campaign for the extension of the franchise and an enthusiastic supporter of the plans to set up Toynbee Hall in Glasgow on the lines of the university settlement already established in the east end of London.[25]

Arnold Toynbee himself had become the symbol and embodiment of the relevance of morality to economics and politics. He had been a product of Jowett's Balliol in the 1870s. Because of ill-health and because he was largely self-educated, he was already twenty-three when he matriculated in 1875. For the same reasons he attempted no more than the pass school three years later but was then immediately appointed a college lecturer. In 1882, having recently been married and on the point of being elected a fellow, he died at the age of thirty-one.

For someone whose life was so brief, he had a considerable influence, for which his romantic appearance and great gifts as a speaker were partly responsible. He seems to have gathered around himself a circle of undergraduates and younger dons who shared his enthusiasms and interests. He was an ardent disciple of T. H. Green and a close friend of Lewis Nettleship (Green's successor as tutor in the college). Alfred Milner (the future high commissioner in South Africa)[26] and Lyttelton Gell (who was to be largely responsible for the publication of Jowett's sermons) were also in his circle. Even as an undergraduate he spent his vacations in the east end of London, trying to live in much the same conditions as working-class people themselves. He worked with Samuel Barnett, a slum clergyman and a friend and former curate of W. H. Fremantle's, and he became a member of the Tower Hamlets Radical Club.[27]

Toynbee's particular interest was economics, not a subject much

---

[25] Jones and Muirhead, p. 114.

[26] Milner wrote the article on Toynbee in the *Dictionary of National Biography*.

[27] [F.C.] Montague, ['Arnold Toynbee', *Johns Hopkins University Studies in Historical and Political Science*, 7 (1889),] p. 24 and L. E. Nettleship, pp. 572f.

studied by Oxford dons. He was savagely critical of the 'old' exponents of political economy, particularly Ricardo. Though he recognised the importance of competition, he believed that the only hope for the future lay in competition controlled by a deliberate and conscious morality.[28] He followed Mill in making a distinction between laws of production operating automatically and laws of distribution, largely controlled by human contrivance. Therefore, he believed, wages were not simply controlled by supply and demand but by all sorts of largely unrecognised factors which might, in the interests of fairness, be adjusted by altering the structure of society.[29] But what marked him out most from conventional political economists was his use of history as an instrument in the critical appraisal of economic theory,[30] and his belief that economic laws were not simply to be noted and accepted—but wrestled with.[31]

Toynbee understood the economic history of Britain in the preceding century as a process by which the working man had lost—through the social changes consequent upon the breakdown of rural communities—the patronage of the wealthy but had not, at first, acquired compensating political rights of his own. He believed that the most important fact of all was that the worker was at that very time acquiring rights which he could never have possessed without the industrial revolution. To encourage that process was the way to build the good society.

As is the case with so many of those whose ideas were shaped at Balliol in the 1870s, it is difficult to be certain whether Toynbee was chiefly influenced by Green, or by Jowett himself, or simply by the general atmosphere of the college. In view of the fact that he was reckoned more radical than Jowett, it is interesting to note the master's own description of Toynbee's political convictions. Though admitting that he only knew him 'as an older person knows one who is much younger than himself', he called him 'a dearly-

---

[28] Montague, p. 34.
[29] Montague, p. 38.
[30] For a very clear example see his critique of the theories of Henry George in the posthumously published [*Lectures on the*] *Industrial Revolution* [*in England*, London 1884,] p. 142.
[31] Lyttleton Gell in an appendix to Montague, p. 57.

beloved friend',[32] and his assessment of Toynbee's political thought reveals a sound grasp of the subject and a good deal of sympathy with his point of view.

Jowett described Toynbee's assessment of the school of Ricardo as follows:

> They assured the poor man freedom of labour, but without education, without the chance of emigration, confined as he was to his original place of abode by the action of the old Poor Law, the freedom granted to him was under ordinary circumstances only a liberty to starve.[33]

And he added that the worker's contract with his employer was so unequal that it gave him no opportunity to share in the increasing wealth of the country. Perhaps Jowett was not always as elitist in politics as he sometimes seemed.

Toynbee's religious beliefs were fervent but undogmatic. He seems to have developed them for himself by reading the Bible and *The Imitation of Christ* rather than through the formal observances of the institutional Church. It is difficult to tell how far he had already acquired them before he come to Balliol and how far he was influenced directly by Green and Jowett. In his very first year at Balliol he described his beliefs in words very reminiscent of Jowett's translation of the passage quoted from Kant in the commentary on Romans.[34] And in a passage which is very like Jowett's sermons of the period, but perhaps better put, he once wrote:

> What the real character of Christ was, what is the truth about certain incidents of his life, we may never be certain, but the ideal Christ, the creation of centuries of Christian suffering and devotion, will be as little affected by historical scepticism as the character of Shakespeare's Hamlet by researches into the Danish chronicles.[35]

If some of Toynbee's ideas of the universe as a manifestation of the life of God were like Green's,[36] in certain respects he was a throwback to Thomas Arnold, as if to prove the legitimacy of the

---

[32] In a memoir printed in the first edition of *The Industrial Revolution in England*, p. v.
[33] Ibid. p. xii.
[34] Montague, p. 18.
[35] Montague, p. 22.
[36] Ibid.

liberal bloodline. For, like Arnold, he was anxious for the practical reform of the established church, recognising that structures are necessary for the survival of ideas even if institutional religion is always a poor echo of real faith. He desired an inclusive national Church of the type advocated by Arnold. Indeed he once said, 'The ideal Church is the State.'[37] A state connection, he thought, was necessary to preserve the independence of the clergy from the tyranny of their congregations no less than from hierarchical tyranny, leaving them free to formulate their faith in terms that were consonant with modern thought. But he also believed in drawing the laity in to participate in planning and running the life of the Church through parochial councils such as Arnold had suggested. Thus it would be possible 'to *secure a form of Christianity in harmony with progress, liberty and knowledge.* . . . By making the Church of England a church of intellectual freedom and a church of the people.'[38]

Toynbee Hall which was founded in his memory in the year after his death embodied many of his ideas and interests. But it has also been shown that the roots of what was achieved there are to be found in experiments already begun in London parishes by clergymen like Fremantle and Barnett in the 1870s.[39] And Fremantle and Barnett had derived their ideas from Oxford liberalism of the 1850s. There was far more continuity, in fact, between the social concern of the very end of the nineteenth century and earlier liberalism than has often been recognised. But Toynbee Hall was, in any case, a great deal more than a social mission. It attempted to provide not merely contact between university undergraduates and the working-class Londoners. It provided educational extension, practical action for health and sanitation, charitable relief, Bible classes, games, and a wide variety of resources of one kind and another.

Social concern, powered by intense if unconventional religion, was characteristic of Balliol under Caird. Indeed the tradition continued long after Caird in the masterships of A. L. Smith and A. D.

[37] *Industrial Revolution*, p. 238.
[38] *Leaflet for Working Men No. 1—The Church and the People*, printed in *Industrial Revolution*, p. xxvi. The italics are in the original.
[39] L. E. Nettleship, pp. 564ff.

Lindsay, becoming gradually more and more concerned with the structure of society and less with charity, social mobility, and elitism. But its characteristics continued to be 'moral convictions strongly held and vigorously defended' and 'an image of a good society'.[40]

R. H. Tawney, whose concerns and interests were very much in the Toynbee pattern, was a later product of this tradition. He became an undergraduate at Balliol in the last year of the nineteenth century, and returned as a fellow from immediately after the First World War until he became Professor of Economic History at London from 1931 to 1949. Like Toynbee his area of interest was the connection between economics, politics, and morality and, in a sense, the motivating force behind his concern was a religious one. But, in spite of the fact that his famous *Religion and the Rise of Capitalism* was to be dedicated to Charles Gore, he was concerned neither with the niceties of orthodox doctrine nor with the institutional Church. He was passionate about social and political morality,[41] and (like Green) he took seriously the practical, even small-scale political activities which could improve the state of the disadvantaged.

A great deal of Tawney's time was given to the Workers Educational Association, which enlisted the support of many younger Christians who believed in the necessity of changing society. He was a member of the WEA executive for over forty years from 1905 and its president from 1928 until 1944. The moving spirit behind the association in its early days was Albert Mansbridge of the Co-operative Wholesale Society who was concerned not only to persuade trade unionists that education was a socially emancipating force but also to ensure that the education offered to them was the kind of education they themselves wanted—not what others thought might be good for them. Since it was hoped that this new kind of education would be offered through existing universities, the movement issued a challenge to Oxford not just to open itself to others besides

---

[40] Davis, p. 266.
[41] See R. H. Preston's essay, 'R. H. Tawney as a Christian Moralist', in *Religion and the Persistence of Capitalism*, London 1979, pp. 83ff.

the middle classes but to change both the manner and the content of its teaching.

Some dons, like A. L. Smith—who had been appointed to Balliol as fellow and tutor in history in 1882, had been one of Jowett's most ardent disciples in his last years,[42] and was to become master himself in 1924—were whole-hearted supporters of the movement. But most senior members of the university did not want Oxford's middle-class life or its traditional pattern of study to be seriously disturbed. When Charles Gore raised the question of university reform in the House of Lords in 1907, he provoked considerable resentment.

The WEA became for a time an important organisation, though its achievements were never as revolutionary as the rhetoric on both sides implied. Virtually every university in the country was persuaded to support a central joint advisory committee to back its work. Summer schools and extension lecture courses made it possible for men and women who had no opportunity to become undergraduates to encounter some of the features of a university education. But it has to be said that the universities themselves, and the kind of education and opportunities they offered, hardly changed at all.

Many of the meetings connected with the life of the WEA were held in Balliol and many of those connected with it were Balliol men. One of these was William Temple (president of the WEA from 1908), in whom, in a remarkable way, all the strands of what might be called the Jowett tradition seem to come together and culminate. He was Tawney's friend and contemporary at Rugby and became an undergraduate at Balliol from the autumn of 1900. Caird, as master, was at his height. He had had time to settle in and gain control but was not yet ailing. And to his genius Temple 'was drawn as by a magnet'.[43]

In one sense, of course, a liberal approach to Christianity was nothing new to the young Temple. In spite of the fact that Jowett

---

[42] Smith published a brief updated memoir of Jowett (*Reminiscences of Jowett* by A.L.S.) which clearly reveals how Jowett was able, even as an old man, to evoke hero-worship from much younger people.

[43] [F. A.] Iremonger, [*William Temple, Archbishop of Canterbury*, London 1948], p. 39.

had regarded Frederick Temple as a traitor to the liberal cause, the archbishop had continued to be receptive to at least some of the ideas of science and criticism. His Bampton lectures of 1884 were cautious and hesitant. He laid great emphasis upon the hypothetical and incomplete character of Darwin's argument. He tended to regard evolution and natural selection as programmed into creation, so that the living beings which emerged from the process could be said to have been intended from the beginning.[44] He refused to believe that Paley's argument from design had been drastically undermined by Darwin.[45] He continued to assert that man was, at least in his moral aspect, a kind of 'special creation'.[46] And he took up some of Herbert Spencer's ideas as a way of incorporating evolution into a religious view of the universe. But the very fact that a bishop of the Church of England could deliver such lectures, accepting evolution and making positive use of critical scholarship in order to do so, was a significant thing. Owen Chadwick has, indeed, asserted that it was Temple's Bampton lectures which marked the final acceptance of evolution as a permissible doctrine among clergymen of the Church of England.[47]

Frederick Temple appears to have been a very powerful and dominating figure in his home. William—even as a late adolescent—was, perhaps, a little too inclined to allow his father to make his mind up for him.[48] At any rate he seems to have acquired from him an openness to liberal ideas tempered by a veneration for the institutional Church and its traditions. Rugby, where he went to school, was still the home of the liberal intellectual tradition established under Arnold, Tait, and Frederick Temple, in spite of a brief attempt by the governors to change things in the aftermath of *Essays and Reviews*.[49] And if Rugby was the school for William, Balliol was inevitably the college. 'Better at Balliol with nothing than at Trinity with an Exhibition', his father insisted.[50]

[44] F. Temple, [*The Relations between Religion and Science*, London 1885], pp. 113f.
[45] F. Temple, pp. 111f.
[46] Ibid. pp. 172ff.
[47] O. Chadwick, *The Victorian Church*, London 1966, ii, p. 23.
[48] Iremonger, p. 3.
[49] Sandford, ii, p. 625f.
[50] Iremonger, p. 37.

At Oxford Temple began to develop a concern for the condition of society. He became involved with boys' clubs, settlements, and—through Tawney's influence—the Workers Educational Association. This last his biographer regarded as the means of his 'emancipation' from the conventionally comfortable background in which he grew up.[51] But there was a sense in which that emancipation was probably never complete. Temple never seemed to develop a satisfactory theory of Christian social action as anything other than a matter of private, individual morality.[52] It is true that his earliest writings contain hints that he held an Hegelian view of the state, in which the individual was of slight importance as compared with corporate society.[53] But this line of thought, which was no doubt part of his inheritance from Caird, Temple never fully developed.

In part, no doubt, this was because it was submerged (as it often was even in Caird himself) by other strands of the liberal theological tradition. The liberals had always tended, after all, to try and make sense of Christian theology in terms of individual, subjective, human experience. That was how Jowett himself had dealt with the atonement. The corporate and the objective aspect of the doctrine was much more difficult. Even the *Lux Mundi* group, with their catholic view of the Church, often seem more at home when they can talk about what lies within the personal experience of the individual. It is not surprising, then, that someone who inherited that tradition should, even in the political sphere, be inclined to individualism. Even Green and Caird had been somewhat ambiguous on the subject of society. They had said a great deal about the importance of each man serving the whole but there remained much that was strongly individualistic about their thinking.

The influence of Caird's Idealism Temple never threw off entirely. He owed his first introduction to formal philosophy to the

[51] Iremonger, pp. 73ff.

[52] P. Hinchliff, 'Can the Church "Do" Politics?, *Theology*, 84 (1981), pp. 345f. On Temple's political thought see also A. Suggate, 'William Temple and the challenge of Reinhold Niebuhr', *Theology*, 84 (1981), pp. 413ff.

[53] See e.g. *The Education of Citizens*, a published address of 12 pages, dated 1905. There is a copy in Lambeth Palace library. I am indebted to Stephen Spencer, a former pupil of mine now working on Temple's social thought, for drawing my attention to this pamphlet and its significance.

master and it coloured all his later thought. It is difficult now to judge his significance as a philosopher. Nor is it entirely easy to say how far he was really to develop into an independent thinker. Though he clearly moved away from the line of thought derived from Kant and Hegel by the Idealists and returned more directly to Plato, the shift in his thought often seems to be as much the result of a reconciliation with orthodox Christian doctrine as a specifically *philosophical* development.[54]

Temple became a fellow of Queen's College after taking his degree and then went through a period of wondering whether his beliefs were sufficiently orthodox to enable him to be ordained. The Bishop of Oxford thought they were not but eventually Randall Davidson, Frederick Temple's successor at Canterbury, made him a deacon in 1908. Some lectures, published in 1910,[55] seem to have convinced the archbishop that his theology was sound. Though they reveal very clearly his debt to Caird they also indicate that his thought had begun to move towards a more conventional orthodoxy.

Like Caird, he desired to adopt a 'scientific' approach to religion,[56] and to insist that the world was a single coherent system.[57] But there was also a good deal in the lectures which read like an echo of Jowett. There was an emphasis upon the importance of experience and a very obvious personal devotion to the Jesus of the Gospels: Christ is represented as the culminating point of all religion and ethics. This was something that separated Temple's thought from that of Caird. Whenever he wrote about Jesus Christ, he plainly conceived himself to be discussing a real historical person rather than some kind of demythologised ideal truth. He possessed that same sense of 'friendship' with an actual person which had been such a feature of Jowett's religious life. Temple's treatment of the atonement included a criticism of satisfaction theology which was as sharp as Jowett's, though he recognised—as Jowett had not—that there was something to be

[54] For a contemporary assessment of Temple as a philosopher see Dorothy Emmet in Iremonger, pp. 521ff. and cf. W. R. Matthews, 'William Temple as a Thinker' in *William Temple: An Estimation and Appreciation*, London 1946.
[55] [W. Temple], *The Faith and Modern Thought*, [London 1910].
[56] *The Faith and Modern Thought*, p. 2.
[57] Ibid. p. 3.

said for it. On the basis of the fourth Gospel he insisted that the proper way to consider the atonement was simply as an expression of love. Love works by sacrifice, he said, that is always the mode of its operation.[58] And, finally, he had as strong a sense of the continuous moral progress of humanity as Jowett.[59]

The same line of developing thought can be found in an essay Temple (by this time headmaster of Repton) contributed to the volume called *Foundations* which appeared two years later.[60] The book, satirised by that other Balliol man, Ronald Knox, in 'Absolute and Abitofhell',[61] was edited by B. H. Streeter who had been a colleague of Temple's at Queen's and had played some part in convincing him that he could conscientiously go forward to ordination.[62]

There was an historical irony about the volume. There were seven contributors, just as there had been in the case of *Essays and Reviews*, and all were Oxford men. One of them (Temple himself) was the son of a contributor to *Essays and Reviews*. Two of the others (Neville Talbot and W. H. Moberly) were sons of members of the *Lux Mundi* group. This, no doubt coincidental, coming together of two rather different traditions in liberal theology reflected something of importance in Temple's own life. Most of the contributors to *Foundations* belonged somewhat vaguely in the tradition of liberal Anglo-Catholicism. Perhaps because he shared their political concerns, Temple had already begun to draw closer to members of that group. Scott Holland had been one of those who had helped to persuade him that he was sufficiently orthodox to be ordained.[63] As early as 1908 he had begun to rely on Gore for help and advice. His biography does not explain how this close relationship arose, but it is clear that Temple always consulted Gore when he had an important decision to make. Eventually he came to regard Gore as the person

---

[58] *The Faith and Modern Thought*, pp. 133f. and 136.
[59] Ibid. p. 145.
[60] [B. H. Streeter (ed.),] *Foundations*[: *A Statement of Christian Belief in Terms of Modern Thought*, London 1912.
[61] In the *Oxford Magazine*, Nov. 1912, and reprinted in *In Three Tongues* (ed. L. E. Byres), London 1959, pp. 112ff.
[62] Iremonger, pp. 108f.
[63] Iremonger, pp. 108ff. and n.b. p. 126.

'to whom more than any other (despite great differences) I owe my apprehension of the truth'.[64]

Streeter himself, the editor of the volume, was the odd man out, in the sense of being the least obviously concerned with maintaining traditional orthodoxy. He was, of course, an eminent New Testament scholar but he was also determined that Christian thought should be rendered in terms which he regarded as consonant with contemporary ideas. The volume professed to be a 'statement of Christian belief in terms of modern thought' and the introductory chapter describing 'The Modern Situation' was written by Neville Talbot, chaplain and fellow of Balliol. Talbot was not himself a product of the Jowett/Caird tradition: his chapter reflected the attitudes and thinking of younger Anglo-Catholic 'socialists'. It was self-consciously post-Victorian; arguing that, after Darwin, and in an age when the belief in the inevitability of progress had collapsed, the world was a much wilder and more frightening place. His only reference to *Essays and Reviews* was a somewhat oblique one in a footnote:[65] *Lux Mundi* was not mentioned at all.

Foundations derived some notoriety from Streeter's own essay on the historic Christ which was much influenced by what Albert Schweitzer had written in *The Quest of the Historical Jesus* and adopted a sceptical attitude to the possibility of reconstructing an accurate account of the Jesus of history. Largely because of this essay, the volume made something of a stir but its impact was weakened by an unconvincing optimism. The contributors strove to recapture the immanentist approach of Idealists like T. H. Green which, as Talbot admitted,[66] had already begun to seem out of date. Talbot's opening chapter, in fact, was typical. He insisted that the very morbidity of contemporary society was a sign of hope; 'A knowledge of darkness is needed to urge indolent man upon the quest after light.'[67] It was an optimism of passion, unable to cite any specific evidence to justify itself.

By this time Temple had come to adopt a Christocentric and

[64] Iremonger, p. 488, quoting Temple's dedication to Gore of *Studies in the Spirit and Truth of Christianity*.
[65] *Foundations*, pp. 6f.
[66] *Foundations*, p. 8.
[67] *Foundations*, p. 24.

incarnational emphasis in theology, very reminiscent of *Lux Mundi* and therefore consonant with the optimistic immanentism of much of the volume. His own essay on the divinity of Christ was much more orthodox than Streeter's. It followed the same sort of outline as his chapter on the atonement in *The Faith and Modern Thought*, though it was, perhaps, aimed at a somewhat more academic audience. He maintained that it was wrong to start a consideration of the divinity of Christ from the question whether this historical, human person was also divine. Instead he wished to argue that the correct approach was 'to take Jesus as the embodiment of the Supreme Principle, and to believe that its nature is the character of Jesus'.[68] The whole chapter was based, like the conclusion of his earlier lecture, on the fourth Gospel: its text stood below the chapter heading—'Lord, shew us the Father, and it sufficeth us'. The essay was, in fact, a solid, learned and well-constructed *sermon*, concluding with a triumphant rhetorical flourish in which there were many echoes of Caird. When, Temple proclaimed, all men have been drawn in to the purposes of God and have come to constitute 'One Perfect Man', then 'for the first time will the Divinity of Christ be fully manifest; then for the first time will the God in Christ be fully known.'[69]

Temple's vigorous struggle to reconcile his early liberalism with orthodoxy was best revealed by *Mens Creatrix*, a substantial attempt at a restatement of all the main themes of Christian doctrine. Though the book was not published till 1917 (by which time he had become the incumbent of St James's Piccadilly) he claimed in the preface that he had planned it as early as 1908 and had been working on it ever since. The themes and the approach of *The Faith and Modern Thought* and of the essay in *Foundations* are still easily recognisable. Three years of the war do not seem to have had any very marked influence on the Platonic serenity of his ideas for he could write that 'all history appears as the method of the Divine Love.'[70]

Temple dedicated the book to his father and claimed that St John, Plato, and Browning were 'the master-influences' upon his own

---

[68] *Foundations*, p. 215.
[69] *Foundations*, p. 263.
[70] [W. Temple], *Mens Creatrix*, [London 1917,] p. 290.

thinking.⁷¹ This odd triumvirate reveals that *Mens Creatrix* was, in fact, a book rooted much more firmly in the late nineteenth century—in Jowett's world—than in the last years of the First World War. All three had been favourites of Jowett's. To Plato he had returned after his flirtation with Hegel. St John, he had thought, was able to represent Truth in history in a way Hegel had failed to do and the 'idealised life of Christ' which he had hoped to write would surely have been based more closely on the fourth Gospel than anything else. Browning had been a close friend of Jowett and an honorary fellow of Balliol.⁷² Jowett regarded him as a greater poet than Tennyson,⁷³ and thought his poems, 'Christmas Eve' and 'Easter Day', his 'noblest work': 'The first poem . . . seems to rest on the love of God, which embraces the vulgarest of human beings; the second expresses the beating of the human soul against God and nature, aspiring but unsatisfied.'⁷⁴

It is fairly clear that, whether he knew it or not, William Temple stood in the tradition created by Jowett at Balliol—provided that one remembers that that tradition consisted of the large generalised ideas, rather than the specific details of what Jowett had advocated. As with most traditions, those who belonged to it derived certain principles from it and set themselves to maintain those principles rather than any particular manifestations of them. It was part of the tradition that one should take the results of the natural sciences seriously and adopt a critical approach to the study of scripture. An idealist framework of thought had also become part of the tradition, though it was only tenuously connected with Jowett's enthusiasm for Plato and his early interest in Kant and Hegel. In a similar way, perhaps, a passion for social and political morality—which had developed far beyond Jowett's tentative concern—was part of it, too. And there was—much more directly Jowettian—a vivid sense of the nearness of the divine and a devotion to the person of Christ.

It is even possible that Temple came closer to Jowett's own

---

[71] *Mens Creatrix*, p. viii.
[72] Browning was made an honorary fellow in 1867, before Jowett became master but after he had gained effective control of the college.
[73] Abbott and Campbell, i, pp. 400ff.
[74] Abbott and Campbell, ii, p. 355.

position than did any of the other thinkers whose ideas have been examined. Gore began with a determined adherence to dogmatic orthodoxy which set very specific limits about his 'liberalism'. Green and Caird had been committed to an idealist system which would only permit the acceptance of a Christianity detached from the historical. Temple, like Jowett, aimed, in intention at least, at a genuine and open search for the truth. What he arrived at was, in effect and again like Jowett's, an attempt at a *personal*—even an *ad hoc*—synthesis of faith and enquiry. It had been an essential part of Jowett's approach that religious and theological knowledge was to be obtained by reflection upon experience unrestricted by the demands of a system. Inevitably, what one arrived at would be *one's own* understanding of truth.

But Temple's was also arguably the most satisfactory attempt to give expression to the tradition which Jowett had set himself to create. For one thing he brought liberal theology back into the orthodox mainstream of Anglicanism, without committing himself too firmly to any one particular school of churchmanship as Gore had done. He felt no compulsion to justify every aspect of patristic and 'catholic' orthodoxy, yet it was plainly his intention to come to terms with, reinterpret, and make the best possible case for, the central truths of classical Christian doctrine. This was not wholly different from the way in which Jowett had attempted to deal with the atonement in the 1850s but it had an entirely opposite *direction* from the arguments Jowett had so often enunciated in his sermons as master. While Jowett had always tended to stress the need to be independent of classical dogma and to think for oneself, Temple more commonly attempted to demonstrate that thinking clearly for oneself would bring one back to something like orthodox belief. At the same time, though he abandoned the idealist system developed by Green and Caird, Temple claimed to have a philosophically justifiable methodology and, as a result, his ideas were more coherent, less occasional, less subject to internal contradiction than Jowett's.

William Temple died in 1944, almost exactly a hundred years after Jowett and Stanley had set out on their campaign to make the university of Oxford conform, even in the study of theology, to the principle that education was an enquiry after truth not the transmission of correct answers. Partly because of their efforts, the theological climate had changed almost out of all recognition. Theological enquiry, biblical criticism, and a scientific world-view had all been accepted as perfectly proper concomitants of religious truth. Universities had ceased to be places for the entrenchment of dogmatic orthodoxy—at least in theology. What academics believed in matters of religion had become their own private affair. The strait-jacket in which Jowett had felt his deeply religious beliefs to be constrained would be difficult even to imagine.

Anthony Quinton, writing about the British Idealists, has argued:

> Philosophical movements lead two different lives. On the one hand a body of ideas is formulated, published, accepted, and finally superseded; on the other, at the institutional level, leading positions in the academic system are occupied by the exponents of the movement's ideas. Naturally these two careers are not coincident in time. New ideas are normally produced by unimportant people; the holders of important posts disseminate the ideas they acquired in their comparatively unimportant youth.[75]

He also points out that the Idealists 'continued to be the largest group in the philosophical professoriate until 1945'.[76] Temple's death, therefore, coincided with the end of the institutional dominance of the Idealist school of philosophy. Part of the great success of his theological synthesis was a result of the fact that he worked in a world which was dominated by a philosophy naturally hospitable to religious ideas and one which had grown out of the same tradition which he himself represented.

It is some measure of Jowett's importance in the history of Anglican thought that he initiated a tradition which provided some of the impetus not only for that theology but also for the philosophical context in which it was able to succeed. This is not to ignore the originality of Green, Caird, or Temple, but the fact remains that it was Jowett who first made it possible to develop a positive but liberal theology because he perceived that, to do so, one needed to capture an institution within which to operate. What he was not

---

[75] Quinton, p. 303.
[76] Ibid. p. 304.

ultimately capable of conferring upon it was the respectability necessary for it to pass into the thought of the Church as a whole. For that it needed the philosophical climate created by Idealists like Green and Caird and the ecclesiastical eminence of exponents like Gore and Temple. These last two had both, in different ways, attempted to reunite liberalism with something more like conventional orthodoxy. But they were able to make what they derived from the liberal tradition into something richer and more satisfactory, largely because they were aided by Idealist philosophy. As long as that philosophy was dominant, it was possible to produce a convincing justification for a theology which combined liberal enquiry, basic orthodoxy, and a 'modern' world-view. They made liberalism respectable because they made it successful by showing that faith could be compatible with both integrity and intellectual brilliance.

Bibliography

Abbott, E. and Campbell, L., *The Life and Letters of Benjamin Jowett*, 2 vols., London 1897
Abbott, T. K., *Kant's Critique of Practical Reason*, 4th edition, London 1889
Anonymous, 'Mr Jowett and Oxford Liberalism', *Blackwood's Edinburgh Magazine*, 161 (1897)
Arnold, T., *Principles of Church Reform, With an Introductory Essay by M. J. Jackson and J. Rogan*, London 1962
Barr, J., 'Jowett and the "Original Meaning" of Scripture', *Journal of Religious Studies*, 18 (1982)
—— 'Jowett and the Reading of the Bible "Like Any Other Book"', *Horizons in Biblical Theology*, 4 (1982)
Bebbington, D. W., 'Nonconformity and Electoral Sociology, 1867–1918', *The Historical Journal*, 27 (1984)
Bill, E. G. W., *University Reform in Nineteenth Century Oxford: A Study of Henry Halford Vaughan, 1811–1885*, Oxford 1973
—— and Mason, J. F. A. *Christ Church and Reform, 1850–1867*, Oxford 1970
Brent, R., 'The Emergence of Liberal Anglican Politics: The Whigs and the Church, 1830–1841', Oxford University D. Phil. thesis, 1984
Caird, E., 'The Genius of Carlyle', *Essays on Literature and Philosophy*, Glasgow 1892
—— *The Evolution of Religion*, 2 vols., Glasgow 1893
—— 'Professor Jowett', *International Journal of Ethics*, October 1897
—— *Lay Sermons and Addresses delivered in the Hall of Balliol College, Oxford*, Glasgow 1907
Campbell, L., *On the Nationalisation of the Old English Universities*, London 1901
Carpenter, J., *Gore: A Study in Liberal Catholic Thought*, London 1960
Chadwick, O. *The Mind of the Oxford Movement*, London 1960
—— *The Victorian Church*, 2 vols., London 1966
Cockshut, A. O. J., *Anglican Attitudes: A Study of Victorian Religious Controversies*, London 1959
Copleston, F., *History of Philosophy*, New York 1965

Corsi, P., 'Natural Theology, Methodology of Science and the Question of Species in the Works of the Reverend Baden Powell', Oxford University D.Phil. thesis, 1980
Cosslett, T. (ed.), *Science and Religion in the Nineteenth Century*, Cambridge 1984
Cox, G. W., *Life of John William Colenso DD, Bishop of Natal*, 2 vols., London 1888
Crawfurd, J., 'On Language as a Test of the Races of Man', *Transactions of the Ethnological Society*, New Series, 3 (1865)
—— 'On the Supposed Infecundity of Human Hybrids or Crosses', *Transactions of the Ethnological Society*, New Series, 3 (1865)
Cupitt, D., 'Darwinism and English Religious Thought', *Theology*, 78 (1975)
Davidson, R. T., *Life of Archibald Campbell Tait*, 2 vols., London 1891
Davis, H. W. C., *History of Balliol College*, revised by R. H. C. Davis and R. Hunt, Oxford 1963
Durant, J., *Darwinism and Divinity*, Oxford 1985
Ellis, I., 'Jowett's Dutch Degree' in *Balliol College Annual Record*, 1979
—— *Seven Against Christ*, Leiden 1980
—— 'Pusey and University Reform', in P. Butler (ed.), *Pusey Rediscovered*, London 1983
—— 'Dean Farrar and the Quest for the Historical Jesus', *Theology*, 89 (1986)
Engel, A. J., *From Clergyman to Don: The Rise of the Academic Profession in Nineteenth Century Oxford*, Oxford 1983
Faber, G., *Jowett, a Portrait with Background*, London 1957
Farrar, F. W., *History of Interpretation*, London 1886
—— 'Language and Ethnology', *Transactions of the Ethnological Society*, New Series, 4 (1866)
Foot, M. R. D. and Matthew, H. C. G., *The Gladstone Diaries*, iv, Oxford 1974
Fremantle, W. H., *Recollections of Dean Fremantle, chiefly by himself*, edited by the Master of the Temple, London 1921
Gillespie, N. C., *Charles Darwin and the Problem of Creation*, Chicago 1979
Gore, C., 'The Holy Spirit and Inspiration', *Lux Mundi*, London 1889
—— *Can We Then Believe?*, London 1926
—— *Christ and Society*, London 1928
Greaves, R. W., 'Golightly and Newman, 1824–1845', *Journal of Ecclesiastical History*, 9 (1958)

Griffin, J. R., 'The Radical Phase of the Oxford Movement', *Journal of Ecclesiastical History*, 27 (1976)
—— *The Oxford Movement: A Revision*, Front Royal, Virginia 1980
Harvey, V. A., *The Historian and the Believer*, London 1967
Helfand, M. S., 'T. H. Huxley's "Ethics and Evolution": The Politics of Evolution and the Evolution of Politics', *Victorian Studies*, 20 (1977)
Hinchliff, P., *John William Colenso: Bishop of Natal*, London 1964
—— 'Benjamin Jowett and the Church of England: Or Why really great men are never clergymen.', in John Prest (ed.), *Balliol Studies*, London 1982
—— 'Can the Church "Do" Politics?', *Theology*, 84 (1981)
—— 'Jowett and Gore: Two Balliol Essayists', *Theology*, 87 (1984)
—— 'Ethics, Evolution and Biblical Criticism in the Thought of Benjamin Jowett and John William Colenso', in *Journal of Ecclesiastical History*, 37 (1986)
Hort, A. F., *Life and Letters of Fenton John Anthony Hort*, 2 vols., London 1896
Hort, F. J. A., Review of Jowett's commentaries in *Journal of Classical and Sacred Philology*, 2 (1856)
Howes, G., 'Dr Arnold and Bishop Stanley', in G. J. Cuming (ed.), *Studies in Church History*, ii, London 1965
Huxley, T. H., *Method and Results*, London 1893
—— *Evolution and Ethics and Other Essays*, London 1894
Iremonger, F. A., *William Temple, Archbishop of Canterbury*, London 1948
Jarrett-Kerr, M., 'W. H. Mallock: Radical Tory, Romantic Classicist', *P. N. Review*, 43 (1984)
Jones, H. and Muirhead, J. H., *The Life and Philosophy of Edward Caird*, Glasgow 1921
Jones, J., 'A Contested Mastership: the Election of Jowett's Successor', *Balliol College Annual Record*, 1977
—— 'Sound Religion and Useful Learning: The rise of Balliol under John Parsons and Richard Jenkyns, 1798–1854', in John Prest (ed.), *Balliol Studies*, London 1982
Jowett, B., *The Epistles of St Paul to the Thessalonians, Galatians and Romans*, 2 vols., London 1855
—— *The Epistles of St Paul to the Thessalonians, Galatians, Romans, with critical notes and dissertations*, 2 vols., 2nd edition, London 1859
—— 'On the Interpretation of Scripture', *Essays and Reviews*, London 1860
—— *College Sermons*, ed. W. H. Fremantle, London 1895

―― *Sermons: Biographical and Miscellaneous*, ed. W. H. Fremantle, London 1899

―― *Sermons on Faith and Doctrine*, ed. W. H. Fremantle, London 1901

Kadish, A., *Apostle Arnold, the Life and Death of Arnold Toynbee*, Durham, North Carolina 1986

Knox, R., 'Absolute and Abitofhell', *Oxford Magazine*, November 1912, and reprinted in *In Three Tongues* ed. L. E. Byres, London 1959

Lewis, H. D., 'The British Idealists' in N. Smart, J. Clayton, P. Sherry and S. T. Katz (eds.), *Nineteenth Century Religious Thought in the West*, ii, Cambridge 1985

Liddon, H. P., *The Divinity of Our Lord*, 8th edition London 1878

Lockhart, J. G., *Cosmo Gordon Lang*, London 1949

Mackinnon, D. M., 'Some Aspects of the Treatment of Christianity by the British Idealists', *Journal of Religious Studies*, 20 (1983)

Macquarrie, J., 'Kenoticism Reconsidered', *Theology*, 77 (1974)

Major, S. H., 'Lux Mundi: A Reassessment', *Church Quarterly Review*, 166 (1965)

Mallock, W. H., *The New Republic*, 2 vols., London 1877

―― *Memoirs of Life and Literature*, London 1920

Marsh, P. T., 'The Primate and the Prime Minister: Archbishop Tait, Gladstone and the National Church', *Victorian Studies*, 9 (1965)

Matthews, W. R. et al., *William Temple: An Estimation and Appreciation*, London 1946

Montague, F. C., 'Arnold Toynbee', *Johns Hopkins University Studies in Historical and Political Science*, 7 (1889)

Moore, J. R., *The Post-Darwinian Controversies*, Cambridge 1979

―― 'Herbert Spencer's Henchmen: The Evolution of Protestant Liberals in Late Nineteenth Century America', in Durant, J. (ed.), *Darwinism and Divinity*, Oxford 1985

Nettleship, L. E., 'William Fremantle, Samuel Barnett and the Broad Church Origin of Toynbee Hall', *Journal of Ecclesiastical History*, 33 (1982)

Nettleship, R. L. (ed.), *Works of Thomas Hill Green*, 3 vols., London 1886–90

Newsome, D., *Two Classes of Men: Platonism and English Romantic Thought*, London 1972

―― 'The Assault on Mammon: Charles Gore and John Neville Figgis', *Journal of Ecclesiastical History*, 17 (1966)

Nicholls, D., 'Conscience and Authority in the Thought of W. G. Ward', *Heythrop Journal*, 26 (1985)

Nimmo, D., 'Learning against religion, learning as religion: Mark Pattison and the Victorian crisis of Faith', in K. Robbins (ed.), *Studies in Church History*, xvii, Oxford 1987

Paget, S., *Henry Scott Holland: Memoir and Letters*, London 1921

Paley, W., *Works: Complete in One Volume, to which is Prefixed the Life of the Author*, London 1851

Pals, D. L., *The Victorian 'Lives' of Jesus*, San Antonio 1982

Powell, B., 'On the Study of the Evidences of Christianity', *Essays and Reviews*, London 1860

Prest, J. M., *Jowett's Correspondence on Education with Earl Russell in 1867*, supplement to the Balliol College Record 1965

—— *Robert Scott and Benjamin Jowett*, supplement to Balliol College Record 1966

Prestige, G. L., *Life of Charles Gore*, London 1935

Preston, R. H., *Religion and the Persistence of Capitalism*, London 1979

Quinton, A. M., 'Absolute Idealism', *Proceedings of the British Academy*, 57 (1971)

Ramsey, A. M., *From Gore to Temple*, London 1960

Rogerson, J., *Old Testament Criticism in the Nineteenth Century: England and Germany*, London 1984

Romanes, G. J., *Thoughts on Religion*, ed. C. Gore, London 1896

Rothblatt, S., 'The Student Sub-Culture and the Examination System in Early Nineteenth Century Oxbridge', in L. Stone (ed.), *The University and Society*, Princeton 1974

Rowell, G., *The Vision Glorious: Themes and Personalities of the Catholic Revival in Anglicanism*, Oxford 1983

Ruse, M., 'The Relationship between Science and Religion in Britain, 1830–1870', *Church History*, 44 (1975)

Sandford, E. G., (ed.), *Memoirs of Archbishop Temple*, 2 vols., London 1906

Schmidt, C., 'Classical Studies at Balliol in the 1860's: The undergraduate essays of Gerard Manley Hopkins', in John Prest (ed.). *Balliol Studies*, London 1982

Scott, P. G., 'A. H. Clough: A Case Study in Victorian Doubt', in D. Baker (ed.), *Studies in Church History*, ix, Cambridge 1972

Seth, A. and Haldane, R. B., (eds.), *Essays in Philosophical Criticism*, London 1883

Simon, W. M., 'Auguste Comte's English Disciples', *Victorian Studies*, 7 (1964)

Smith, T., 'The Balliol Trinity Laboratory', in John Prest (ed.), *Balliol Studies*, London 1982

Stanley, A. P., *The Life and Correspondence of Thomas Arnold*, 6th edition, London 1846

Stephen, L., 'Jowett's Life', *Studies of a Biographer*, 2nd edition, 2 vols., London 1910

Stephenson, A. M. G., *The Rise and Decline of English Modernism*, London 1984

Streeter, B. H. (ed.), *Foundations: A Statement of Christian Belief in Terms of Modern Thought*, London 1912

Suggate, A., 'William Temple and the challenge of Reinhold Niebuhr', *Theology*, 84 (1981)

Swanston, H. F. G., *Ideas of Order: Anglicans and the renewal of theological method in the middle years of the 19th century*, Assen 1974

Sykes, S. W., *The Identity of Christianity*, London 1984

Temple, F., *The Relations between Religion and Science*, London 1885

Temple, W., *The Education of Citizens*, London 1905

—— *The Faith and Modern Thought*, London 1910

—— 'The Divinity of Christ', in B. H. Streeter (ed.), *Foundations: A Statement of Christian Belief in Terms of Modern Thought*, London 1912

—— *Mens Creatrix*, London 1917

Toynbee, A., *Lectures on the Industrial Revolution in England*, London 1884

Vincent, A. and Plant, R., *Philosophy, Politics and Citizenship: The Life and Thought of the British Idealists*, Oxford 1984

Ward, W., *William George Ward and the Oxford Movement*, London 1889

—— *William George Ward and the Catholic Revival*, London 1893

Ward, W. R., *Victorian Oxford*, London 1965

—— 'Oxford and the Origins of Liberal Catholicism in the Church of England', in C. W. Dugmore and C. Duggan (eds.), *Studies in Church History*, i, London 1964

Wiles, M. F., *Faith and the Mystery of God*, London 1982

Index

Abercrombie, Lady 203
Aberdeen, Lord 26, 33
Adullam, Cave of 102
Africa 189–90
All Souls College 146, 207
Anglo-Catholics 34, 119, 168, 172, 176, 177, 226, 227
Arches, Court of 92
Arnold, T. 8, 9, 10, 16, 17, 26, 27, 28, 31, 32, 46, 47, 48, 49, 69, 71, 73, 76, 219–20, 223
atonement, doctrine of 55, 61, 62, 63, 64, 86, 116, 122, 126, 131, 136, 139, 174
Authorised Version 45

Balliol College 1, 7, 9, 14, 15, 16, 27, 40, 43, 44, 64, 71, 72, 77, 78, 80, 88, 92, 95, 101, 104, 107, 109–10, 118, 121, 147, 148, 149, 150, 157, 158, 161, 165, 167, 174–5, 176, 177, 192, 207, 209, 210, 216, 219, 221, 222, 223
Bandinel, Dr 92
Barnett, S. 217, 220
Baur, F. C. 54, 84, 160–1
belief 58–61
Bentham, J. 17, 99
Beza, T. 45
biblical criticism 20, 31, 38, 54, 55, 75, 84, 108, 126, 129, 130–3, 137, 142, 143, 144, 160, 162, 168–9, 171, 177, 206, 223, 231
Blackwood's Magazine 71
Blundell's School 7, 16, 27, 35
Broad Churchmen 21, 26, 27, 69, 72, 98, 99, 108, 148, 207
Brodie, B. 22, 23, 25, 37, 58, 145, 183
Browning, R. 229
Bunsen, Baron von 72
Butler, Bishop 141

Caird, E. 88, 90, 100, 108, 149, 157, 165, 209–16, 220, 222, 224, 225, 228, 230, 231
Caird, J. 211
Campbell, L. 149, 191
Camperdown, Lord 95, 203
Carlisle cathedral 19
Carlyle, T. 211
catechetical lectures 4, 5, 114
Chambers, R. 23, 183
chapel, college 108, 110–11, 114, 115, 116, 134, 147, 171
chapel services 147–9, 196–7
Christ, life of 115, 124, 137–9
Christ Church 93
Christology 75, 109, 123, 126, 130–2, 137, 139, 140, 168, 228
Church, R. 7
civil service: British 26, 37; Indian 26, 36, 93, 153, 193
Cleveland, Duke of 192
Clough, A. H. 158–9, 212
Colenso, J. W. 20, 71, 76, 96, 102, 107, 108, 112, 169, 189–91
Coleridge, S. T. 76
Commissions, Royal 7, 26, 29, 32, 34, 37, 151, 192–3
Comte, A. 77, 78, 199
convocation of Canterbury 91
Copleston, E. 8, 9, 10
Court of Arches 92
court of the university 92
creeds 178

Darwin, C. 23, 119, 163, 173, 183–92, 199, 200, 208, 223, 227
Davidson, R. 225
deism 22, 23, 58, 81, 140, 183, 185
Derby, Lord 34, 103
dialectic, Hegelian 82
Disraeli, B. 190
dissenters 9, 14, 29, 34, 37, 38, 104

dogma 132, 133, 178, 207, 230
dons 6, 15, 192, 222

eclecticism 88–9, 188
economics 217–19, 221
education 103–6, 217, 221–2
education of women 217
Eliot, George 78, 113, 202
Erasmus 45
Erastianism 98–9
Essays and Reviews 8, 23, 68, 69–76, 84, 89, 90, 91, 94, 106, 108, 109, 110, 111, 114, 118, 122, 133, 134, 138, 153, 167, 168, 181, 182, 183, 223, 226, 227
Evangelicals 18, 19, 62, 69, 90, 97, 134, 152, 153, 174, 194
evolution 23, 141, 183–92, 186, 214
Ewald, H. 54
examination system 3, 4, 6, 28, 29, 32

Farrar, F. W. 194
Fichte, J. G. 79, 84
Foundations 226–8, 227
Fox, C. J. 4
freedom 163–4
Fremantle, W. H. 122, 123, 126, 146, 149, 152–4, 156, 179–80, 207, 208, 217, 220
Froude, H. 10, 12, 13, 15

Gell, L. 217
German theology 78, 79, 86, 87–8, 89–90, 113
Gladstone, W. F. 5, 34, 35, 36, 37, 38, 39, 41, 66, 95–7, 100, 101, 102, 104, 106, 110, 151, 177, 192, 200, 201, 203
God, Israelite concept of 127–9
God-consciousness 83, 88
Golightly, C. P. 16, 63, 64, 66, 90
Goodwin, C. 72
Gore, C. 167–82, 207–8, 221, 222, 226, 230
grammar schools 24, 99, 104
Greats (Literae Humaniores) 4, 5, 6, 32, 163, 210
Green, T. H. 27, 76, 100, 149, 150, 156, 157–67, 172, 180, 181, 193, 202, 209, 211, 217, 218, 219, 221, 224, 230, 231

Hadleigh Rectory 12, 13
halls 29, 33, 37, 150
Hamilton, Sir W. 5
Hampden, R. D. 6, 8, 14, 70
Hare, J. C. 65
Harrow School 171
Hawkins, E. 8, 9
hebdomadal board 16, 19, 33, 36
hebdomadal council 38
Hegel, G. W. F. 33, 36, 54, 65, 77, 79, 80–3, 82, 85, 87–8, 116, 123–4, 159, 163, 165, 173, 175, 177, 210, 224, 225, 229
Heywood, J. 38, 49
High Churchmen 10, 11, 13, 62, 69, 179, 208
Hinds, Bishop 33
Holland, H. S. 116, 118, 119, 156, 167, 172, 177, 226
Home Rule (Irish) 100, 203
Homer 96, 97, 102
Hopkins, G. M. 156, 174
Hort, F. J. A. 46
House of Commons 12, 37
Hume, D. 199, 206
Huxley, Mrs 201
Huxley, T. H. 78, 102, 184, 199–202

Idealism 77, 80, 81, 89, 157, 160, 167, 224–5, 227, 231–2
Imitatio Christi 124, 219
India 153
inspiration 46, 47, 73, 75
interpretation of scripture 47, 48, 67, 68, 72–6, 82, 178, 198

Jenkyns, R. 6, 7, 8, 10, 14, 15, 34, 39, 41
Jesus of history, the 59, 87, 122, 130, 133–4, 137–8, 142, 144, 160, 161, 162, 175, 196, 198–9, 201, 215, 219, 225, 227
John, St. 82, 162, 214, 228–9
Johnson, G. H. S. 33, 38
Jowett B. 6, 14, 16, 17, 18, 19, 21, 39, 40, 41, 42, 90, 106, 146, 172, 222, 224, 225–6, 229, 230, 231; and Arnold 46–9, 73; and the atonement 61–3; and

atonement, doctrine of 129; and Balliol 1, 2, 3, 14, 15, 108, 145, 165; and belief 141–2, 145; and Caird 209–11; and eclecticism 83–4; and education 24, 26, 28, 29, 36, 37, 103–6, 199; and female friendship 113; and Florence Nightingale 113–14; and Fremantle 146–9, 152–4; and friendship 1, 5, 16, 20, 26, 27, 55, 65, 97–8, 111–12, 134–7; and the German language 79, 80, 85; and German theology 87–8, 91; and Gladstone 35, 95–7, 101, 102, 106; and 'God's personality clothed in laws' 51, 52, 57, 123–24, 128, 185, 206; and Gore 168–78; and Green 165–6; and Hegel 80–3, 123; and his parents 1, 79; and his pupils 1, 107, 109, 115, 121–2, 135, 145, 146–8, 152–9, 167–8, 172–182, 215; and history 75, 82, 87, 124, 134, 137–9, 141–2; and holiness 142; and Huxley 199–202; and interpretation of scripture 48, 67, 72–6, 88, 114, 115, 126, 127, 129; and Kant 49–54; and morality 3, 24, 49, 59, 60, 65, 85, 100, 106, 108, 117, 143, 185, 187–8, 197–8; and natural science 24, 25, 191, 199–202; and ordination 22, 63, 64, 67, 84, 107; and other religions 153; and paradox 89, 143; and Pauline Commentaries 45–66; and philology 46, 56; and politics 99–102, 103, 104, 203–5; and prayer 197; and preaching 114–20; and preferement 107; and Pusey 66, 92–3; and religious controversy 90, 92; and religious tests 43–4, 63–4, 67, 108; and Schleiermacher 83–4, 86; and Scott 42, 43, 66, 106–7; and Semler 84–5; and snobbery 101, 155, 183; and society 24, 59, 103, 164; and Stanley 27, 28, 32, 45–7, 70, 71, 73; and 'systems' 122, 143, 176; and Tait 70, 98; and Temple 35, 36, 39, 111; and theology 3, 8, 14, 15, 19, 20, 21, 22, 23, 31, 32, 40, 55–63, 65, 74, 84, 105–6, 108, 109, 110, 111, 121–2, 125, 133, 143–5, 147–8, 154, 193, 205–7; and Toynbee 218–20; and university extension 150; as a classicist 105; as a college preacher 115, 116; as master of Balliol 209; as professor of Greek 45, 75, 93–4; as vice-chancellor 191–3, 197; election as master of Balliol 95, 106; malicious remarks of 97–8; on the ideal tutor 154–5; sermons of 125–46, 154, 156, 158, 166–7, 171, 177, 183–4, 186, 194–6, 206, 217

Judical Committee of the Privy Council 92, 107

Kant, I. 49–54, 77, 79, 81, 85, 86, 89, 159, 163, 165, 175, 206, 211, 219, 225, 229
Keble, J. 10, 12, 13, 38
kenotic theology 169, 175
King's College, London 3
Kneller Hall 35, 39
Knox, R. 226

laboratories 25, 191
Lachmann, K. 45
laissez-faire 163, 202
Lake, W. C. 34, 41
Lambeth Conference 71
Lang, C. G. 195–6, 207–8
Latitudinarianism 20, 21
Lay Sermons 216
Lewes, G. H. 113, 202
liberal protestantism 122, 133, 137, 171
liberalism, political and religious 99
Liberals (political) 99, 100, 101, 102, 177, 202–3
liberals (religious) 12, 13, 14, 15, 16, 17, 18, 20, 33, 34, 35, 39, 43, 48, 52, 69, 70, 71, 77, 90, 92–3, 96, 98, 102, 108, 148, 149, 158, 159, 207, 224, 231–2
library, college 78, 79, 85
Liddell, H. G. 93–4
Liddon, H. P. 169–70
Life of Christ 194
Lightfoot, J. B. 46, 62, 63
Lindsay, A. D. 221
Locke, J. 48, 76, 77, 163, 166–7
love, Christian 136
Lowe, R. 5, 95, 96, 97, 101, 102, 103, 106
Luther, M. 61
Lux Mundi 167–71, 224, 226, 227, 228

Mallock, W. H. 118–20, 155
Manchester College 214
Mansbridge, A. 221
Mansel, H. L. 91
Marylebone Literary Institute 189
master, election of Scott as 39–45
Maurice, F. D. 3, 69, 76, 96
Mazzini, G. 99–100, 162
metaphysics 25, 52, 53, 54, 65, 82, 86, 87, 123, 124, 126, 159, 160–1, 165, 173, 206
middle classes 164
Mill, J. S. 17, 33, 78, 79, 163, 218
Milner, Lord 217
miracles 55, 59, 81, 105, 109, 118, 141–2, 146, 161, 182–3
missions 189–90
Moberly, W. H. 226
morality 52, 161, 204, 221
morality, political 101, 103, 163–4, 224
mysticism 132, 134, 139, 156

Napoleon III 99, 162
natural science 5, 10, 11, 23, 24, 25, 55, 57, 58, 59, 72, 80, 81, 105, 132, 142, 182, 183–5, 199, 202, 229
natural selection 190
natural theology 8, 10, 11, 54, 57
Nettleship, R. L. 156–7, 172, 195, 217
New Testament 46, 48, 54, 55, 73, 75, 78, 84, 90, 126, 127, 129, 130–1, 134, 142, 161, 169, 198
Newman, J. H. 10, 11, 15, 16, 17, 63, 140, 141, 157
Nightingale, F. 43, 71, 89, 97, 98, 101, 102, 106, 111, 112, 113–14, 165, 173, 202, 203
Noetics 8, 9, 10, 77, 82

Oakeley, F. 16
Old Testament 127, 128, 129, 169, 170, 178
Oriel College 7, 8, 10, 11, 14, 15, 27, 158
Oxford Society of Historical Theology 215

Paley, W. 54, 57, 223
Palmerston, Lord 34, 93, 97

paradox 52–4
Parsons, J. 6, 7, 8, 14, 15
Pattison, M. 28, 72, 79, 96
Paul, St 161, 214
Pauline Commentaries 26, 30, 31, 35, 40, 45–66, 80, 122, 142, 159, 185, 219
Peel, Sir R. 41, 100
Philo 133
philology 24, 47, 55
Plato 25, 33, 80, 81, 89, 116, 123–4, 126, 164, 173, 225, 228, 229
Poole-Hughes, W. W. 180
Powell, Baden 9, 10, 11, 23, 24, 33, 72, 183, 199
Prayer, Book of Common 110–11
Priestley, J. 66
professors 28, 29, 33, 35, 36, 38, 149
providence 81
Public Worship Regulation Act 69
Pusey, E. B. 37, 38, 64, 66, 92, 93, 94, 97, 102, 132, 148, 169, 170, 174
Pusey House 170, 175, 179

Queen's College, the 226

reform university 2, 4, 7, 8, 14, 15, 26–39, 99, 102, 104–5, 106, 149–51, 192, 221–2, 230–1
religion in Oxford 2, 3
religion of Christ 140
religious census (1851) 38
religious tests 2, 3, 12, 29, 38, 39, 43, 44, 63, 64, 67, 69, 75, 92, 102, 103, 104, 106, 107, 108, 110, 151, 172
research 28
revelation 11, 48, 52, 72, 73, 74, 82, 88, 90, 142
Ricardo, D. 218–19
Roman Catholicism 203
Romanes, Mrs 208
Romanes, G. J. 200, 208
Romanes lecture 200–6
Rugby School 9, 16, 26, 27, 28, 31, 35, 41, 71, 111–12, 157, 158, 222, 223
Russell, Lady 103
Russell, Lord J. 33, 37, 38, 39, 41, 97, 101, 103, 106

Schelling, F. W. J. 79, 85, 87
Schleiermacher, F. D. E. 79, 83, 85, 86, 99, 116, 131, 132, 175
Schweitzer, A. 227
science of religion 212–15
Scott, R. 9, 16, 17, 28, 39, 40, 41, 42, 43, 44, 64, 66, 90, 91, 92, 93, 95, 104, 106–7, 115, 150, 152, 164, 203
Seeley, Sir J. R. 109, 137
Semler, J. S. 84–5
sermons 58, 59, 81, 89, 114–20, 121–2, 123, 125–46, 149, 154–5
settlements, slum 164
Seymour, E. 197–8, 203
Shaftesbury, Lord 97
Smith, A. L. 220, 222
Smith, Goldwin 29, 39, 41, 98
Snell Exhibition 18, 44, 210
Socrates 135
Spencer, H. 163, 165, 185–7, 202, 223
Stanley, A. P. 19, 20, 26, 27, 28, 29, 31, 32, 33, 37, 38, 41, 43, 45, 46, 47, 48, 63, 65, 66, 70, 71, 73, 76, 79, 80, 82, 91, 96, 107, 111, 158, 199, 230
Stanton, Fr. 170
Stephen, L. 145
Strauss, D. F. 113
Streeter, B. H. 226, 227
suicide 118–20
survival of the fittest 184–5, 186–7, 204–5

Tait, A. C. 16, 17, 18, 19, 20, 21, 22, 27, 33, 35, 44, 63, 69, 72, 83, 91, 98, 99, 107, 109, 111, 112, 113, 118, 126, 146, 165, 223
Talbot, E. S. 177
Talbot, N. 226, 227
Tavistock, Lady 196
Tawney, R. H. 221–2, 224

Temple, F. 27, 29, 35, 39, 41, 72, 73, 79, 80, 91, 96, 100–1, 111–12, 146, 186, 191, 199, 208, 223
Temple, W. 222–32
Tennyson, Lord 179
textus receptus 45
theology, German 85
theology, school of 31–2, 93
Thirty-nine Articles 9, 19, 28, 32, 38, 39, 43, 44, 63, 64, 66, 67, 70, 75, 108
Tories 4, 12, 13, 99, 101, 152, 155
Toynbee, A. 217–20
Toynbee Hall 217, 220
Tractarians 2, 10, 12, 14, 15, 16, 17, 19, 20, 37, 92, 93, 96, 98, 148, 157, 168, 170, 174, 176, 177
tutors 4, 5, 6, 28, 34, 149, 161, 165
tutors, private 6, 95

Unionists 203
University College 30
Utilitarianism 99, 163

Vaughan, H. H. 33

Wall, H. 39
Ward, W. G. 15, 16, 17, 18, 20, 41
welfare state 157
Wellington, Duke of 14
Westcott, B. F. 170
Whateley, R. 8, 9
Whigs 4, 8, 9, 12, 14, 99, 101, 155
Wilberforce, S. 70, 91, 108, 112, 126, 184, 190, 199, 201
Williams, R. 72, 91–2, 107
Wilson, H. B. 72, 91–2, 107, 108
Workers Educational Association 221–2, 224
working classes 164, 217–19